New Directions in American
Indian History

The D'Arcy McNickle Center Bibliographies in American
Indian History

New Directions
in American Indian History

Edited by Colin G. Calloway

University of Oklahoma Press : Norman and London

By Colin G. Calloway

Crown and Calumet (Norman, 1987)
(Editor) *New Directions in American Indian History* (Norman, 1988)
The Western Abenakis of Vermont, 1600–1800 (Norman, 1990)

970, 10072
N532c
1988

Library of Congress Cataloging-in-Publication Data

New directions in American Indian history / edited by Colin G.
  Calloway.—1st ed.
      p.   cm.—(The D'Arcy McNickle Center bibliographies in
  American Indian history)
      Includes index.
      (alk. paper)
      1. Indians of North America—Historiography.   2. Indians of North
  America—History—Bibliography.   I. Series.
  E76.8.N48   1988   88-5424
  970.004'97'00720—dc19
  ISBN 0-8061-2147-5 (hard cover), 0-8061-2233-1 (paperback)

New Directions in American Indian History is Volume 1 of The D'Arcy
McNickle Center Bibliographies in American Indian History.

The paper in this book meets the guidelines for permanence and durability
of the Committee on Production Guidelines for Book Longevity of the
Council on Library Resources, Inc.♾

2   3   4   5   6   7   8   9   10   11   12   13   14   15   16   17   18

Contents

Introduction to the Series

FREDERICK E. HOXIE, GENERAL EDITOR

During the 1970s the scholarly world witnessed a rapid expansion of interest in the history of Native Americans. Spurred by public sympathy, political pressure, and a recognition that the subject had been ignored for too long, academics from many disciplines began producing a flood of books and articles. Indian studies programs and journals began to appear, and a new generation of students received specialized training in the Native American past. By the middle of the 1980s the field of Indian history had begun to build its own infrastructure: organizations, networks of individuals, and institutions now supported a variety of educational and publishing activities, from new survey courses to prizewinning monographs. This infrastructure also assured the production of hundreds of scholarly publications each year.

When the Newberry Library established the Center for the History of the American Indian in 1972, Director D'Arcy McNickle and his colleagues believed that a bibliographical series was essential to the development of serious scholarship in the field. In 1972 there was substantial interest in Indian history but inadequate knowledge of the existing scholarship, a scholarship that spread across (and beyond) the traditional disciplines of history, anthropology, and literature. There was a need to make the work of past scholars readily accessible to students. The product of McNickle's concern was the Newberry Library Center for the History of the American Indian Bibliographical Series, a collection of thirty short volumes published by Indiana University Press and designed to provide newcomers to the field with an introduction to selected topics in Indian history. This series, together with the two volumes of bibliographies on Indian-white relations by Francis Paul Prucha, has enabled a generation of readers to translate their curiosity into serious scholarly endeavor.

Despite our progress, however, it has become apparent as we approach the 1990s that the volume of new material being produced each year makes it necessary to contemplate yet another bibliographical tool. The D'Arcy McNickle Center Bibliographies in American Indian History will provide comprehensive coverage of new publications in the field with two types of publications: indexed bibliographical lists organized by topic and volumes of bibliographical essays. The bibliographical lists will be issued every six years and will provide researchers with a complete list of publications in Indian history. The lists will be arranged topically and will be made up of publications in the disciplines of history, anthropology, sociology, literature, economics, religious studies, and linguistics. The first volume in this series is scheduled for completion in 1991. It will cover material published from 1985 through 1990.

The second type of publication will be volumes of bibliographical essays. Prepared by a cross-section of scholars from a variety of disciplinary and regional backgrounds, these essays will both review recent trends in historical scholarship and point to areas where further research needs to be done. Beginning with this volume, *New Directions in American Indian History,* these publications will provide students of the Native American past with a guide to recent research and a variety of suggestions for new areas of inquiry. The bibliographical essays will also appear every six years, but they will appear between volumes of the bibliographical lists. Thus a new volume in the series will appear about every three years, and the publications will alternate between the two types of guides.

The D'Arcy McNickle Center Bibliographies should provide students at all levels with comprehensive, ongoing guides to a field that has established itself as a permanent part of American intellectual life. We hope they will contribute to wider dissemination of scholarship in American Indian history and to continued growth in the field.

Editor's Preface

A senior professor at a recent meeting of historians observed that, despite fluctuations in the popularity of Indian history among students, we will "never go back" to the period of the 1950s when Native American history was a tiny piece of the academic agenda. The demand for information and materials that began to rise two decades ago has reached a sustained, if occasionally shifting, level.

The persistence of Indian history creates a new set of needs among students and teachers. Principal among these is the need for guides to current literature. More than five hundred books and articles on Indian history appear each year, but which are the most significant? Where is there particular activity among authors and students? What areas are being overlooked? The essays in this volume provide some answers to these questions. They examine aspects of recent scholarship in American Indian history and provide commentary on its quality—its strengths as well as its weaknesses.

New Directions in Indian History contains two parts. Part one, "Recent Trends," contains six essays that review six areas of the field where there has been a significant amount of interest and activity. The essays in part one organize and evaluate recent publications on those six topics in an effort to provide readers with guides to rapidly expanding areas of study. Part two, "Emerging Fields," contains essays on aspects of Indian history that remain undeveloped. The authors of the three essays in part two have presented readers with a sharper critique of current scholarship and have sketched an agenda for future inquiry. This book thus contains essays that respond to two meanings of the label, "new directions." First, they describe what new directions have been pursued recently by historians of the Indian experience. And second, they point out some new directions that remain to be pursued.

Scholars and the Indian Experience: Critical Reviews of Recent Writings in the Social Sciences, edited by W. R. Swagerty and published for the D'Arcy McNickle Center in 1984, presented a volume of essays intended to bring readers "up to date" on material published before 1983. The emphasis in all of the essays in the present volume is on work that has appeared since then, but some authors—particularly those in part two—have necessarily reached back to earlier scholarship to complete their arguments. As a general rule, dissertations are not listed. However, in areas where much of the new scholarship has yet to be published, some dissertations have been included.

Preparation of this volume was supported by a grant from the Education Division of the National Endowment for the Humanities. The Newberry Library has also provided vital human and institutional support for the project. Particularly significant contributions of time and encouragement came from Jeff Auld, Marilyn Deberry, and Rosemarie White of the library's Word Processing Services; Jay Miller, McNickle Center Editor and Assistant Director; Rose Summers, administrative assistant, and Newberry Library Academic Vice President Richard H. Brown.

Colin G. Calloway

Laramie, Wyoming

New Directions in American
Indian History

PART ONE

Recent Trends

Just as visitors to a new city need maps and guidebooks to direct them, students of American Indian history can benefit from directions about points of interest and centers of activity. The chapters in this section focus on six aspects of American Indian history that have received considerable attention in recent years. In each case, the chapter authors describe the published literature on a topic and ask, "Are scholars pursuing significant questions and adopting valuable techniques?" We recognize the quantity of material in each area, but what of its quality? The following six chapters answer that question in six different ways.

CHAPTER 1

Indians and the Numbers Game: Quantitative Methods in Native American History

MELISSA L. MEYER AND RUSSELL THORNTON

Despite the massive outpouring of writing on Indian history in recent years, much of the historical literature follows traditional and well-worn paths. Historians continue to devote more attention to Indian-white conflict, Indian resistance leaders, and federal policy than they do to such questions as Indian family life, economic activity, cultural persistence, and political change. Quantitative methods have not been adopted as readily by historians of American Indians as they have by other social historians.

The few scholars of Indian history who have turned their attention to new questions and new sources of data have found tremendous scope for their inquiry and research. Because Indians occupied a unique position as federal wards, the government produced a mass of records about them—census rolls, ration lists, allotment schedules, birth and death registers, personnel and medical records, and so on. These records—most of which are available on microfilm—provide the basis for a new Indian history. Sophisticated studies of tribal social structure, reservation culture, and labor patterns will lead us away from a preoccupation with past conflict and policy to a fuller picture of the Indians' historical experience.

In this first chapter, a young historian and a Cherokee sociologist collaborate to provide a comprehensive review of recent scholarship employing quantitative methods in the study of American Indian history. Melissa L. Meyer and Russéll Thornton evaluate the literature in areas where quantitative research is being carried out. They also suggest fields where opportunities and challenges exist for further study and show that historians who acquire the necessary skills of statistical reasoning and computing thereby gain access to significant sources of underused data.

Quantitative methods of history range from a simple reporting of data to the variety of methodological techniques used to secure, evaluate, and organize data to mathematical and statistical operations performed upon data. They also include, as defined here, the development of models, often mathematical ones, to generalize or predict data. Quantitative methods encompass such methodological and statistical techniques as survey research, multivariate analysis, population projections, life table construction, correlation, and linear regression. All of these techniques are included in the studies reported here, to one degree or another, as are various other methods and statistics.

The Scope of Quantitative Methods

The quantitative study of American Indian history per se is, however, greatly underdeveloped. Within wider history, there abound a variety of uses of quantitative methods, often quite sophisticated ones, as in the case of economic history or social history. Historians who focus on American Indians have generally not used such methods. Consequently, few of the papers and books included in this survey were written by historians as such. It seems that most quantitative work on American Indians has been done by social scientists in other disciplines. As shown by the works included here, the majority of quantitative efforts focused on American Indians come from anthropologists, physical anthropologists and archaeologists, sociologists and/or demographers, and historical demographers. Scholars in these areas concerned with American Indians have surpassed their counterparts in history in the use of quantitative methods. This situation may now be changing, as evidenced by this chapter, but at present quantifying has not taken hold among historians of American Indians.

Historical Demography and Epidemiology

American Indian historical demography and epidemiology probably represent the forefront of quantitative approaches to American Indian history: the topics lend themselves naturally to quantification, and historic data on them abound. Such studies also comprise a large body of literature in our survey, even though we have limited it. Some of the recent research in this area has been summarized by S. Ryan Johansson in her "The Demographic History of the Native Peoples of North America: A Selective Bibliography" [32] and by Henry F. Dobyns in a chapter in William R. Swagerty's *Scholars and the Indian Experience* [15]. We do not wish to duplicate this literature here; with several notable exceptions, the works discussed below were either published in the past few years or published earlier but not cited by Johansson or Dobyns.

Scholars still direct much research toward establishing the size of pre-Columbian American Indian populations. Russell Thornton and Joan Marsh-Thornton, in "Estimating Prehistoric American Indian Population Size for United States Area" [83], mathematically project the nineteenth-century American Indian population decline backward in time. This enables them to make an estimate of aboriginal population size for the United States area. The paper also lowers by several million Henry Dobyns's [13] earlier population estimate for North America by using a more accurate nadir population figure than he used. Russell Thornton also discusses the aboriginal population of California in "Recent Estimates of the Prehistoric California Indian Population" [75].

In the controversial *Their Number Become Thinned* [14], Henry F. Dobyns attempts, in part, to establish the size of the aboriginal American Indian population north of Mesoamerica; however, he focuses particularly on the southeast coast of North America. He employs several methodologies, including an epidemiological model whereby depopulations are projected backward in time to establish aboriginal size. Dobyns also postulates what appear to be excessively large numbers of aboriginal American Indians based upon his assessment of the carrying capacity of the ecosystems involved, given possible natural resources and American Indian technologies.

Many of the works surveyed focus more on population decline than on aboriginal population size. They include *American Indian Holocaust and Survival: A Population History Since 1492* [82], by Russell Thornton. A population history of North American Indians from pre-European contact to the present, it contains a variety of data, particularly information obtained from published U.S. census reports. It also presents a new aboriginal population size for North

America. A detailed analysis of the native populations of Mexico and California is contained in the third volume of Sherburne F. Cook and Woodrow Borah's *Essays in Population History* [12]. Cook and Borah use a variety of data, including revenue payments, possible food production, and mission registers, and several methodological and statistical techniques to establish population sizes and other demographic characteristics during the sixteenth and seventeenth centuries.

Florence C. Shipek's "A Native American Adaptation to Drought" [66] reports an analysis of records from Mission San Diego. She shows population decline of the Kumeyaay during the late eighteenth century, primarily through lowered birth rates and in response to recurrent droughts. Robert H. Jackson's "Causes of Indian Population Decline in the Pimería Alta Missions of Northern Sonora" [28] traces population decline and changes in other demographic characteristics as a result of epidemics during the very late seventeenth, the eighteenth, and the nineteenth centuries. Russell Thornton's "Social Organization and the Demographic Survival of the Tolowa" [79] and "History, Structure, and Survival: A Comparison of the Yuki (*Ukomno'm*) and Tolowa (*Hush*) Indians of Northern California" [80] both consider depopulation and demographic survival.

Lawrence E. Aten [2] also considers aboriginal population sizes and their decline during the eighteenth and nineteenth centuries along what is now the upper Texas coast; S. Alan Skinner's "Aboriginal Demographic Changes in Central Texas" [68] develops a model for determining such "prehistoric" changes.

Donald J. Lehmer examines population losses resulting from nineteenth-century epidemics in his "Epidemics Among the Indians of the Upper Missouri" [42]. In "The Fur Trade and Native American Population Growth" [36], Jeanne Kay documents that, following initial declines caused by European diseases and warfare, the populations of the Foxes, Sauks, Menominees, and Winnebagos all increased from about 1700 through 1840. She argues that this growth resulted from their involvement in the fur trade and the increased resources it provided. Russell Thornton, in "Cherokee Population Losses During the Trail of Tears" [78], uses mathematical projections of the nineteenth-century Cherokee population trends to provide both a new perspective on population losses during the Cherokee removal and a new estimate of these losses. He illustrates that the losses might have been twice the generally accepted figure of four thousand. Using linear regression on a variety of population figures for the mid-eighteenth century through the early nineteenth century, J. Anthony Paredes and Kenneth J. Plante [56] show that Creek population increased rapidly during the late eighteenth century and early nineteenth century, the Creeks having reached their population nadir earlier than other American Indian groups.

June Helm uses census data to argue for high levels of female infanticide among the nineteenth-century Mackenzie Denes in her "Female Infanticide, European Disease, and Population Levels Among the Mackenzie Dene" [22]. She argues moreover, that failure to recognize female infanticide has led scholars erroneously to attribute the depopulation of the Denes to European diseases. Shepard Krech's "The Influence of Disease and the Fur Trade on Arctic Drainage Lowlands Dene, 1800–1850" [38] covers some of the same time period but emphasizes the importance of disease in the aboriginal depopulation of the area.

Several important works have been published recently on the epidemiology of disease. A volume edited by Jane E. Buikstra, *Prehistoric Tuberculosis in the Americas* [6], contains various papers on the epidemiology of this disease in both aboriginal North and South America. Steadman Upham, in "Smallpox and Climate in the American Southwest" [86], develops a model of smallpox infection and argues that unreported smallpox epidemics likely occurred in the Southwest before 1540, between 1541 and 1581, and perhaps again during the 1600s. Stephen J. Kunitz's *Disease Change and the Role of Medicine* [39] examines demographic and epidemiologic changes among the Navajos during the present century using a variety of data and techniques. Also examining the Navajos, David W. Broudy and Philip A. May [5] use various data to argue that the Navajos may be considered in the transitional stages of demographic and epidemiologic flux.

Some works surveyed used quantitative methods to describe "prehistoric" and historic American Indian populations. Many of the essays in *Progress in Skeletal Biology of Plains Populations* [31], edited by Richard L. Jantz and Douglas H. Ubelaker, fall into this category. Other descriptive works include the well-known "The Cherokees in Transition: A Statistical Analysis of the Federal Cherokee Census of 1835" [44] by William G. McLoughlin and Walter

M. Conser, Jr.; a paper by S. Ryan Johansson and S. H. Preston, "Tribal Demography: The Hopi and Navaho Population as Seen Through Manuscripts from the 1900 U.S. Census" [33]; a paper by Dori Penny, "Demographic Contrasts Among Cheyenne Bands" [57]; James M. Goodman's *The Navajo Atlas* [18]; and Melissa L. Meyer's detailed demographic examination of the White Earth Ojibwas, "The Historical Demography of White Earth Indian Reservation: The 1900 U.S. Federal Manuscript Census Considered" [47]. Eric Abella Roth has reconstructed historic village populations in his "Demography and Computer Simulation in Historic Village Population Reconstruction" [63].

Several scholars have examined contemporary or possible future American Indian populations. William R. Swagerty and Russell Thornton [71] report 1980 census figures for American Indians. *Les Populations amerindiennes et inuit du Canada: Aperçu demographique* [52] contains numerous demographic studies not only of contemporary Native Americans in Canada but also of historic Native American populations. *Population Projections of Registered Indians, 1982 to 1996* [58], also concerned with Native Americans in Canada, projects future populations for regions, districts, and bands as well as all of Canada.

The construction of life tables from skeletal recoveries, currently in vogue in "prehistoric" demography, seeks to analyze past aboriginal and historic American Indian populations, particularly their life expectancies. Such attempts in part represent efforts to provide more sophisticated measures than the often-used "average age at death." Two recent papers have examined the populations of Pecos Pueblos in this regard: Charles M. Mobley's "Demographic Structure of Pecos Indians: A Model Based on Life Tables" [49], and Christopher B. Ruff's "A Reassessment of Demographic Estimates for Pecos Pueblo" [64]. John W. Lallo and Jerome C. Rose's "Patterns of Stress, Disease and Mortality in Two Prehistoric Populations from North America" [40] examines populations from the Dickson Mounds site in Illinois, as does "An Ecological Interpretation of Variation in Mortality Within Three Prehistoric American Indian Populations from Dickson Mounds" [41], by John Lallo, Jerome Carl Rose, and George J. Armelgos. However, as S. Ryan Johansson and S. Horowitz illustrate in "Estimating Mortality in Skeletal Populations" [34], such life tables are based on unrealistic assumptions that no migration or population growth or decline occurred within the populations in question. Moreover, they argue that obtaining reasonable mortality estimates from skeletal populations requires an independent measure of growth rate.

Scholars of historical demography and epidemiology may also examine various implications of depopulation and disease for American Indian populations, including American Indian responses to them. In this regard, Russell Thornton has examined the nineteenth-century Ghost Dances as religious responses to depopulation. His "Demographic Antecedents of a Revitalization Movement: Population Change, Population Size, and the 1890 Ghost Dance" [76] examines differential participation in this revitalization movement and relates depopulation and other demographic variables to Ghost Dance participation. "Demographic Antecedents of Tribal Participation in the 1870 Ghost Dance Movement" [77] replicates his earlier study by focusing on tribes of the first Ghost Dance movement. *We Shall Live Again: The 1870 and 1890 Ghost Dance Movements as Demographic Revitalization* [81] reports Thornton's larger study from which these papers were drawn. In it he examines differential participation in greater detail and also assesses the implications of Ghost Dance participation upon *subsequent* American Indian population change.

Much further work could be done regarding American Indian responses to depopulation and disease that would also link demography and epidemiology to wider historical concerns. Social and revitalization movements other than the Ghost Dances, for example, might be linked to depopulation. The same holds true for other changes in American Indian societies and cultures. D. H. Ubelaker and P. Willey have examined changes in the mortuary practice of an American Indian people in their "Complexity in Arikara Mortuary Practice" [85]. They argue that while the Arikaras have historically been described as burying their dead soon after death, various historical, archaeological and even entomological evidence indicates an earlier period of scaffolding before burial. The incidence of various epidemics among the Arikaras may have led to a change in burial practices. The Arikaras may have changed from a scaffolding style of burial to direct interment to avoid the hazard of increased exposure to corpses infected with epidemic disease.

A few scholars are beginning to investigate the impact of epidemic diseases on burial practices and religious institutions, but in general, scholars have only begun to consider the social and cultural implications of widespread depopulation.

Some researchers concern themselves with methodological considerations in the study of historical demography and epidemiology. Included here are Cary W. Meister's often-cited "The Misleading Nature of Data in the Bureau of the Census Subject Report on 1970 American Indian Population" [45] and "Methods for Evaluating the Accuracy of Ethnohistorical Demographic Data of North American Indians: A Brief Assessment" [46]. These papers show that demographic data should not be accepted uncritically and offer tests for assessing their utility. From a broader perspective, William Petersen's "A Demographer's View of Prehistorical Demography" [60] is a critique of research in this area, as is a review essay by Russell Thornton [74]. Douglas H. Ubelaker's "Approaches to Demographic Problems in the Northeast" [84] discusses methods and data that pertain to the demography of American Indians in the Northeast region of what is now the United States.

Numerous sources of data exist for the study of American Indian populations, some more accessible than others. U.S. census reports on the American Indian population are important among these. They vary in content, but typically contain both demographic and social information about American Indians. Published reports based on the regular decennial censuses of 1890 [91], 1910 [94], 1930 [95], and 1970 [96] are readily available. The manuscript forms of the 1900 and 1910 censuses have been microfilmed but not used to any great extent. Also, the U.S. Bureau of the Census issued several special reports on specific American Indian tribes or groups of tribes during the 1890s: the Six Nations [87], the Eastern Band of Cherokees [88], the Pueblos [89], the Moqui Pueblos [90], and the so-called Five Civilized Tribes [92]; also issued was a 1907 report on the population of Oklahoma and Indian Territory [93]. Special censuses of American Indian tribes are also available, such as the 1835 census of the Cherokees. The Indian Office and the later Bureau of Indian Affairs have compiled censuses annually since the mid-1800s. They are microfilmed and serve as the basis for statistics included in the *Annual Reports of the Commissioner of Indian Affairs* [1]. State censuses have sometimes enumerated nonreservation American Indians. Another important, often-used source of population data is the various records of Spanish missions before the establishment of U.S.

jurisdiction. Noteworthy, but largely untapped, are the Mormon archives in Salt Lake City, containing various genealogical records [17] and open to the public. These sources are not exhaustive but merely a sample of more well known source material available to scholars.

A review of the studies cited herein forces the conclusion that some scholars publishing in the area remain unaware of fundamental demographic assumptions, basic demographic processes of human populations, the nature of demographic data, and the methods and techniques of demography. These are obviously serious shortcomings that must be remedied if scholars are to achieve full credibility within the wider fields of historical demography and demography, or even history and anthropology. The discipline of demography must be brought much more fully into the study of American Indian historical demography and epidemiology.

Archaeology

Archaeologists have long employed quantitative methods in their research. Typically, they collect materials from excavations, enumerate items and assemblages, and analyze artifacts and floral and faunal remains spatially to determine their density and patterning.

Archaeologists are currently asking new questions and reviewing recovered materials in new ways. "Ethnoarchaeologists" increasingly seek to relate material remains to human social behavior instead of concentrating only on their categorization. They use historical documents in conjunction with material remains to ask how the patterning of artifacts relates to the cultural behavior of the groups that produced them. Inter- and intragroup relations thus become the focus.

Timothy K. Perttula and James E. Bruseth quantify remains found in midden heaps and calculate their nutritional value to shed light on subsistence patterns in "Early Caddoan Subsistence Strategies, Sabine River Basin, East Texas" [59]. In "Growth and Aggregation at Canyon Creek Ruin: Implications for Evolutionary Change in East-Central Arizona" [19], Michael W. Graves dates tree rings to hypothesize that population growth through both natural increase and immigration accounted for the timing of Pueblo room construction. Quantification of the archaeological record can also illuminate trade relations both among Indians, as in Katherine A. Spielmann's "Late

Prehistoric Exchange Between the Southwest and Southern Plains"
[69], and between Indians and Europeans, as Charles E. Orser demonstrates in "Trade Good Flow in Arikara Villages: Expanding Ray's
Middleman Hypothesis" [53]. Studies contained in *Peopling the
New World* [16], by Jonathon E. Ericson, R. E. Taylor, and Rainer
Berger, offer quantitative evidence pushing back the clock for human
entrance into North America by way of Beringia to as early as forty
thousand years ago.

   Historians have had difficulty using the insights of archaeology, a
technical discipline steeped in its own language and methods. Because archaeology involves a massive outlay of time, energy, and
training, historians rely primarily on published archaeological reports. However, archaeologists must often resort to salvage projects
for financial reasons. Few projects focus on the more recent historical era, especially the late nineteenth and twentieth centuries. Many
archaeologists often publish their analyses in obscure places, if at
all; are constrained by financial considerations in their choice of research topics; and write in a technical language that few historians
have mastered. This impasse poses significant problems because the
archaeological record can validate, modify, and expand the documentary record.

Economics

Several scholars have employed quantitative methods in ecological
studies of American Indians' economic subsistence systems. Using
linear regression, Alan J. Osborn, in "Ecological Aspects of Equestrian Adaptations in Aboriginal North America" [55], demonstrates
that ecological models better explain variability in aboriginal horse-
herd size than do simple diffusion models. In "The Inland Shore
Fishery of the Northern Great Lakes: Its Development and Importance in Prehistory" [10], Charles E. Cleland reconstructs relative
fish yields in the Great Lakes to emphasize the historical importance
of the inland shore fishery to the Indian groups there. Tallying fur
returns for a Connecticut River valley trader between 1650 and 1670,
Peter A. Thomas challenges the standard interpretation that over-
hunting and European encroachment undermined native societies in
all situations. In "The Fur Trade, Indian Land and the Need to Define Adequate 'Environmental' Parameters" [73], he argues that

these Connecticut Valley tribes exchanged land as part of a strategy to maintain social and cultural needs and obligations.

Other historians focus on Indians' involvement in various agricultural enterprises, an area that warrants further attention. James A. Vlasich documents the increasing use by Pueblo Indians of more mechanized agricultural technology in the mid-twentieth century in "Transitions in Pueblo Agriculture, 1938–1948" [99]. Employing economic theory and sophisticated quantitative methods, Leonard A. Carlson analyzes Indian responses to the late-nineteenth-century allotment program. As illustrated in *Indians, Bureaucrats, and Land: The Dawes Act and the Decline of Indian Farming* [7], and two shorter articles [8, 9], Indian farming actually decreased, as historians have long suspected. Further extending his analysis, he finds that allotment actually benefited neighboring non-Indians instead of Indians. The easing of restrictions and sale of land corresponded to boom and bust cycles in American agriculture, with government officials opening Indian lands as prices reached their zenith.

Other studies employ computer technology to help establish parameters to guide research in areas where documents have always been scarce. R. Brooke Jacobsen and Jeffrey L. Eighmy, in "A Mathematical Theory of Horse Adoption on the North American Plains" [29], suggest a new explanation for the adoption of the horse on the Plains. They argue the utility of an S-curve model—one in which initial high demand tapered off quickly then declined less dramatically. In a similar vein, Charles E. Orser and Larry J. Zimmerman's "A Computer Simulation of Euro-American Trade Good Flow to the Arikara" [54] offers a simple computer simulation model to account for the initial flow of European trade goods to the Arikaras. Their model suggests that Arikara "needs" could have been saturated far earlier than previously believed.

Increasingly, scholars have turned their attention to the impact of energy exploitation on Indian communities and economic development, as evidenced in *Native Americans and Energy Development* [35] and *The Southwest Under Stress: National Resource Development in a Regional Setting* [37]. This topic lends itself readily to quantitative techniques, especially in a comparative context. The authors compare the relative benefits derived by various tribes and the multinational corporations anxious to extract the minerals from their lands. They assess how tribes will fare in the future as unlimited exploitation depletes reserves of nonrenewable resources, which are mined in line with the needs of the dominant society. More important, they examine how the environmental devastation will affect the long-term health and welfare of reservation residents.

Quantitative methods can contribute further to historical studies of American Indians' economic experiences. Although pioneering studies like Arthur J. Ray and Donald B. Freeman's *"Give Us Good Measure"*: *An Economic Analysis of Relations Between the Indian and the Hudson's Bay Company Before 1763* [62] have made extensive use of fur trade company records, the potential of such documents still remains great. The records of the Hudson's Bay Company, located in Winnipeg, Manitoba, and trade records housed in archives and historical societies across the country continue to support sophisticated research.

Unlike Russell Lawrence Barsh and Katherine Diaz-Knauf in "The Structure of Federal Aid for Indian Programs in the Decade of Prosperity, 1970–1980" [3], few have undertaken historical studies of Indian financing. Historians have scarcely touched accounting records of the Bureau of Indian Affairs housed at the National Archives and various regional centers, perhaps because their unwieldy nature hinders their use. However, more convenient financial statistics appended to the *Annual Reports of the Commissioner of Indian Affairs* [1] have received only limited attention. Paul Stuart in *The Indian Office: Growth and Development of an American Institute* [70] and Francis Paul Prucha in *The Great Father: The United States Government and the American Indians* [61] excerpt portions of these published statistics to analyze federal spending on Indian affairs. More localized studies might assess the financial contributions made by various Indian groups. Facile generalizations about American Indians' dependence on welfare gratuities from the U.S. government have masked the fact that some groups essentially financed their own "assimilation" through the sale of their land and resources. Lingering Indian Claims Commission cases dealing with issues of financing may alert scholars to the potential of these documents as they continue to serve as consultants and expert witnesses.

Politics

In mainstream U.S. history, the analysis of voting behavior and political constituencies has become almost commonplace. The fact that significant numbers of American Indians were not enfranchised until 1924 hampers analysis of Indian voting patterns, but these techniques may have utility in other areas. Over the years, substantial politicking, reflective of regional and party coalitions, contributed to Congress's formulation of U.S. Indian policy. Frederick E. Hoxie, in *A Final Promise: The Campaign to Assimilate the Indians, 1880–1920* [25], offers a glimpse of the potential of such studies. He analyzes regional voting blocs by tallying roll call votes recorded in the *Congressional Record* [11]. Similar studies of congressional voting behavior should be possible at all time periods after the founding of the republic.

Court records will permit more localized studies of policy toward American Indians. Such records provide quantifiable evidence of American Indians' offenses and subsequent treatment that can reveal a great deal about the context of Indian-white relations at the time. Although she does not employ quantitative methods per se, Kathleen Joan Bragdon's treatment of "Crime and Punishment Among the Indians of Massachusetts, 1675–1750" [4] suggests the utility of these documents.

Studies of the internal politics of Indian communities can also profit from a quantitative approach. Any documents in which leaders' names appear grouped together are potential targets for such analysis. These include treaties, reports of special commissions, censuses of eligible voters, tribal council minutes, petitions, and other forms of correspondence. Linking names of leaders through several such documents can produce even greater breadth of information about individuals, perhaps revealing band, clan, or kinship affiliations that often underlie political associations. In the case of political factionalism, the composition and relative strength of constituencies can be assessed.

Social History

Perhaps the greatest potential for quantitative methods in Indian history lies in the realm of social history. Only a few scholars have ventured into this area. This inattention appears curious considering the current popularity of mainstream social history. New generations of historians have turned with enthusiasm to studies of ethnic enclaves and communities, family life, social mobility, workers, blacks, women, and immigrants. Yet American Indians' experiences remain largely insulated from such attention, and thus their histories are prevented from being integrated fully into renditions of the national experience. Such oversight represents a significant omission. As the only indigenous peoples in the western hemisphere, American Indians possess separate land bases and are regulated by an intrusive colonial bureaucracy, which differentiates their experiences from those of all other racial and ethnic groups in their relationships with the federal government. Inclusion of their social experiences may produce important revisions and refinements in the interpretation of the history of the American people.

Explanations offered for this failure to study Indians' social experiences have rested on the paucity of documentation. However, this reasoning can only apply before the early nineteenth century. Beginning in the mid-nineteenth century, the U.S. government, in its self-imposed role as guardian of Indians' affairs, created an abundance of documentation relevant to Indian social history. As the colonial bureaucracy of the United States controlled, managed, and attempted to change Indian cultures, it generated reams of serially organized paperwork that lie in the national and regional archives, virtually untouched by scholars. Censuses, annuity lists, tribal rolls, allotment records, ration lists, rosters of employees, economic statistics, financial and accounting records, medical and health records, birth and death registers, school records, parish records, and a wealth of more idiosyncratic materials exist for federally recognized tribes throughout the country. Edward E. Hill's *Guide to Records of the National Archives of the United States Relating to American Indians* [24] describes these records. Regional branches of the National Archives also publish guides to their holdings. Numerous statistics are also appended to the *Annual Report of the Commissioner of Indian Affairs,* published regularly in the Congressional Serial Set [1]. This wealth of serial data means that American Indians are among the best-documented populations in the world; yet these resources have gone largely unnoticed.

The failure to exploit such materials perhaps stems more from attitudes toward the "proper" topics for research than on the existence of the necessary documentary material. With notable exceptions, many Indian historians are still preoccupied with predictable subjects that reflect popular tastes. Colorful Indian leaders, warfare, and U.S. policy toward Indians retain their hold on the public's imagination. Vague terms like *acculturation* and *ethnohistory* permeate the literature as scholars continue to search for elusive "world views." Such romantic preoccupations have caused historians to ignore materials from which they can derive the actual behavior of Indian people and bring their research more in line with innovations in the larger field. Twentieth-century American Indians' experiences, a topic of little attention, would especially profit from a reorientation of research issues. Redirecting questions toward topics like fertility and mortality rates, household sizes and types, marriage patterns, age structures, social mobility, migration, and economic trends could allow historians to generate the data necessary to bring American Indians' diverse experiences into a broader comparative framework.

Besides colonial militias and armies, local courts, and traders, few agencies before the mid-nineteenth century produced serial data on a regular basis. However, several scholars have recently shown great ingenuity in mining previously underutilized sources to create quantifiable material for the early colonial period. Alden T. Vaughan and Daniel K. Richter, in "Crossing the Cultural Divide: Indians and New Englanders, 1605–1763" [97], employ sources recording New England captives taken in military encounters to examine the general issue of transculturation. Using data on the age, sex, race, social status, hometown, place of capture, length of captivity, and ultimate fate of those captured, they show that few captives, other than the very young, simply abandoned their cultures.

In "Western Dakota Winter Counts: An Analysis of the Effects of Westward Migration and Culture Change" [23], Elizabeth R. P. Henning quantifies symbols in western Dakota winter counts and analyzes their patterning. She breaks the winter counts, which span the years 1790 to 1850, into two thirty-year periods and categorizes the symbols according to inter- and intratribal relations, warfare, religion, resource procurement, natural phenomena, and interaction with whites. Analyzing their frequency of occurrence, she discerns changes over that period. Dakota concerns shifted from a preoccupation with whites and warfare to intragroup concerns, especially religion and the procurement of resources. She hypothesizes that this shift reflected their internal adaptation to rapidly changing conditions of life.

In "Malhiot's Journal: An Ethnohistoric Assessment of Chippewa

Alcohol Behavior in the Early 19th Century" [100], Jack O. Waddell excerpts data on alcohol distribution and consumption from an early-nineteenth-century Wisconsin fur trader's journal. Waddell then develops the notion of culturally and temporarily restricted drinking behavior on the part of neighboring Indians. He finds that comments about pervasive drunken debauchery reflect the trader's location at the fur post, a primary locus for otherwise restricted drinking behavior.

Local town records may provide detail on migration patterns and the integration of individual Indians into the regional area. Marriage records, land records, church records, occasional censuses, and tax lists may enumerate Indians who chose to live apart from a federally recognized tribe or reservation. Linking names through several sets of documents promises to reveal information about the nonreservation Indian population that has proven so elusive to scholars.

Census materials regarding American Indians have utility for social historians beyond demography or population history. Albert L. Hurtado uses an 1846 census of John Sutter's California rancho to explore conditions for native workers there. As he argues in " 'Saved So Much As Possible for Labour': Indian Population and the New Helvetia Work Force" [27], an unusual age structure indicates that native women resorted to infanticide to provide their newborn children with a form of "escape" from intolerable conditions of enslavement. Hurtado uses 1860 federal census materials for California to examine the conditions Indian laborers faced working in white households in " 'Hardly a Farm House—A Kitchen Without Them:' Indian and White Households on the California Borderland Frontier in 1860" [26]. He reasons that in addition to genocide and epidemics, the California Indian population declined because of the inability of native men and women to achieve productive unions, as evidenced in an uneven sex ratio. Cardell K. Jacobsen uses existing census reports from the early twentieth century to analyze the transformation of Indians into wage laborers in "Internal Colonialism and Native Americans: Indian Labor in the United States from 1871 to World War II" [30]. Anastasia M. Shkilnyk in *A Poison Stronger than Love: The Destruction of an Ojibwa Community* [67], assembles statistics from published sources to explore the social consequences of mercury poisoning for the Ojibwa people who live among the lakes and rivers at Grassy Narrows in southern Ontario.

The subsequent undermining of fishing as the main commercial and subsistence activity took a social toll in the form of increasing rates of alcoholism and suicide. Other scholars have excerpted aggregate statistics from various published sources to explore other social issues concerning American Indian groups [20, 21, 43, 65]. During the past several years, John H. Moore and his students at the University of Oklahoma have analyzed allotment records for information on the composition and settlement patterns of Cheyenne bands. Moore devised what he termed "nearest neighbor" techniques to convert geographic distance between allotment selections to a measure of social distance. He demonstrates in "Aboriginal Indian Residence Patterns Preserved in Censuses and Allotments" [50] that when these selections are geographically mapped by computer, clustering patterns indicate closer social affinity than a dispersed pattern. Moore's students have refined and expanded his research, some of them focusing on Osage allotment selections as well [51, 72, 98].

One technique that scholars have not yet fully utilized is the computer-assisted linkage of serial records. Record linkage can create a range of information on individuals and trace them temporally. The serial records available in the late nineteenth and twentieth centuries have special utility for historians. The manuscript forms of the 1900 and 1910 U.S. federal censuses were the first to enumerate reservation populations and directed a special set of inquiries toward American Indians. They are organized according to residence and will also permit the construction of fertility estimates based on "own children" techniques, as termed in the demographic literature. The Bureau of Indian Affairs also produced "censuses" of reservation populations annually from the mid-1800s into the twentieth century that are less detailed but may include variables not enumerated in the federal censuses. Allotment records and, potentially, any of the serial records mentioned earlier can be linked by computer with these censuses to reveal more detail about reservation populations than has previously been possible. This technique will enable historians to explore residence patterns and their relationship to allotment patterns, both intra- and extra-reservation marital patterns, off-reservation migration as well as individual persistence, political factionalism, and changes in occupations, literacy, and naming patterns. Documents must be carefully evaluated for each reservation population, but the possibilities are impressive.

Conclusion

Such bright prospects should not be allowed to mask the difficulties inherent in applying quantitative methods to documents dealing with American Indian populations. Specific cultural naming practices and variable phonetic translations of names will pose formidable obstacles to record linkage. In addition, historians must critically evaluate serial records and statistics with the same rigor they apply to all of their source materials. Lifting statistics from appendices to the *Annual Reports of the Commissioner of Indian Affairs* without evaluating how local officials generated those statistics can impair the quality of the measures drawn and comparisons made. For example, Leonard A. Carlson, in "Land Allotment and the Decline of American Indian Farming" [8], assumed that figures given for the White Earth Reservation accurately reflected economic conditions at the reservation without fully considering the massive fraud that had occurred during the allotment process. How can decreasing acres of Indian farmland reflect Indian responses to economic incentives when legislation beneficial to outside corporations allowed them to acquire 90 percent of the reservation land base within ten years of its allotment? Overreliance on aggregate statistics can obscure local peculiarities.

Problems also arise in the interpretation of statistics. In "Off the White Road: Seven Nebraska Indian Societies in the 1870s—A Statistical Analysis of Assimilation, Population and Prosperity" [48], Clyde A. Milner II draws correlation coefficients for a number of variables to determine relationships between economic indicators and measures of "assimilation." He then links successful "assimilation" with growing population and prosperity. He concludes that "times must be good before people will accept change in order to make them better" (p. 52). One is left wondering how people dealing with poverty and a decreasing population could respond well to *anything*, assimilationist programs notwithstanding. Numbers may be seductive, but they are no more reliable than the written word. Statistics yield the best results when critical standards are upheld and when they are combined with other documents for reinforcement.

Uninformed dabbling can imperil quantitative measures taken and the interpretations drawn from them. Historians must acquaint themselves with the assumptions of statistical reasoning and develop the computing skills necessary to undertake this work. These prerequisites pose a formidable task. The mastery of more than rudimentary quantitative techniques requires a large outlay of time and energy, which can be a tall order for scholars who have already ranged widely to develop research skills appropriate to their subjects. Indian historians have explored linguistics, archaeology, anthropology, physical anthropology, ecological analysis, oral history, geography, and demography, among other disciplines, to get at the historical experiences of people who left few written records of their own. Perhaps this partially explains why they have shown such reluctance to branch into this new area of inquiry.

The requirements attending the reorientation of research advocated here are weighty, but the potential is too great to be ignored any longer. A conference at the Newberry Library in February 1987 provided a forum for beginning this process. The conference brought together quantifiers and potential quantifiers working in and outside of Indian history to encourage dialogue and dissemination of quantitative techniques throughout the field of American Indian history. Through such efforts, scholars of American Indian experiences can develop the framework to integrate their field into mainstream disciplines.[1]

References

1. *Annual Report of the Commissioner of Indian Affairs.* U.S. Congressional Serial Set. Washington, D.C.: Government Printing Office.
2. Aten, Lawrence E. 1983. *Indians of the Upper Texas Coast.* New York: Academic Press.
3. Barsh, Russell Lawrence, and Katherine Diaz-Knauf. 1984. "The Structure of Federal Aid for Indian Programs in the Decade of Prosperity, 1970–1980." *American Indian Quarterly* 8:1–35.
4. Bragdon, Kathleen Joan. 1981. "Crime and Punishment Among the Indians of Massachusetts, 1675–1750." *Ethnohistory* 28:23–32.
5. Broudy, David W., and Phillip A. May. 1983. "Demographic and Epidemiologic Transition Among the Navajo Indians.' *Social Biology* 30:1–16.
6. Buikstra, Jane E., ed. 1981. *Prehistoric Tuberculosis in the Americas.* Evanston, Ill.: Northwestern University Archaeological Program.
7. Carlson, Leonard A. 1981. *Indians, Bureaucrats, and Land: The*

[1] The authors gratefully acknowledge the research assistance of David L. Smith, the bibliographic assistance of Velma S. Salabiye of the American Indian Studies Center Library at UCLA, and the word processing assistance of Gloria DeWolfe of the Department of Sociology at the University of Minnesota.

Dawes Act and the Decline of Indian Farming. Westport, Conn.: Greenwood Press.

8. ———. 1981. "Land Allotment and the Decline of American Indian Farming." *Explorations in Economic History* 18:128–54.

9. ———. 1983. "Federal Policy and Indian Land: Economic Interests and the Sale of Indian Allotments, 1900–1934." *Agricultural History* 57:33–45.

10. Cleland, Charles E. 1982. "The Inland Shore Fishery of the Northern Great Lakes: Its Development and Importance in Prehistory." *American Antiquity* 47:761–84.

11. *Congressional Record.* Washington, D.C.: Government Printing Office.

12. Cook, Sherburne F., and Woodrow Borah. 1979. *Essays in Population History: Mexico and California.* Vol. 3. Berkeley: University of California Press.

13. Dobyns, Henry F. 1966. "Estimating Aboriginal American Population: An Appraisal of Techniques with a New Hemisphere Estimate." *Current Anthropology* 7:395–416.

14. ———. 1983. *Their Number Become Thinned: Native American Population Dynamics in Eastern North America.* With the assistance of William R. Swagerty. Knoxville: University of Tennessee Press.

15. ———. 1984. "Native American Population Collapse and Recovery." Pp. 17–35 in William R. Swagerty, ed., *Scholars and the Indian Experience.* Bloomington: University of Indiana Press.

16. Ericson, Jonathon E.; R. E. Taylor; and Rainer Berger, eds. 1982. *Peopling the New World.* Los Altos, Calif.: Ballena Press.

17. "Genealogical Records in the United States." Rev. 1977. Series B, no. 1. Salt Lake City, Utah: Genealogical Department, Church of Jesus Christ of Latter-day Saints.

18. Goodman, James M. 1982. *The Navajo Atlas.* Norman: University of Oklahoma Press.

19. Graves, Michael W. 1983. "Growth and Aggregation at Canyon Creek Ruin: Implications for Evolutionary Change in East-Central Arizona." *American Antiquity* 48:291–315.

20. Grinde, Donald A., Jr., and Quintard Taylor. 1984. "Red vs. Black: Conflict and Accommodation in the Post Civil War Indian Territory, 1865–1907." *American Indian Quarterly* 8:211–29.

21. Haan, Richard L. 1981. " 'The Trade Do's Not Flourish as Formerly': The Ecological Origins of the Yamassee War of 1715." *Ethnohistory* 28:341–58.

22. Helm, June. 1980. "Female Infanticide, European Disease, and Population Levels Among the Mackenzie Dene." *American Ethnologist* 7:259–85.

23. Henning, Elizabeth R. P. 1982. "Western Dakota Winter Counts: An Analysis of the Effects of Westward Migration and Culture Change." *Plains Anthropologist* 27:57–65.

24. Hill, Edward E. 1981. *Guide to Records of the National Archives of the United States Relating to American Indians.* Washington, D.C.: National Archives and Records Service, General Services Administration.

25. Hoxie, Frederick E. 1984. *A Final Promise: The Campaign to Assimilate the Indians, 1880–1920*. Lincoln: University of Nebraska Press.
26. Hurtado, Albert L. 1982. " 'Hardly a Farm House—A Kitchen Without Them': Indian and White Households on the California Borderland Frontier in 1860." *Western Historical Quarterly* 13:245–70.
27. ———. 1982. " 'Saved So Much as Possible for Labour': Indian Population and the New Helvetia Work Force." *American Indian Culture and Research Journal* 6:63–78.
28. Jackson, Robert H. 1983. "Causes of Indian Population Decline in the Pimería Alta Missions of Northern Sonora." *Journal of Arizona History* 24:405–29.
29. Jacobsen, R. Brooke, and Jeffrey L. Eighmey. 1980. "A Mathematical Theory of Horse Adoption on the North American Plains." *Plains Anthropologist* 25:333–41.
30. Jacobsen, Cardell K. 1984. "Internal Colonialism and Native Americans: Indian Labor in the United States from 1871 to World War II." *Social Science Quarterly* 65:158–71.
31. Jantz, Richard L., and Douglas H. Ubelaker, eds. 1981. "Progress in Skeletal Biology of Plains Populations." Part 2. *Plains Anthropologist (Memoir 17)* 26(94):1–106.
32. Johansson, S. Ryan. 1982. "The Demographic History of the Native Peoples of North America: A Selective Bibliography." *Yearbook of Physical Anthropology* 25:133–52.
33. ———, and S. H. Preston. 1978. "Tribal Demography: The Hopi and Navajo Population as Seen Through Manuscripts from the 1900 U.S. Census." *Social Science History* 3:1–33.
34. ———, and S. Horowitz. 1986. "Estimating Mortality in Skeletal Populations: The Influence of the Growth Rate on the Interpretation of Levels and Trends During the Transition to Agriculture." *American Journal of Physical Anthropology* 71:233–50.
35. Jorgensen, Joseph G.; Richard O. Clemmer; Ronald L. Little; Nancy J. Owens; and Lynn A. Robbins. 1978. *Native Americans and Energy Development*. Cambridge, Mass.: Anthropology Resource Center.
36. Kay, Jeanne. 1984. "The Fur Trade and Native American Population Growth." *Ethnohistory* 31:265–87.
37. Kneese, Allen V., and F. Lee Brown. 1981. *The Southwest Under Stress: National Resource Development Issues in a Regional Setting*. Baltimore, Md.: Johns Hopkins University Press.
38. Krech, Shepard, III. 1983. "The Influence of Disease and the Fur Trade on Arctic Drainage Lowlands Dene, 1800–1850." *Journal of Anthropological Research* 39:123–46.
39. Kunitz, Stephen J. 1983. *Disease Change and the Role of Medicine: The Navajo Experience*. Berkeley: University of California Press.
40. Lallo, John W., and Jerome C. Rose. 1979. "Patterns of Stress, Disease and Mortality in Two Prehistoric Populations from North America." *Journal of Human Evolution* 8:323–35.
41. ———, Jerome Carl Rose, and George J. Armelgos. 1980. "An Ecological Interpretation of Variation in Mortality Within Three Prehistoric

American Indian Populations from Dickson Mounds." Pp. 203–38 in David L. Browman, ed. *Early Native Americans: Prehistoric Demography, Economy, and Technology.* The Hague: Mouton Publishers.

42. Lehmer, Donald J. 1977. "Epidemics Among the Indians of the Upper Missouri." *Reprints in Anthropology* 8:105–11.
43. McBeth, Sally J. 1983. *Ethnic Identity and the Boarding School Experience of West Central Oklahoma American Indians.* Washington, D.C.: University of America Press.
44. McLoughlin, William G., and Walter H. Conser, Jr. 1977. "The Cherokees in Transition: A Statistical Analysis of the Federal Cherokee Census of 1835." *Journal of American History* 64:678–703.
45. Meister, Cary W. 1978. "The Misleading Nature of Data Obtained from the Bureau of the Census Subject Report on 1970 American Indian Population." *Indian Historian* 7:12–19.
46. ———. 1980. "Methods for Evaluating the Accuracy of Ethnohistorical Demographic Data on North American Indians: A Brief Assessment." *Ethnohistory* 27:153–68.
47. Meyer, Melissa L. 1982. "The Historical Demography of White Earth Indian Reservation: The 1900 U.S. Federal Manuscript Census Considered." *American Indian Culture and Research Journal* 6:29–62.
48. Milner, Clyde A., II. 1981. "Off the White Road: Seven Nebraska Indian Societies in the 1870s—A Statistical Analysis of Assimilation, Population and Prosperity." *Western Historical Quarterly* 12:37–52.
49. Mobley, Charles M. 1980. "Demographic Structure of Pecos Indians: A Model Based on Life Tables." *American Antiquity* 45:518–30.
50. Moore, John H. 1980. "Aboriginal Indian Residence Patterns Preserved in Censuses and Allotments." *Science* 207:201–202.
51. Nespor, Robert. 1980. "Spatial Dimensions of Southern Cheyenne Sociopolitical Organization Represented in Allotment Records of 1892: A Preliminary Analysis." *Papers in Anthropology* (Department of Anthropology, University of Oklahoma) 21:19–36.
52. Normandeau, Louise, and Victor Piche, eds. 1984. *Les Populations amerindiennes et inuit du Canada: Aperçu demographique.* Montreal: Les Presses de l'Université de Montréal.
53. Orser, Charles E., Jr. 1984. "Trade Good Flow in Arikara Villages: Expanding Ray's Middleman Hypothesis." *Plains Anthropologist* 29: 1–12.
54. ———, and Larry J. Zimmerman. 1984. "A Computer Simulation of Euro-American Trade Good Flow to the Arikara." *Plains Anthropologist* 29:199–209.
55. Osborn, Alan J. 1983. "Ecological Aspects of Equestrian Adaptations in Aboriginal North America." *American Anthropologist* 85:563–91.
56. Paredes, J. Anthony, and Kenneth J. Plante. 1982. "A Reexamination of Creek Indian Population Trends: 1738–1832." *American Indian Culture and Research Journal* 6:3–28.
57. Penny, Dori. 1980. "Demographic Contrasts Among Cheyenne Bands." *Papers in Anthropology* (Department of Anthropology, University of Oklahoma) 21:61–69.

58. Perreault, J.; L. Paquette; and M. V. George. 1985. *Population Projections of Registered Indians, 1982 to 1996*. Ottawa: Statistics Canada.
59. Perttula, Timothy K., and James E. Bruseth. 1983. "Early Caddoan Subsistence Strategies, Sabine River Basin, East Texas." *Plains Anthropologist* 28:9–21.
60. Petersen, William. 1975. "A Demographer's View of Prehistoric Demography." *Current Anthropology* 16:227–45.
61. Prucha, Francis Paul. 1984. *The Great Father: The United States Government and the American Indians*. 2 vols. Lincoln: University of Nebraska Press.
62. Ray, Arthur J., and Donald B. Freeman. 1978. *"Give Us Good Measure": An Economic Analysis of Relations Between the Indians and the Hudson's Bay Company Before 1763*. Toronto: University of Toronto Press.
63. Roth, Eric Abella. 1981. "Demography and Computer Simulation in Historic Village Population Reconstruction." *Journal of Anthropological Research* 3:279–301.
64. Ruff, Christopher B. 1981. "Reassessment of Demographic Estimates for Pecos Pueblo." *American Journal of Physical Anthropology* 54:147–51.
65. Shepardson, Mary. 1982. "The Status of Navajo Women." *American Indian Quarterly* 6:149–69.
66. Shipek, Florence C. 1981. "A Native American Adaptation to Drought: The Kumeyaay as Seen in the San Diego Mission Records 1770–1798." *Ethnohistory* 28:295–312.
67. Shkilnyk, Anastasia M. 1985. *A Poison Stronger Than Love: The Destruction of an Ojibwa Community*. New Haven, Conn.: Yale University Press.
68. Skinner, S. Alan. 1981. "Aboriginal Demographic Changes in Central Texas." *Plains Anthropologist* 26:111–18.
69. Spielmann, Katherine A. 1983. "Late Prehistoric Exchange Between the Southwest and Southern Plains." *Plains Anthropologist* 28:257–72.
70. Stuart, Paul. 1979. *The Indian Office: Growth and Development of an American Institution*. Ann Arbor, Mich.: UMI Research Press.
71. Swagerty, William R., and Russell Thornton. 1982. "Preliminary 1980 Census Counts for American Indians, Eskimos and Aleuts." *American Indian Culture and Research Journal* 6:92–93.
72. Swan, Daniel. 1980. "Spatial Patterns in Osage Homestead Selections: A Preliminary Analysis of the Relationship Between Band and Village in Osage Socio-Political History." *Papers in Anthropology* (Department of Anthropology, University of Oklahoma) 21:77–91.
73. Thomas, Peter A. 1981. "The Fur Trade, Indian Land and the Need to Define Adequate 'Environmental' Parameters." *Ethnohistory* 28:359–79.
74. Thornton, Russell. 1979. "American Indian Historical Demography: A Review Essay with Suggestions for Future Research." *American Indian Culture and Research Journal* 3:69–74.

75. ———. 1980. "Recent Estimates of the Prehistoric California Indian Population." *Current Anthropology* 21:702–704.
76. ———. 1981. "Demographic Antecedents of a Revitalization Movement: Population Change, Population Size, and the 1890 Ghost Dance." *American Sociological Review* 46:88–96.
77. ———. 1982. "Demographic Antecedents of Tribal Participation in the 1870 Ghost Dance Movement." *American Indian Culture and Research Journal* 6:79–91.
78. ———. 1984. "Cherokee Population Losses During the 'Trail of Tears': A New Perspective and a New Estimate." *Ethnohistory* 31: 289–300.
79. ———. 1984. "Social Organization and the Demographic Survival of the Tolowa." *Ethnohistory* 31:187–96.
80. ———. 1986. "History, Structure, and Survival: A Comparison of the Yuki (*Unkomno'n*) and Tolowa (*Hush*) Indians of Northern California." *Ethnology* 25:119–30.
81. ———. 1986. *We Shall Live Again: The 1870 and 1890 Ghost Dance Movements as Demographic Revitalization*. New York: Cambridge University Press.
82. ———. 1987. *American Indian Holocaust and Survival: A Population History Since 1492*. Norman: University of Oklahoma Press.
83. ———, and Joan Marsh-Thornton. 1981. "Estimating Prehistoric American Indian Population Size for United States Area: Implications of the Nineteenth Century Population Decline and Nadir." *American Journal of Physical Anthropology* 55:47–53.
84. Ubelaker, D. H., 1981. "Approaches to Demographic Problems in the Northeast." Pp. 175–94 in Dean R. Snow, ed., *Foundations of Northeast Archaeology*. New York: Academic Press.
85. ———, and P. Wiley. 1978. "Complexity in Arikara Mortuary Practice." *Plains Anthropologist* 23:69–74.
86. Upham, Steadman. 1986. "Smallpox and Climate in the American Southwest." *American Anthropologist* 88:115–28.
87. U.S. Bureau of the Census. 1892. *Indians: The Six Nations of New York. Extra Census Bulletin*. Washington, D.C.: U.S. Census Printing Office.
88. ———. 1892. *Indians. Eastern Band of Cherokees. Extra Census Bulletin*. Washington, D.C.: U.S. Census Printing Office.
89. ———. 1893. *Report on the Condition of 15 Pueblos of New Mexico in 1890. Extra Census Bulletin*. Washington, D.C.: U.S. Census Printing Office.
90. ———. 1893. *Moqui Pueblo Indians of Arizona and Pueblo Indians of New Mexico. Extra Census Bulletin*. Washington, D.C.: U.S. Census Printing Office.
91. ———. 1894. *Report on Indians Taxed and Indians Not Taxed in the United States (Except Alaska) at the Eleventh Census: 1890*. Washington, D.C.: U.S. Government Printing Office.
92. ———. 1894. *The Five Civilized Tribes in Indian Territory. Extra Census Bulletin*. Washington, D.C.: U.S. Government Printing Office.

93. ———. 1907. *Population of Oklahoma and Indian Territory: 1907.* Bulletin 89. Washington, D.C.: U.S. Government Printing Office.

94. ———. 1915. *Indian Population of the United States and Alaska, 1910.* Washington, D.C.: U.S. Government Printing Office.

95. ———. 1937. *The Indian Population of the United States and Alaska.* Washington, D.C.: U.S. Government Printing Office.

96. ———. 1973. *1970 Census of the Population. Subject Report. American Indians. Final Report PC (2)-IF.* Washington, D.C.: U.S. Government Printing Office.

97. Vaughan, Alden T., and Daniel K. Richter. 1980. "Crossing the Cultural Divide: Indians and New Englanders, 1605–1763." *Proceedings of the American Antiquarian Society* 90:23–99.

98. Vehik, Susan C. 1980. "The Osage Allotment: A Preliminary Analysis of Land Selection Patterns." *Papers in Anthropology* (Department of Anthropology, University of Oklahoma) 21:93–105.

99. Vlasich, James A. 1980. "Transitions in Pueblo Agriculture, 1938–1948." *New Mexico Historical Review* 55:25–46.

100.Waddell, Jack O. 1985. "Malhiot's Journal: An Ethnohistoric Assessment of Chippewa Alcohol Behavior in the Early 19th Century." *Ethnohistory* 32:246–68.

CHAPTER 2

American Indian Women: Reaching Beyond the Myth

DEBORAH WELCH

Perhaps no stereotype has been more pervasive and persistent than that applied to American Indian women. In film, fiction and history, Indian women have been portrayed in one-dimensional, inaccurate, and insulting terms, their roles in Native American society neglected and trivialized by an obsession with male warriors and chiefs. Changes for the better began in the sixties and gathered pace in the seventies, and Rayna Green's survey of the literature produced in that period showed that the study of Native American women was flowering by the early eighties.

Building on Green's Native American Women: A Contextual Bibliography *(Bloomington: Indiana University Press, 1983), Deborah Welch surveys the rich and growing field of literature about the history of Indian women. Much of this literature has come from the pens of female writers, and the advances they have made in a number of key areas contribute significantly to our better appreciation of the roles, experiences, and influences of American Indian women in their historical and cultural contexts. However, there are areas that remain to be examined, and Welch predicts that in the history of American Indian women the best writing may be still to come.*

Not long ago, a colleague commented that Indian women's history had truly flowered in the last decade, engaging the talents of a wide array of historians, anthropologists, sociologists, and feminist writers. While it is true that political and social developments over the past twenty years have spurred new and needed attention to all fields of minority studies, the flower is still in bud. The promise for the future is rich as current scholars, many of whom are at an age when their most productive years still lie ahead, are joined by growing numbers of younger colleagues. The next decade should indeed be a time for exciting new directions in the research and writing of Indian women's history. Equally important, we look forward to increased attention being paid to Indian women by all writers concerned with the American past as well as by faculty anxious to incorporate the new scholarship into their teaching.

Not all Indian women's history has been the product of recent years, of course. As Rayna Green, a leading writer in Indian women's studies, has observed, "My review of the literature has left me with the conviction that Native American women have neither been neglected nor forgotten. They have captured hearts and minds, but . . . the level and substance of most passion for them has been selective, stereotyped, and damaging" [32]. Recent scholars have assumed the burden of correcting those stereotypes and emphasizing the important role Indian women have played and continue to play as members of enduring cultures. Modern writers also urge us forward in new directions of research and study, further enriching our understanding of this field.

This chapter provides a review of that current scholarship with consideration given to the context of the past. Also included is an overview of available books and articles designed for use by writers and teachers seeking referral to general works and specific topics in the history of American Indian women. While space constraints have limited the number of works considered here, every effort has been made to cite studies which include excellent bibliographies.

Six areas are considered here. The first, biography and autobiography of American Indian women, examines one of the earliest forms of study and an approach still used by historians, including this one. Early biographies which concentrated on the Indian heroine—Pocahontas, Sakakawia (Sacajawea)—led naturally to studies on the role of these women in American westward expansion, with particular emphasis on American Indian women and the fur trade.

The growth, early in this century, of anthropological study of Indian women within their traditional tribal cultures focused attention on women's cultural roles. Ranging from the early "custom" studies, which appeared to confine Indian women's concerns to the "three

Ms" (menstruation, marriage, and maternity rituals), to new studies
on the importance of women to tribal organization and cultural continuity, this category includes numerous studies and is therefore one
of the largest considered here.

The work of American Indian women writers offers one of the
richest resources for information. The most current literature by and
about Indian women writers is reviewed in section four. The fifth
category reviews current scholarship dealing with Indian women's
leadership on tribal and national levels. Finally, this chapter will
consider new directions in Indian women's history before turning to
an overview of general and bibliographic works currently available
to scholars in section six.

Biography and Autobiography

Some of the earliest literature on Native American women appeared
as biographies of Indian heroines (defined by their right-thinking al-
legiance to Anglo western heroes). The Pocahontas and Sakakawia
myths are an important component of American history and have
been popularized, trivialized, and debated in countless studies [8,
31, 33]. The work of Flora Warren Seymour, western historian and
first woman member of the Board of Indian Commissioners, presents a useful example of this sexual stereotyping. In her biographical series, written primarily for young readers in the 1930s and '40s,
all of the western heroes are Anglo (Kit Carson, John Frémont,
Meriwether Lewis), while her heroines are Indian (Sakakawia, Pocahontas) [65, 66]. Two modern studies which do a good job of eradi-
cating these earlier biases and present well-researched analyses of
these women's place in history are Philip L. Barbour's *Pocahontas
and Her World* [12] and Ella Elizabeth Clark and Margot Edmonds's
Sacajawea of the Lewis and Clark Expedition [26].

In the last two decades, Indian women, especially those who made
their deeds known and voices heard in Anglo society, have continued
to attract biographers. Studies of Indian women leaders are discussed
in section five, but Indian women have also made their mark by their
artistic achievements.

In *This Song Remembers: Self Portraits of Native Americans in
the Arts* [43], Jane B. Katz offers a biographical compilation, drawn
primarily from oral interviews, of the work of twenty-one Indian
artists, including Laguna author and poet Leslie Silko and Navajo

weaver Pearl Sunrise. Similarly, Jamake Highwater's *The Sweet Grass Lives On* [38] examines the work of fifty artists. Both books are well illustrated, though Katz's photos are limited to black and white prints.

Historians' and anthropologists' fascination with Indian art forms and artists like Pueblo potter Maria Martinez and Inuit Pitseolak arose rapidly in the 1920s and continues today. Susan Peterson's *The Living Tradition of Maria Martinez* [54] offers an in-depth look at the contribution of Martinez to art and Pueblo society. Pitseolak's *Pictures Out of My Life* [57] is a beautifully illustrated autobiography of the Inuit artist's life and work.

Pitseolak's book, published in 1971, was among the first of a series of autobiographies of Indian women which greatly enhances our understanding of women's lives and concerns. Maria Campbell's *The Half-Breed* [23] struggles with questions of identity and conflicts between the Indian and Anglo world of Elizabeth Qoyawayma. Polingaysi's *No Turning Back* [58] offers an especially moving account of the effect of the modern Anglo world and Christianity upon the lives of the Hopis she describes. Elizabeth Colson's *Autobiographies of Three Pomo Women* [27] and Irene Stewart's *A Voice in Her Tribe: A Navajo Woman's Own Story* [70] are valuable additions to our autobiography resources.

Finally, no review of the available resources in autobiographical literature would be complete without mention of Nancy Lurie's classic account, *Mountain Wolf Woman* [46], still among the finest narratives in Indian women's history.

American Indian Women and the Fur Trade

Early preoccupation with the American Indian heroine and the conquering Western hero naturally focused historical attention on the fur trade of the eighteenth and early nineteenth century. Again, much of the early writing deals with the myth and reality of Sakakawia [65] of the Lewis and Clark Expedition and Madame Dorion, friend to the Astorians [13]. These biased studies, based almost wholly on male accounts, entrenched a shallow and denigrating stereotype of Indian women which was reproduced, but rarely reexamined, in much of the literature which followed, even in the 1960s and 1970s. Fortunately there have appeared over the last five years a number of studies which seek to correct longstanding misconceptions. One of the best monographs currently available is Jennifer S. H. Brown's *Strangers in Blood: Fur Trade Families in Indian Country* [22], which emphasizes the economic and familiar relations established between American Indian women and British and French fur traders. In her 1985 essay, "Commodity, Exchange and Subordination: Montagnais-Naskapi and Huron Women, 1600–1650" [7], Karen Anderson focuses on the role of Montagnais-Naskapi and Huron women, whose seventeenth-century northeastern communities acted as intermediaries in the French fur trade. Anderson disputes earlier theories that it was the advent of the fur trade (that is, growing Indian involvement in commodity production) which eradicated traditional gender equality in Native American societies and brought about male dominance. As a case study, she contrasts the Huron and Montagnais-Naskapi experiences. Both groups were deeply involved in the fur trade, and both were proselytized by Jesuit missionaries. Yet while Montagnais-Naskapi women were compelled to assume subordinate roles, Huron women preserved their independence because they retained access to the benefits of trade and because a gender-specific as well as kinship-based societal organization survived.

Jacqueline Peterson's 1981 dissertation, "The People in Between: Indian-White Marriage and the Generation of a Métis Society and Culture in the Great Lakes Region, 1680–1830" [53], offers an in-depth look at the lives of Indian women who married Anglo-European trappers and the subsequent rise of a new generation of mixed-blood children. The sex roles assigned and assumed by mixed-blood women is the primary focus of Sylvia Van Kirk's *Many Tender Ties: Women in Fur-Trade Society, 1670–1870* [74]. Van Kirk brings a detailed research into primary and secondary sources to an examination of the alliances formed between Indian women and Anglo-European traders specifically in western Canada. Van Kirk deals with important issues encountered especially by the mixed-blood female offspring of these "country marriages" who lost their cultural heritage and much of their independence as the nineteenth century progressed. The advance of the Anglo-American frontier brought new threats of displacement from these women's important roles as producers and trade negotiators as well as the racism of an encroaching Anglo society which could muster only contempt for women of mixed blood.

Women's Cultural Roles

A welcome shift in Indian women's history from a concentration on
the Indian princess/saint/heroine of early biographical material occurred in the first decade of this century when scholars, primarily
anthropologists, undertook a series of studies dealing with Indian
women's menstrual, marriage, and child-rearing rituals and traditions. Many of these early studies may frustrate modern readers
through their narrow preoccupation with rituals surrounding women's
bodies to the exclusion of any consideration of women's other concerns. Nonetheless, they played an important role in establishing
the importance of viewing Indian women in the context of their different cultures.

Many of the biases which marred earlier studies of female ceremonies and customs have been corrected by modern scholars. A
good example is Marla N. Powers's 1980 article, "Menstruation and
Reproduction: An Oglala Case" [59]. Powers demonstrates how female puberty ceremonies and menstrual "taboos" are more accurately viewed as symbols celebrating the importance of the female
reproductive role rather than as signs of women's defilement. Powers's new book, *Oglala Women: Myth, Ritual and Reality* [60], analyzes the role of women in past and present Oglala society. In the
first part of the book she describes in detail traditional Oglala attitudes towards marriage, childbearing, and kinship, analyzes the
complementary nature of relationships and the division of labor between men and women, and portrays "the mythic superiority of
womanhood" in the early Oglala cosmology.

Another area of interest which first appeared in this century and
continues in modern scholarship deals with cross-sexual roles and
the acceptance of transvestite behavior among many Indian peoples.
Sue-Ellen Jacobs provides an overview of existing studies in her
1977 article "Berdache: A Brief Review of the Literature" [41].
Paula Gunn Allen discusses the role traditionally reserved for cross-
sexual females in "Beloved Women: Lesbians in American Indian
Culture" [1]. In her 1984 article, "Sexuality and Gender in Certain
Native American Tribes: The Case of Cross-Gender Females," Evelyn Blackwood also takes to task earlier anthropological studies
which explained the berdache as a mixed sexual role. Blackwood
insists that the physical identity of the berdache remained unchanged
in the eyes of her community, therefore enabling many tribal groups

to accept these women in terms of the social responsibilities they assumed [17]. Blackwood agrees that the impact of Anglo society led to the demise of the cross-sexual role. The first full-length study of the berdache tradition, Walter L. Williams's *The Spirit and the Flesh*, has recently been published [77].

A rapidly growing body of literature dealing with the lives and concerns of modern Indian women has emerged in recent years. The first issue of the *American Indian Quarterly* in 1982 was devoted to articles about Navajo women. This issue is especially commendable for its efforts to include essays on women in a wide variety of circumstances and endeavors. The problems of urban women and relocation away from the reservation are examined in "Navajo Women in the City: Lessons from a Quarter-Century of Relocation," by Ann Metcalf, and in Joyce Griffen's "Life is Harder Here: The Case of the Urban Navajo Women." Reservation life and women's roles are described in "Ladies, Livestock, Land and Lucre: Women's Networks and Social Status on the Western Navajo Reservation," by Christine Conte; "The Status of Navajo Women," by Mary Shepardson; and Nancy J. Parego's "Navajo Sandpaintings: The Importance of Sex Roles in Craft Production." Other articles and poems enhance this very fine issue [52]. The second half of Powers's *Oglala Women* [60] examines how Oglala women have adjusted to changed circumstances and suggests that they have adapted to the modern world with far greater success than have Oglala men.

The changing roles of American Indian women as examined through autobiographies and narrative resources are the subject of Gretchen M. Bataille and Kathleen Mullen Sands's *American Indian Women: Telling Their Lives* [15]. In addition to presenting these women's narratives, the authors demonstrate varying techniques of employing oral history and provide an extensive annotated bibliography.

Janet A. McDonnell examines the impact of late-nineteenth-century acculturation policies on traditional female work and responsibility in "Sioux Women: A Photographic Essay" [48]. McDonnell's narrative is highlighted by a wonderful collection of photographs from the late nineteenth and early twentieth centuries. The article's look at Sioux women adds a new resource to a field sometimes overly concerned with southwestern and northeastern Indian women.

Another useful resource in the study of women's roles and the impact of Anglo expansion on traditionally accepted gender models is a collection of essays in Patricia Albers and Beatrice Medicine's *The Hidden Half: Studies of Plains Indian Women* [5]. Like Karen Anderson [7], Albers uses a case study to examine government attempts to subordinate the role of women and create new male-dominated societies. Medicine's essay brings renewed attention to the subject of sex role alternatives among Plains Indian women. She concludes that cross-sexual females were accepted by tribal communities before the imposition of Anglo societal mores.

Albers and Medicine, like Bataille and Sands, have devoted a good deal of their energies and writings to providing needed correction to previously biased accounts of the traditional role of Indian women. Beth Brant also labors to dispel old stereotypes in her book, *A Gathering of Spirit* [21]. Brant draws upon narratives, poetry, letters, photographs, and art to present a wide range of modern Indian women's views. The evidence collected here is convincing testimony to the importance of Indian women as sources of cultural continuity and strength.

Indian Women's Literature

Nowhere is the importance of women to cultural continuity more strongly and movingly expressed than in the poems, stories, and novels of modern Indian women writers. Fortunately, a number of outstanding works are now in print, and I urge all students seeking an orientation to the field of Indian women's history to begin with these writers.

One of the earliest female activists who published stories about the Indian past and her early life as a young Sioux girl during a time of rapid transition for Indian peoples is Gertrude Bonnin, or Zitkala-Sa. Taken from her mother's home on the South Dakota Yankton reserve at age eight, Zitkala-Sa received her advanced education at Earlham College in Richmond, Indiana. A talented poet and writer, Zitkala-Sa sought to educate Anglo America on the value of American Indian culture through a series of short stories, most of which were printed in *The Atlantic Monthly* and other leading magazines of turn-of-the-century America. Many of these stories were subsequently gathered for publication in two books, *American Indian Stories* [19] and *Old Indian Legends* [18]. Fortunately both books were reprinted by the University of Nebraska Press in 1985.

An excellent review to acquaint interested readers with contemporary themes in Indian literature is contained in Paula Gunn Allen's article, "The Grace That Remains: American Indian Women's Literature" [2]. Elaine Jahner's study of Paula Gunn Allen, David Remley's analysis of the Sakakawia literature, and Caren J. Deming's essay on miscegenation are contained in *Women and Western American Literature* [69]. Michael Castro's *Interpreting the Indian: Twentieth-Century Poets and the Native American* looks at the work of Indian and non-Indian writers of Native American literature [25]. Alan R. Velie's book, *Four American Indian Literary Masters* [75], provides a useful introduction to the work of Laguna poet and writer Leslie Marmon Silko, together with that of N. Scott Momaday, James Welch, and Gerald Vizenor. Silko's work, along with that of other Indian women writers, is also discussed in Dexter Fisher's *The Third Women: Minority Women Writers of the United States* [28]. Kenneth Rosen's *The Man to Send Rain Clouds: Contemporary Stories by American Indians* [62] is another good source for modern poetry and short stories. Silko's novel, *Ceremony*, should be read by all students of American Indian peoples [67].

Unlike Zitkala-Sa, who wrote for an Anglo reading public in the early 1900s, modern Indian women writers also labor to enhance Indians' understanding of themselves. In "Answering the Deer," Paula Gunn Allen analyzes the work of current writers whose contemporary themes nonetheless bear the mark of past history: "The impact of genocide in the minds of American Indian poets and writers cannot be exaggerated. It is an all-pervasive feature of the consciousness of every American Indian . . ." [3].

An intriguing selection of the poems and stories of American Indian women writers is offered in Rayna Green's *That's What She Said: Contemporary Poetry and Fiction by Native American Women* [34]. Aside from an introduction, Green allows the eloquence of the works to speak for themselves. Included there are the writings of Paula Gunn Allen (Laguna/Sioux/Lebanese), Diane Burns (Chemehuevi/Ojibwa), Gladys Cardiff (Eastern Cherokee), Charlotte de Clue (Osage), Nora Dauenhauer (Tlingit), Louise Erdrich (Turtle Mountain Chippewa), Rayna Green (Cherokee), Joy Harjo (Creek), Linda Hogan (Chickasaw), Wendy Rose (Hopi/Miwok), Carol Lee Sanches (Laguna Pueblo/Sioux), Jaune Quick-to-see-Smith (Salish-Kootenai), Mary TallMountain (Athabaskan), Judith Mountain Leaf

Volborth (Apache/Comanche), Annette Arkeketa West (Oto-Creek), Roberta Hill Whiteman (Oneida), and Shirley Hill Witt (Tuscarora).

Paula Gunn Allen's most recent publication, *The Sacred Hoop* [4], ties together a number of her essays to produce a strong and unyielding demand for the recognition of American Indian women and the continuity of their roles in tribal cultures. Allen's book provides one of the strongest resources now available to debunk the old stereotypes of Indian women.

American Indian Women Leaders

A renewed interest in women's leadership on both the tribal and national levels is one of the exciting new directions in Indian women's history. The articulate Omaha LaFlesche family, in particular physician and activist Susan LaFlesche, have been the focus of many studies. Norma Kidd Green's article, "Four Sisters: The Daughters of Joseph LaFlesche" [29], as well as her book, *Iron Eye's Family: The Children of Joseph LaFlesche* [30], are still among the most widely used sources. Some isolated studies specifically examining tribal women's leadership roles, such as Leslie Scott's article on female tribal councilors [63] and Robert Anderson's "The Northern Cheyenne War Mothers" [9], appeared in the 1940s and the 1950s. However, only in the last ten years has a steady stream of books and articles appeared offering individual and tribal studies of women's power.

Laurence Hauptman's "Alice Jemison: Seneca Political Activist" [36] turned historical attention to Indian women active on the national level and continues to prompt new research into the lives of twentieth-century Indian women leaders. This well-researched study explores Jemison's opposition to John Collier and reveals the scurrilous tactics used by John Collier to silence Jemison. Kenneth Philp's revisionist study of Collier also provides a long-needed correction to the slander perpetuated against Jemison [56].

L. G. Moses and Raymond Wilson's *Indian Lives: Essays on 19th and 20th Century Native American Leaders* includes essays on four prominent women [50]. Laurence Hauptmann examines the life of Iroquois Minnie Kellog, H. A. Vernon discusses Marie Bryant Pierce, Ronald McCoy studies Nampeyo, and Valerie Sherer Mathews writes on Susan LaFlesche Picotte.

The 1979 American Ethnological Society annual meeting included a session on Native American political organization which addressed women's roles [73]. Helen Tanner's "Coocoochee, Mohawk Medicine Woman" examines the important role of the medicine women within historical tribal societies [72].

Robert Lynch presents a contemporary view of the women's leadership of a tribal council as it existed on the Nevada Northern Paiute reserve in the late 1960s in "Women in Northern Paiute Politics" [47]. This case study of the Brownsville Indian community, where for one year the tribal council was composed entirely of women, offers new insight into tribal politics as well as a blatant example of a government agent's resistance to women's ascendancy. Another very good resource for students of contemporary leadership is Irene Stewart's autobiographical account, *A Voice in Her Tribe: A Navajo Woman's Own Story* [70]. Finally, Clara Sue Kidwell's article, "The Power of Women in Three American Indian Societies" [44], explores the avenues to power traditionally available to Indian women in three case studies. Marla Powers's *Oglala Women* [60] illustrates the important roles played by women as professionals and community leaders at Pine Ridge. Taken together, these studies provide a long overdue recognition of Indian women's tribal leadership.

Gae Whitney Canfield's biography of Sarah Winnemucca [24] presents new insights into the life and leadership of the famous Northern Paiute activist reformer. Hazel Hertzberg's pathbreaking study, *The Search for an American Indian Identity* [37], contains a good deal of information on the important roles assumed by a number of Indian women active in twentieth-century pan-Indian movement, especially the Society of American Indians. My own study of Yankton Sioux author and activist Gertrude Bonnin (Zitkala-Sa), secretary of the SAI and editor of its quarterly journal, *The Amerian Indian Magazine*, explores Bonnin's leadership on both the national and tribal levels [76].

The leadership of American Indian women is but one aspect of the subject that promises a number of interesting works in the future. Other avenues of new research include a fresh look at Indian women's education. Margaret Szasz explores eighteenth-century instruction in " 'Poor Richard' Meets the Native American: Schooling for Young Indian Women in Eighteenth-Century Connecticut" [71]. Contemporary educational opportunities and problems facing young Indians are discussed in Ethel Krepps's "Equality in Education for Indian Women" [45].

James Axtell's *The Indian Peoples of Eastern America: A Documentary History of the Sexes* [10] provides a good overview of Anglo/European views of Indian women and men. Interaction between Indian and Anglo peoples on the frontier and the changing Anglo perceptions of Indian peoples which resulted from contact has been the focus of two recent works, Glenda Riley's *Women and Indians on the Frontier, 1825–1915* [61] and Sherry Smith's dissertation study of army officers' reflections on Indians in the trans-Mississippi west [68]. Both examine the preconceptions of Indians brought to the frontier by Anglo men and women and how those attitudes and their subsequent behavior changed. Both authors provide a rich collection of memoirs and experiences which document the establishment of relationships and sympathy between Indian and Anglo individuals. Finally, both Smith and Riley address the issue of how Anglo women's increased understanding of Indian women influenced their attitudes toward themselves. Smith goes further and examines the changes in Anglo male perceptions of both Indian and Anglo women. Riley, on the other hand, insists that while Anglo women's views were modified by their frontier experiences, Anglo men remained far more hostile and unchanged in their original biases.

Contemporary research into the role of Anglo women who lived and worked on reservations in the late nineteenth and early twentieth centuries also adds to our resources on women's and Indian history. In "'Holy Women' and Housekeepers: Women and Teachers on South Dakota Reservations, 1885–1906," Susan Peterson examines the work of women who attempted to innundate Sioux society with Anglo middle-class cultural values [55]. Similarly, the appointment of Indian Service field matrons to the reservations was warmly endorsed by reformers of the late nineteenth and early twentieth centuries as an important step toward breaking the roles of Indian women as agents of cultural continuity. Instead, Anglo women would instill acceptable character and virtues in their Indian female charges. The work of these field matrons between 1891 and the 1930s is examined in Helen Bannan's *"True Womanhood" on the Reservation: Field Matrons in the United States Indian Service* [11].

Finally, Beatrice Medicine offers a review of past historical and anthropological approaches to Indian women's history and suggests new directions in *The Native American Woman: A Perspective* [49]. Alison Bernstein also reviews past historical stereotyping as well as

current studies and calls for new approaches in "Outgrowing Pocahontas: Toward a New History of Indian Women" [16].

Overviews and Suggested Biographies

The Medicine and Bernstein essays provide useful citations of studies in Indian women's history past and present. Gretchen Bataille's
bibliographic essay in *Concerns* offers additional sources [14]. Linda
Hogan has compiled a collection of writings by both Indian and non-
Indian women in a 1982 special issue of *Frontiers* containing poems,
stories, and a discussion of current issues [39].

A good resource for secondary school instruction in precontact Indian women's history is "Native American Women in Pre-
Columbian America" in *U.S. History* [51]. Short biographies of
noted Indian women are contained in Marion Gridley's reprinted *Indians of Today* series from the 1930s and 1940s [35]. Other useful
biographical sources include Edward T. James's edition, *Notable
American Women, 1607–1950* [42] and annual issues of *American
Women: The Official Who's Who Among the Women of the Nation* [6].

The leading bibliographer of Indian women is Rayna Green. Her
1980 article, "Native American Women: A Review Essay" provides
a chronological discussion of Indian women's studies including both
the good and the bad [32]. Green's *Native American Women: A Contextual Bibliography* [33] is an invaluable resource containing almost
seven hundred citations of available studies succinctly annotated in
Green's enjoyably straightforward style.

Conclusion

As this essay indicates, some of the best modern scholarship about
women is being carried forward by women, Indian and non-Indian.
Equally obvious is the conclusion that studies in Indian women's history, past and present, have been primarily the work of anthropologists, sociologists, and scholars of literature. Only recently have
growing numbers of historians assumed responsibility for research
and writing in this field. This apparent gap is not surprising, given
the sparseness of written evidence, particularly before the twentieth century. Few historians will venture forth without a paper trail
to follow.

The simultaneous advance of women's history and an increasing interest in twentieth-century Indian history has prompted fresh attention to the resources available on twentieth-century Indian women. Contemporary biographies on Indian male leaders like Peter Iverson's *Carlos Montezuma and the Changing World of American Indians* [40] and Raymond Wilson's *Ohiyesa: Charles Eastman, Santee Sioux* [78] are excellent examples of an increasing awareness among historians that Indian history did not end at Wounded Knee. Moreover, Iverson and Wilson's studies suggest both sources and an approach to materials which can be adapted with equal effectiveness to twentieth-century Indian women's leadership roles.

The records of congressional hearings on Indian questions, journals, correspondence, and pamphlets of twentieth-century pan-Indian organizations; agency files; and the Bureau of Indian Affairs records housed in the National Archives are just a few examples of the available and sizeable resources we have not yet begun to explore fully for the information they contain on women. The exciting lives of Indian women important to modern history, such as Dora B. Mc-Cauley, Alice H. Denomie, Nora McFarland, Emma Johnson Goulette, and Margaret Frazier, compel our attention. We need more information on the roles played by women such as Chippewa Marie Baldwin, one of the first two Indian female attorneys in the United States. Baldwin's early feminist activities must attract the interest of feminist historians keeping in mind that most, if not all, Indian women subordinated questions of their status as women to the larger context of their place and responsibilities as Indians. Nonetheless, the lives of these twentieth-century Indian women raise intriguing questions about the views of themselves and their relationships with each other. Did they transcend tribal boundaries to recognize and act upon a sisterhood of common interests and concerns? How did their traditional heritage and the impact of Anglo assimilationist policies combine to shape the roles these women chose (or were compelled) to play both in inter- and intratribal settings?

These questions are only one example of the many opportunities for research which will be pursued in the years ahead. Already, modern contributions to the field provide clear evidence that all aspects of Indian history, like Anglo history, are incomplete without careful attention to the roles and contributions of women. While early-twentieth-century Anglo observers were busy documenting the demise of Indian peoples, Native Americans continued to survive as Indians. Women worked in numerous roles, using different means to ensure cultural continuity. Contemporary Indian voices acknowledge this central strength and responsibility of women, as is made clear in the writings of Paula Gunn Allen, Rayna Green, Leslie Silko, and, finally, Anna Lee Walters:

> *Listen my sons! Listen to a song for life.*
> *The words are good. The song is old.*
> *Hear me now! Inside each of you, there*
> *beats a drum. Drums that are never silent. . . .*
>
> *I wish that your grandmothers could see*
> *you now. I wish they could reach out and*
> *touch you. For they were the ones who*
> *gave their drums to you.* [1]

References

1. Allen, Paula Gunn. 1981. "Beloved Women: Lesbians in American Indian Culture." *Conditions* 7:67–87.
2. ———. 1981. "The Grace That Remains: American Indian Women's Literature." *Book Forum* (Special Issue on American Indians Today) 13:376–83.
3. ———. 1982. "Answering the Deer." *American Indian Culture and Research Journal* 6(3): 35–45.
4. ———. 1986. *The Sacred Hoop: Recovering the Feminine in American Indian Traditions.* Boston: Beacon Press.
5. Albers, Patricia, and Beatrice Medicine, eds. 1983. *The Hidden Half: Studies of Plains Indian Women.* Lanham, Md.: University Press of America.
6. *American Women: The Official Who's Who Among the Women of the Nation.* Los Angeles: Richard Blank Publishing Co.
7. Anderson, Karen. 1985. "Commodity Exchange and Subordination: Montagnais-Naskapi and Huron Women, 1600–1650." *Signs: Journal of Women in Culture and Society* 11(1):48–62.
8. Anderson, Marilyn. 1979. "The Pocahontas Legend." *Indian Historian* 12(2):54–64.
9. Anderson, Robert. 1956. "The Northern Cheyenne War Mothers." *Anthropological Quarterly* 29(3):82–90.
10. Axtell, James, ed. 1981. *The Indian Peoples of Eastern America: A Documentary History of the Sexes.* New York: Oxford University Press.
11. Bannan, Helen. 1984. *"True Womanhood" on the Reservation: Field Matrons in the United States Indian Service.* Working Paper no. 18. Southwestern Institute for Research on Women, University of Arizona.

[1] Anna Lee Walters, "Come, My Sons," *The Man to Send Rain Clouds: Contemporary Stories by American Indians,* ed. Kenneth Rosen (New York: Vintage Books, 1975), pp. 15–26.

12. Barbour, Philip L. 1970. *Pocahontas and Her World*. New York: Houghton Mifflin.
13. Barry, J. Neilson. 1929. "Madame Dorion of the Astorians." *Oregon Historical Quarterly*, September.
14. Bataille, Gretchen. 1980. "Bibliography on Native American Women." *Concerns* (Summer): 16–27.
15. ———, and Kathleen Mullen Sands. 1984. *American Indian Women: Telling Their Lives*. Lincoln: University of Nebraska Press.
16. Bernstein, Alison R. 1981. "Outgrowing Pocahontas: Toward a New History of Indian Women." *Minority Notes* (Spring–Summer): 3–8.
17. Blackwood, Evelyn. 1984. "Sexuality and Gender in Certain Native American Tribes: The Case of Cross-Gender Females." *Signs: Journal of Women in Culture and Society* 10:27–42.
18. Bonnin, Gertrude Simmons [Zitkala-Sa]. 1901. *Old Indian Legends*. Boston: Ginn & Company.
19. ———. 1921. *American Indian Stories*. Glorieta, N. Mex.: The Rio Grande Press.
20. ———, Charles A. Fabens, and Mathew K. Sniffen. 1924. *Oklahoma's Poor Rich Indians*. Philadelphia: The Indian Rights Association.
21. Brant, Beth, ed. 1984. *A Gathering of Spirit: Writing and Art by North American Indian Women*. Rockland, Maine: Sinister Wisdom Books.
22. Brown, Jennifer S. H. 1981. *Strangers in Blood: Fur Trade Families in Indian Country*. Vancouver: University of British Columbia Press.
23. Campbell, Maria. 1973. *The Half-Breed*. Toronto: McClelland and Stewart.
24. Canfield, Gae Whitney. 1983. *Sarah Winnemucca of the Northern Paiutes*. Norman: University of Oklahoma Press.
25. Castro, Michael. 1983. *Interpreting the Indian: Twentieth-Century Poets and the Native American*. Albuquerque: University of New Mexico Press.
26. Clark, Ella Elizabeth, and Margot Edmonds. 1980. *Sacajawea of the Lewis and Clark Expedition*. Berkeley: University of California Press.
27. Colson, Elizabeth, ed. 1974. *Autobiographies of Three Pomo Women*. Berkeley: University of California Press.
28. Fisher, Dexter, ed. 1980. *The Third Women: Minority Women Writers of the United States*. Boston: Houghton-Mifflin Co.
29. Green, Norma Kidd. 1964. "Four Sisters: Daughters of Joseph LaFlesche." *Nebraska History* 45 (June): 165–76.
30. ———. 1969. *Iron Eye's Family: The Children of Joseph LaFlesche*. Lincoln: University of Nebraska Press.
31. Green, Rayna. 1975. "The Pocahontas Perplex: The Image of Indian Women in American Culture." *Massachusetts Review* 16 (4):698–714.
32. ———. 1980. "Native American Women: A Review Essay." *Signs: Journal of Women in Culture and Society* 6:248–68.
33. ———. 1983. *Native American Women: A Contextual Bibliography*. Bloomington: Indiana University Press.
34. ———. 1984. *That's What She Said: Contemporary Poetry and Fiction by Native American Women*. Bloomington: Indiana University Press.

35. Gridley, Marion, comp. 1974. *American Indian Women*. New York: Hawthorne Books.
36. Hauptman, Laurence. 1979. "Alice Jemison: Seneca Political Activist," *Indian Historian* 12(2):15–40.
37. Hertzberg, Hazel W. 1971. *The Search for an American Indian Identity: Modern Pan-Indian Movements*. Syracuse: Syracuse University Press.
38. Highwater, Jamake. 1980. *The Sweet Grass Lives On: Fifty Contemporary North American Indian Artists*. New York: Lippincott and Crowell.
39. Hogan, Linda, ed. 1982. *Frontiers*. Special Issue on Native American Women 6(2).
40. Iverson, Peter. 1982. *Carlos Montezuma and the Changing World of American Indians*. Albuquerque: University of New Mexico Press.
41. Jacobs, Sue-Ellen. 1977. "Berdache: A Brief Review of the Literature." *Colorado Anthropology* 1:25–40.
42. James, Edward T., ed. 1971. *Notable American Women 1607–1950*. 3 vols. Cambridge: Harvard University Press.
43. Katz, Jane B., ed. 1980. *This Song Remembers: Self Portraits of Native Americans in the Arts*. Boston: Houghton Mifflin Co.
44. Kidwell, Clara Sue. 1979. "The Power of Women in Three American Indian Societies." *Journal of Ethnic Studies* 6(3):113–21.
45. Krepps, Ethel. 1980. "Equality in Education for Indian Women." *Indian Historian [Wassaja]* 13(2):8–9.
46. Lurie, Nancy, ed. 1961. *Mountain Wolf Woman, Sister of Crashing Thunder, a Winnebago Indian*. Ann Arbor: University of Michigan Press.
47. Lynch, Robert N. 1986. "Women in Northern Paiute Politics." *Signs: Journal of Women in Culture and Society* 11(2):352–66.
48. McDonnell, Janet A. 1983. "Sioux Women: A Photographic Essay," *South Dakota History* 13(3) (Fall):227–44.
49. Medicine, Beatrice. 1978. *The Native American Woman: A Perspective*. Albuquerque: ERIC/CRESS.
50. Moses, L. G., and Raymond Wilson, eds. 1985. *Indian Lives: Essays on Nineteenth and Twentieth Century Native American Leaders*. Albuquerque: University of New Mexico Press.
51. "Native American Women in Pre-Columbia America." 1980. *US History: Teacher Guide and Student Book*. Newton, Mass.: WEEA Publishing Center.
52. "Navajo Women." 1982. *American Indian Quarterly*. Special Issue.
53. Peterson, Jacqueline L. 1981. "The People In Between: Indian-White Marriage and the Generation of a Métis Society and Culture in the Great Lakes Region, 1680–1830." Ph.D. diss., University of Illinois.
54. Peterson, Susan. 1977. *The Living Tradition of Maria Martinez*. Tokyo: Kodanska International.
55. ———. 1983. "'Holy Women' and Housekeepers: Women Teachers on South Dakota Reservations, 1885–1906." *South Dakota History* 13 (Fall):245–60.

56. Philp, Kenneth. 1977. *John Collier's Crusade for Indian Reform, 1920–1954*. Tucson: University of Arizona Press.
57. Pitseolak. 1971. *Pictures Out of My Life*. New York: Oxford University Press.
58. Polingaysi, Qoyawayma. 1977. *No Turning Back*. Albuquerque: University of New Mexico Press.
59. Powers, Marla N. 1980. "Menstruation and Reproduction: An Oglala Case." *Signs: Journal of Women in Culture and Society* 6(1):54–65.
60. ———. 1986. *Oglala Women: Myth, Ritual and Reality*. Chicago: University of Chicago Press.
61. Riley, Glenda. 1984. *Women and Indians on the Frontier, 1825–1915*. Albuquerque: University of New Mexico.
62. Rosen, Kenneth, ed. 1975. *The Man to Send Rain Clouds: Contemporary Stories by American Indians*. New York: Vintage Books.
63. Scott, Leslie M. 1941. "Indian Women as Food Providers and Tribal Councilors." *Oregon History* 42:208–19.
64. Seymour, Flora Warren. 1930. *Women of Trail and Wigwam*. New York: The Woman's Press.
65. ———. 1945. *Bird Girl: Sacajawea*. New York: The Bobbs-Merrill Co.
66. ———. 1946. *Pocahontas: Brave Girl*. New York: The Bobbs-Merrill Co.
67. Silko, Leslie Marmon. 1977. *Ceremony*. New York: Viking Press.
68. Smith, Sherry. 1984. "'Civilization's Guardians': U.S. Army Officers' Reflections on Indians and the Indian Wars in the Trans-Mississippi West, 1848–1890." Ph.D. diss., University of Washington.
69. Stauffer, Helen, and Susan Rosowski, eds. 1982. *Women and Western American Literature*. Troy, N.Y.: Whitson Publishing Co.
70. Stewart, Irene. 1980. *A Voice in Her Tribe: A Navajo Woman's Own Story*. Socorro, N. Mex.: Ballena Press.
71. Szasz, Margaret Connell. 1980. "'Poor Richard' Meets the Native American: Schooling for Young Indian Women in Eighteenth-Century Connecticut." *Pacific Historical Review* 49(2):215–35.
72. Tanner, Helen Hornbeck. 1979. "Coocoochee, Mohawk Medicine Woman." *American Indian Culture and Research Journal* 3(3):23–42.
73. Tooker, Elisabeth, ed. 1983. *1979 Proceedings of the American Ethnological Society: The Development of Political Organization in Native North America*. Washington: The American Ethnological Society.
74. Van Kirk, Sylvia. 1983. *Many Tender Ties: Women in Fur-Trade Society, 1670–1870*. Norman: University of Oklahoma Press.
75. Velie, Alan R. 1982. *Four American Indian Literary Masters: N. Scott Momaday, James Welch, Leslie Marmon Silko, and Gerald Vizenor*. Norman: University of Oklahoma Press.
76. Welch, Deborah. 1985. "An American Indian Leader: The Story of Gertrude Bonnin, 1876–1939." Ph.D. diss., University of Wyoming.
77. Williams, Walter L. 1986. *The Spirit and the Flesh: Sexual Diversity in American Indian Culture*. Boston: Beacon Press.
78. Wilson, Raymond. 1983. *Ohiyesa: Charles Eastman, Santee Sioux*. Urbana: University of Illinois Press.

CHAPTER 3

Riel, Red River, and Beyond: New Developments in Métis History

DENNIS F. K. MADILL

Until recently, Métis historiography has been dominated by Louis Riel's rebellions in Red River and Saskatchewan. Traditional historical writing saw the rebellions as episodes in the building of the Canadian nation and paid little attention to the Métis themselves. The 1985 centenary of the Saskatchewan rebellion obviously encouraged the historian's preoccupation with Riel and produced an outpouring of new literature on the subject.

The new literature is not, however, just more of the same. More sophisticated studies provide new insights into Riel and the nature of the rebellions. In addition, recent writing on Métis history has become broader in scope and interdisciplinary in nature. Riel and the rebellions continue to loom large in Métis history, but historians have progressed into new areas. Enquiries into the complex nature of societies that grew out of the fur trade, the regional diversity of the Métis experience, Métis land claims, historical developments after 1885, and constitutional issues demonstrate that historians have shed their "Red River myopia" and are now looking into exciting new areas for further research in an important aspect of both Canadian and American history.

The gradual emergence of Métis history as a separate field of study can be attributed to several recent developments. In the last five years, the tempo of Métis research has increased dramatically to encompass a wider range of topics and disciplines. Until recently, studies of the Métis in Canada and the northern United States were left largely to historians who focused generally on traditional concerns such as the history of the Red River Settlement and the role of Louis Riel in the two rebellions. Arthur J. Ray states in "Reflections on Fur Trade Social History and Métis History in Canada" [59] that historians have approached these traditional concerns from a narrow base, usually from the "centralist" perspective of the building of the Canadian nation rather than that of the Métis. Because of the preoccupation with Red River and Riel, there were few new in-depth insights into Métis economy and society. There is evidence now that Métis research is becoming more interdisciplinary and the field of investigation much wider. Anthropologists, economists, and archaeologists have been influenced by the works of other disciplines and are assuming a larger and more sensitive role in examining, analyzing, and reassessing Métis history. Because of a more holistic approach, historians are finally overcoming the "Red River myopia" which has characterized Métis historiography since Marcel Giraud's classic *Le Métis Canadien: Son role dans l'histoire des provinces de l'oeust* [31] (recently published in English by the University of Alberta Press with translation by George Woodcock), was released in 1945.

The history of the fur trade has emerged perhaps as the most innovative field of study. It has raised several questions regarding certain aspects of Métis history and exemplifies the interdisciplinary trend of recent Métis historiography. The publication in 1980 of two seminal works on the foundations of fur trade society entitled *'Many Tender Ties': Women in Fur-Trade Society, 1670–1870* [68], by Sylvia Van Kirk, and *Strangers in Blood: Fur Trade Company Families in Indian Country* [6], by Jennifer S. H. Brown, reflect the range, direction, and depth of fur trade historiography since the lifting of restrictions on the use of Hudson's Bay Company records during the tercentenary of the parent company in 1970 and the transfer of the Hudson's Bay Company Archives from Beaver House in London to the Provincial Archives of Manitoba in 1974. Generally, Van Kirk and Brown have reassessed the determinants that shaped fur trade society and have suggested that Red River Settlement society was more complex than traditional historical studies have indicated. They have concentrated on the social interaction between Indians and Europeans to reveal a complex society with origins in the different traditions of the Northwest and Hudson's Bay companies. While these two pathbreaking studies focus somewhat narrowly on Red River in the period before 1870 and the upper classes of fur traders, they have generated much interest in fur trade social history and Métis history. They have laid the groundwork for further studies by broadening our perspectives on the problems of tracing Métis roots and have introduced a range of questions, including the emergence of distinct Métis groups. There are indications already that social scientists in general are responding to some of the questions raised in these two landmark publications as reflected in recent fur trade and Métis conferences.

The conference at the Newberry Library Center for the History of the American Indian in Chicago in 1981, for example, honored the pioneering work of Marcel Giraud and attempted to synthesize the research achievements of the 1970s. It also acknowledged the pathbreaking studies of Van Kirk and Brown and reflected the continuation of work on the process of ethnogenesis in North America. The research presented at the conference resulted in the publication of a special Métis issue of the *American Indian Culture and Research Journal* and a book, edited by Jacqueline Peterson and Jennifer S. H. Brown, entitled *The New Peoples: Being and Becoming Métis in North America* [56]. The latter work contains a collection of twelve essays from Canadian and American authors who employ new approaches, adopt fresh perspectives, and illustrate the increasing depth and breadth of recent directions in Métis scholarship. It also reflects the multidisciplinary nature of Métis studies regarding current concerns such as the problem of tracing Métis roots; the establishment of distinctive Métis communities that had diverse origins and histories; and the economic, political, and cultural forces that compelled the Métis to express their identity in various forms.

Another important development which has served to draw attention to the Métis is reflected by the increasing amount of land claims research conducted by the Native Council of Canada, the Métis National Council, and the provincial and territorial organizations. Since 1965, Métis and nonstatus associations and federations have been established in every Canadian province and in the Great Lakes and Northern Plains regions of the United States. Research into Métis land claims by the Manitoba Métis Federation has recently been stimulated by the application of new techniques of analysis being developed in quantitative (rather than qualitative) history. Qualifi-

cation documents, used to establish Métis legal status, have been
hitherto neglected by scholars, but they are now becoming important
sources of new information, encouraging novel approaches to the
study of Métis land claims. John E. Foster has suggested that the
quantification approach was the direct result of the difficulties of
historians, essentially "middle-class" and/or English-speaking, in
perceiving experiences of substance in the lives of the Métis. This
sense of inadequacy in analyzing documents focusing on the Métis
led some historians to search out new perspectives.

There are other noteworthy avenues of research that have enhanced significantly the growing field of Métis history. The localized
emergence of Métis communities in areas such as the southern Great
Lakes, the central and western subarctic, the Mackenzie River valley, British Columbia, and the Maritimes has been discussed in recent studies by various social scientists. The constitutional affirma-
tion and recognition of aboriginal rights under the Canadian Charter
of Rights and Freedoms has prompted much legal and historical
work regarding the position of the Métis in Canada's new constitution. Finally, Métis research has been stimulated by the commemoration of the centenary of the North-West Rebellion in 1985.

Much of the pre-1982 literature concerning fur trade social history
and Métis history has been summarized by Sylvia Van Kirk in "Fur
Trade Social History: Some Recent Trends" [67], critically evaluated by Arthur J. Ray in "Reflections on Fur Trade Social History
and Métis History in Canada" [59], analyzed by Dennis Madill in
Select Annotated Bibliography on Métis History and Claims [43],
and reviewed extensively by Jacqueline Peterson and John Anfinson
in "The Indian and the Fur Trade: A Review of Recent Literature."
The most recent version of the article by Peterson and Anfinson,
which focused on Canadian studies, appeared in *Manitoba History*
[55] in 1985. An earlier version gave greater attention to American
material [57].

Hence, this chapter will concentrate mainly on post-1982 publications and will be structured upon eight categories which represent
the most current directions in Métis scholarship, reflect a wide variety of interests and interpretations, and exemplify Métis history as
an emerging field of study. They are Métis origins, regional studies,
the North-West Rebellion, Métis claims, biographical studies, Métis
culture, Métis history since 1885, and constitutional issues.

Métis Origins

Jennifer S. H. Brown has recently defined Métissage, in the North American context, as the meeting and mingling of Indian and white racial groups. This process has experienced a complex history over a period of several generations, and as it continues people of mixed ancestry are deciding which of their ancestral roots they wish to tap in defining a contemporary identity. Scholars of Métis history are now focusing on the process or processes of the origins of the Métis and its complications. John E. Foster has provided a useful introduction to the emergence of a distinct Métis identity in the fur trade areas of Rupert's Land and the Great Lakes region and has outlined the two dominant Métis traditions that derived from the Hudson Bay and Saint Lawrence trading systems in two of his earlier articles, "The Métis: The People and the Term" [27] and "The Origins of the Mixed Bloods in the Canadian West" [26]. Much research, however, remains to be conducted before the complexities of the Métis experience can be fully understood. Some progress has been made regarding clarification of some of the complications and obscurities.

The mixing of the races in the New World under particular conditions is discussed by Olive P. Dickason in "From 'One Nation' in the Northeast to 'New Nation' in the Northwest: A Look at the Emergence of the Métis" [15]. France sought to assimilate Amerindians "by trying to use racial intermixing as an instrument of empire," but its original concept of "one people" had over a period of time produced a race of mixed ancestry in the Northeast, the Old Northwest, the Far Northwest, and the Northwest Coast. Only certain conditions, however, allowed for the development of a Métis group consciousness or the spirit of the "New Nation," including isolation, slowness of settlement, and the enduring importance of the fur trade. In Acadia, the tensions of intercolonial warfare polarized the racial situation, causing children of mixed marriages to identify with the French or Amerindians and thereby preventing the establishment of a separate Métis identity. In the Old Northwest the rush of settlement impeded its development; on the Northwest Coast it was essentially the relative brief duration of the fur trade and the absence of symbiotic relationsips between European and Amerindian.

A more detailed examination of Métis roots in the Old Northwest, around and beyond the Great Lakes, and the antecedents of the Red

River Métis and the "New Nation" are provided by the pioneering work of Jacqueline Peterson. The seminal publication in the rediscovery of the American Métis in the southern Great Lakes region is her article "Prelude to Red River: A Social Portrait of the Great Lakes Métis" [52]. Variations on the same theme are presented in *The People In Between: Indian-White Marriage and the Genesis of a Métis Society and Culture in the Great Lakes Region, 1680–1830* [53] and in her most recent effort, "Many Roads to Red River: Métis Genesis in the Great Lakes Region, 1680–1815" [54]. Until recently, the process of Métissage was linked primarily with the western Canadian plains, with only vaguely defined Eastern antecedents and almost no counterpart in the United States. The political maturation of the Red River Métis was the culmination of almost two centuries of ethnic formation rooted along the Saint Lawrence and in the Upper Great Lakes and resulted in the formation of fur trade communities including Detroit, Chicago, Green Bay, and Michilimackinac.

The fate of these communities and the attitudes towards Métis groups in the United States during the period of Indian removal and rampant "manifest destiny" is discussed by R. David Edmunds in "'Unacquainted with the Laws of the Civilized World': American Attitudes Toward Métis Communities in the Old Northwest" [20] and Robert E. Bieder in "Scientific Attitudes Toward Indian Mixed-Bloods in Early Nineteenth Century America" [4]. Edmunds asserts that the policy of forced acculturation, adhered to by federal authorities in the early decades of the nineteenth century, resulted in the dispersal and submergence of the descendants of the Great Lakes Métis and the suppression of a separate Métis identity in the Old Northwest. In a supporting article, Bieder examines the prevailing social attitudes and indicates that the position of the mixed-bloods in American society after 1820 became associated with that of the Indian race as continued discrimination forced them to identify with Indian tribes rather than seek a separate Métis consciousness in a hostile American society.

The fur trade served as a vehicle for the emergence of the Métis in the Old Northwest and on the western Canadian plains. While the establishment of a Métis identity was suppressed in the upper Great Lakes region, it continued to nourish itself on the Northern Great Plains. The nature of the origins of a Métis identity and nationality on the Northern Great Plains and the divergent paths followed by the children of the many fur traders remains complicated. In "Some Questions and Perspectives on the Problem of Métis Roots," [29] John E. Foster attempts to broaden our perspectives on the problems of tracing Métis roots. He urges the increased application of new techniques being developed in quantitative and oral history. He maintains also that it is useful to subdivide each of the two basic populations associated with the Hudson Bay and Saint Lawrence– Great Lakes trading systems.

In the Northern Plains, for example, evidence would suggest distinction between the buffalo hunters of the prairie and parkland and the hunter-trappers of the boreal forest. In the context of the Saint Lawrence–Great Lakes fur trade on the Northern Plains, it was the "freemen" who saw themselves distinct from the indigenous Indian and from the society of the trading post. In "The Plains Métis" [30], Foster elaborates on the roles of the "freemen" and the origins of a Métis sense of separateness. He indicates that more recently social scientists have viewed Métis communities as an infrequent, if not unique, sociocultural product of particular events and circumstances. It was on the Canadian plains that the Métis flourished, and their survival appears to be related to alterations in the circumstances of the fur trade which constituted new opportunities. Future studies should focus more directly on Métis origins in terms of their responses to the challenges of their environments.

Much of recent scholarship on the historiography of the Métis has reassessed the determinants that shaped fur trade society and has suggested that Red River Settlement society was more complex than traditional historical studies have indicated. In 1981, Fritz Pannekoek noted in "The Historiography of the Red River Settlement, 1830–1868" [49] that various authors were focusing more on "the internal dynamics" (that is, religious, social, and economic factors) that shaped the community's early development and change and the growing tensions that ultimately led to its disintegration. Since then, writers have continued to analyze the distinct political and cultural identity of the Red River Colony and have offered more perspectives.

Sylvia Van Kirk, for example, provides a case study of a prominent British-Indian family of Red River in " 'What if Mama is an Indian?' The Cultural Ambivalence of the Alexander Ross Family" [69]. She argues that the Anglophone mixed-bloods lacked a distinct cultural identity based on the duality of their heritage, and this made it difficult for them to build upon their uniqueness as a people of mixed racial ancestry. In "The Métis and Mixed-Bloods of Rupert's Land Before 1870" [63], Irene M. Spry, in contrast to more recent scholarship, stresses the solidarity and communal spirit that linked the various mixed-blood groups of the Red River Settlement as expressed in intermarriages, linguistic and cultural blendings, and shared businesses and occupations.

A study of the economic, cultural, and symbolic roles of women should be pursued in the context of a variety of social science and humanistic disciplines to broaden our insights regarding the consequences of Métissage. In "Woman as Centre and Symbol in the Emergence of Métis Communities" [7], Jennifer S. H. Brown suggests possible avenues for research relating to women in Métis history that would help in clarifying some of the complexities and obscurities of the Métis experience. We should examine, for example, the nature and extent of aboriginal matriorganization in emergent Métis groups. The implications of what Brown has called patrifocality that characterized some upper-level fur trade families in the late eighteenth to early nineteenth centuries would also be a worthwhile project. Several company officer fathers made commitments of resources and affection to their Native families, often selectively, favoring certain children to education and a "civilized" upbringing. Some preliminary research has already been conducted by Brown on the implications of patrifocality in "Diverging Identities: The Presbyterian Métis of St. Gabriel Street, Montreal" [8].

Regional Studies

The common usage of the term *Métis* to refer to people of Indian-white ancestry anywhere in Canada or the United States poses problems for regional studies. In becoming a label which represents many diverse cultural heritages of blended ethnicities located in Canada and the United States, the term does not reflect the origin, the variety of social types of "Métis," or the regional differences. More specifically, just as the term *Indian* denies the diverse heritage or ethnic divisions of such groups as Haidas, Iroquois, or Cheyennes, the term *Métis* does not reveal the separate identities of those who did not share a social or historical connection with the Métis groups at Red River, such as communities located at Moose Factory or near Jasper, Alberta. The Métis, while assuming a common contemporary identification, were historically very different and have been referred to as half-breeds, non-Natives, "borderline Indians," nontreaty, non-status, and mixed-bloods.

Recently Arthur Ray has suggested that future studies on the Métis should focus less on the colony of Red River and more on other Métis settlements. He indicates that Métis historiography has matured immensely during the last decade, but if it is to continue progressing one must look past the blinkers of Red River to appreciate better the historical roots of present patterns of Indian, Métis, and white interaction. That several writers have responded to Ray's suggestion is reflected in several excellent regional studies that trace the local development of Métis populations in many areas across North America. Research is now beginning to concentrate on admixed populations that developed in the Maritimes and the Great Lakes region (see the section on Métis origins) as well as the James Bay area, the Mackenzie River valley, the central and western subarctic, British Columbia, Montana, and North Dakota. Some of these populations predate Red River, while others were contemporaneous but geographically and culturally isolated from it.

Carol Judd's most recent publication, "Moose Factory Was Not Red River: A Comparison of Mixed-Blood Experiences" [36], is a perceptive study of the small, isolated mixed-blood community of Moose Factory, located on the coast of James Bay, compared with the three distinguishable groups of mixed-bloods at Red River: Métis, native children of high-ranking Hudson's Bay Company officers, and native offspring of English-speaking Hudson's Bay Company servants. Her central theme is that geographical and historical realities contributed to extremely varied mixed-blood "experiences" at Moose Factory and may have also contributed to the vast differences in collective behavior between the mixed-bloods of Red River and those of Moose Factory.

That the timing of the fur trade, white attitudes toward Natives, missionary activities, and the policies of the federal government contributed to the varied patterns of mixed-blood development in the Canadian North is evident in "More Than a Matter of Blood: The Federal Government, the Churches and the Mixed Blood Populations of the Yukon and the Mackenzie River Valley, 1890–1950" [10], by K. S. Coates and W. R. Morrison. The specific development of the mixed bloods in the Yukon, where they were forced to choose between an Indian or white society, differed from the experience of the "New Nation" and was closer to the North American norm. The absence of external intervention allowed regional social forces to determine patterns of association and identification. In the Mackenzie watershed, however, various government policies, particularly the imposition of treaties, tampered with the social realities of Native society by establishing legal distinctions between Indians and Métis. Coates and Morrison conclude with the hope that "the study of conditions in the Yukon and Northwest Territories will encourage others to examine the extent to which the formation of Indian and Métis societies was more than a matter of blood."

Another study of a Métis community which had no social or historical connections with the Red River Métis is provided by Trudy Nicks and Kenneth Morgan in their insightful study "Grande Cache: The Historic Development of an Indigenous Alberta Métis Population" [48]. The community of Grande Cache is an indigenous development of subarctic west central Alberta, with roots that were contemporary with, but independent of, the Métis groups at Red River. It descended from independent trappers or "freemen," including several Iroquois and Métis, who settled in the area in the early nineteenth century. Following confederation, they were commonly called halfbreeds by outsiders, and their own adoption of the term Métis seems to be related to the recent urban and industrial development of the Grande Cache area. Identifying themselves as Métis ensures their continued distinctiveness in a social, political, and economic environment currently dominated by Euro-Canadian immigrants.

Another unique Métis culture flourished in the Pacific drainage region in the first half of the nineteenth century at Fort Vancouver near present-day Portland, Oregon. By the time the fort was established in 1824, there was considerable intermarriage of traders from John Jacob Astor's abortive fur trade enterprise and Nor-Westers with women whose native cultures differed substantially from that east of the Rocky Mountains. A study of this unique Métis society is presented in "A Most Remarkable Phenomenon-Growing Up Métis: Fur Traders' Children in The Pacific Northwest" [58], by Julliet Pollard. As Pollard indicates, most of the children in her study founded new communities in British Columbia, Washington, Oregon, and Montana.

With the failure of the Manitoba Act in 1870 to meet the political and legal goals of the Métis, and as a result of the two Riel rebellions, much of the Métis population dispersed to the North-West Territories, British Columbia, and the northwestern regions of the

United States. There are clusters of Métis families throughout British Columbia which exemplify the westernmost extremity of the Red River Métis diaspora. A study of one such cluster is provided by Gerry Andrews in *Métis Outpost: Memoirs of the First Schoolmaster at the Métis Settlement of Kelly Lake, B.C., 1923–1925* [1]. Until recently, Louis Riel and the Red River Métis were viewed essentially as a Canadian and not an American phenomenon. An appreciation of Louis Riel and the Métis as an integral part of the history of the north-central part of the United States is presented by Thomas Flanagan in his informative article "Louis Riel and the Dispersion of the American Métis" [24]. He maintains that the 49th parallel as a political boundary was artifically imposed on the Métis social reality and that the history of the Métis cannot be fully understood unless it is followed on both sides of the border. As Flanagan indicates, Riel spent about half his adult life in the United States and after the Red River Rebellion took refuge in Saint Joseph, Dakota Territory. The influence of Riel after the exodus of the Métis from the Red River valley, regarding the development of a distinct Métis identity, was insignificant. He made no attempt, for example, to assert any Métis rights against the American government, in contrast to his politics on Canadian soil, where he was active in advocating a doctrine of aboriginal rights to land. Historically, the Métis probably had as much of a claim to the Dakota and Montana prairies as they did to the Canadian northwest.

Flanagan also analyzes the social dispersion of the Pembina/Saint Joseph Métis, who were once a cohesive and distinct society, and their submergence within the larger American society. In the United States, the dispersal of the Métis has coincided with the loss of legal identity. It remains to be seen whether constitutional developments in Canada, where the Métis have achieved an identity distinct from the Indians, will have some repercussions on ethnic politics in the United States, encouraging the Métis there to reemerge as a distinct and acknowledged group.

More specific studies on the Montana and North Dakota Métis and their futile fight for an adequate land base are contained in "Waiting for a Day That Never Comes: The Dispossessed Métis of Montana" [19], by Verne Dusenberry and "The Turtle Mountain Chippewa, 1882–1905," by Stanley N. Murray [46]. The former, originally published in 1958 in *Montana: The Magazine of Western History* and reprinted in 1985 in *The New Peoples: Being and Becoming*

Métis in North America, is a synthesis of oral and documentary material on the "Landless Indians of Montana." From the 1880s they were increasingly people in between—neither white nor Indian—an outside community of American Métis seeking a land settlement with the U.S. government. They are still, as an Indian agent stated in 1903, "waiting for a day that never comes." The theme of landlessness, with reference to the full-bloods, the Canadian mixed-bloods, and those mixed-bloods who considered themselves American citizens, is also discussed by Murray.

While considerable progress has been made in tracing the local development of admixed populations over a much broader geographical area, further studies are required in five essential classifications: (1) those mixed-blood peoples that descended from the Red River Métis who reside on Indian reserves in Canada or on reservations in the United States; (2) clusters of Métis families who dispersed after the two Métis rebellions and now live in different sociocultural environments such as northern regions of the prairie provinces, the Northwest Territories, British Columbia, northern Montana, or the Pembina area of North Dakota; (3) those mixed-bloods who possess no social or historical connection with the Red River Métis, such as the Scots-Cree near Prince Albert, Saskatchewan; (4) those mixed-bloods who still maintain close relationships with the more traditional Indian bands, such as the Oglala Sioux at Pine Ridge, South Dakota; and (5) those mixed-bloods who have moved to the cities.

The North-West Rebellion

The centenary of the 1885 Saskatchewan rebellion has prompted a plethora of literature on this much-studied subject. The interpretation of the North-West Rebellion developed by George F. G. Stanley dominated the literature for generations. He viewed the rebellion as the result of government indifference in resolving the problems of the Métis of the North-West. Recent historiography on the North-West Rebellion has modified some of the traditional assumptions regarding the Indian-Métis uprising and represents widely divergent evaluations and revisionist scholarship.

An "1885 and After" conference held at the University of Saskatchewan in May 1985 resulted in the publication of an impressive book, edited by F. L. Barron and James B. Waldram, entitled *1885 and After: Native Society in Transition* [2], which represents a benchmark of scholarship on the subject. The compilation of papers presented in that volume includes such topics as the Indian view of the uprising; an anthropological account of the rise and fall of Louis Riel and the Métis nation; a comparison of two frontiers in transition, Nova Scotia (1713–63) and the North-West (1869–85); and an evaluation of the role of the Indian agent as a cause of the uprising. These papers introduce new insights and interpretations and offer a more balanced view of the roots of the uprising and its aftermath. No longer are the Métis and the Indians who were involved in the uprising viewed simply as rebels raging against the encroachments of white society. Also, Sir John A. Macdonald and other government authorities are no longer uncritically accepted as passive guardians of the national interest. As Barron and Waldram suggest, we have only begun to understand the important issues of the rebellion and its consequences, and more work is still required in this area.

Thomas Flanagan's revisionist and controversial study, *Riel and the Rebellion: 1885 Reconsidered* [23], is the first scholarly work to challenge the standard interpretation that responsibility for the causes of the rebellion lay directly with an indecisive federal government. Flanagan's thesis is that Métis land claims were seriously considered by the Canadian government and that the Métis were unrealistic in their expectations. Riel, as Flanagan asserts, was not as concerned with local issues as he was with the larger claims based on a theory of aboriginal rights. Here, Flanagan has introduced some pathbreaking research on Riel's theory of Métis aboriginal land rights.

Don McLean has also offered new perspectives on certain aspects of the North-West Rebellion. His recent publication, *1885: Métis Rebellion or Government Conspiracy?* [41], documents the role of Lawrence Clarke, the Hudson's Bay Company's chief factor at Fort Carleton, in the Métis uprising. He asserts that when the Canadian Pacific Railway Company was struggling in the mid-1880s, Sir John A. Macdonald used Clarke to provoke a rebellion that would dramatize the utility of the railway and encourage subsidization. While McLean's book is an interesting view of the events leading up to the rebellion, it fails to prove convincingly and definitively that the rebellion was in fact a conspiracy by Macdonald and his agents. It raises, however, some hitherto neglected questions about the rebellion's causes and provides useful information about Lawrence Clarke, a figure about whom little has been written.

Prairie Fire: The 1885 North-West Rebellion [3], by Bob Beal and Rod Macleod, attempts to demonstrate that the rebellion represented a wider discontent and disillusionment. The authors claim also that their study is "the first comprehensive history of the rebellion" and that they "undertook the project in the belief that the definitive history of the rebellion . . . had yet to be written." While their book is an excellent narrative, they fail to take into account several of the revisionist interpretations of Louis Riel and the rebellion and the controversial areas that are now the subject of debate among Canadian historians.

They refuse to accept or reject, for example, Thomas Flanagan's interpretation of Louis Riel as a messianic prophet and his views of the causes of the rebellion. The interpretations of Louis Riel and the rebellion and the sections on the causes of Indian unrest and the role of Indian leaders in the uprising, moreover, should be read in conjunction with Hugh Dempsey's biography, *Big Bear: The End of Freedom* [14], and John Tobias's recent article, "Canada's Subjugation of the Plains Cree, 1879–1885" [66]. Both these studies have revised traditional interpretations concerning the causes of Indian unrest and the role of Big Bear and the Cree nation in the North-West Rebellion. The record of the Canadian government in fulfilling treaty obligations is not one of fairness as the traditional interpretation portrays. Tobias, in particular, argues convincingly that the Saskatchewan Rebellion provided federal authorities with the instrument they required to establish control over the Crees and destroy their movement for treaty revision. Both Dempsey and Tobias demonstrate that Big Bear was powerless to prevent the violence at Frog Lake in 1885 and that the so-called Indian uprising was merely an outburst of a few young warriors in the Cree and Assiniboine bands in central Saskatchewan.

A welcome addition to the historiography of the Battle of Batoche is *The Battle of Batoche: British Small Warfare and the Entrenched Métis* [35], by Walter Hildebrandt. He suggests that previous scholarly and popular studies on the Battle of Batoche concentrated primarily on the significance and consequences of the battle but the actual military actions were not clearly defined. Compiling the findings of several years of archaeological and archival research, Hildebrandt analyzes Métis military strategy in greater detail. Also, he revises the traditional interpretation of Major-General Sir Frederick Middleton (commander of the Northwest Field Force) by examining him in the context of British small war tactics.

That the small hamlet of Batoche, located on the south branch of the Saskatchewan River, survived and prospered after the North-West Rebellion is portrayed most effectively in "Batoche after 1885: A Society in Transition" [51], by Diane Payment. She argues, contrary to standard interpretations, that its population did not disperse after the rebellion but rather regrouped and enjoyed a period of relative economic prosperity. Payment's work on Batoche breaks with the "Canadian" or "centralist" perspective, which sees the significance of the rebellion in terms of Canada's domination of the North-West. John E. Foster has noted that because of the centralist perspective an enduring theme in the literature on the Métis has been the "primitiveness" of the Métis as a factor in historical explanation, and not the cultural values that derived from a century and a half of adaptive experiences in the fur trade on the Canadian plains. More studies like Payment's should be encouraged in order to present a more balanced view of the rebellion and its aftermath.

In "The Charismatic Pattern: Canada's Riel Rebellion of 1885 as a Millenarian Protest Movement," [45] German author Manfred Mossman uses the theoretical framework of Michael Adas's *Prophets of Rebellion* (Chapel Hill, 1979) to provide a reinterpretation of the North-West Rebellion as a millenarian prophet-inspired protest. Mossmann also compares Riel's protest movement to similar situations in India, Burma, New Zealand, and Brazil.

Métis Claims

Various Métis organizations and social scientists have been conducting research on three basic categories of Métis and nonstatus Indian claims. There are claims that the distribution of land and scrip, especially under the Manitoba Act, was unjustly and inefficiently administered. The Manitoba Act, passed in 1870 by the Canadian government, made provision for the distribution of 1,400,000 acres of land to the children of Métis heads of families in Manitoba and accorded statutory recognition to Métis's aboriginal title. Also, there is a general claim that this form of compensation was inadequate to extinguish Métis aboriginal title, particularly since few of them gained from scrip, and it only applied to the western interior of Canada. Métis outside the North-West are generally making claims jointly with status Indians in several regions of Canada. Finally, there is the third type of claim which relates to the constitutional status of the Métis and nonstatus Indians under the Constitution Act of 1982.

The most innovative and promising work on Métis claims has been undertaken by the Manitoba Métis Federation. Until recently, historians of the Métis relied almost exclusively upon the analysis of documents that generated qualitative data. With the appearance of studies such as *The Genealogy of the First Métis Nation* [61], by D. N. Sprague and R. P. Frye, various techniques of quantification are now being employed. That book, which focuses on the Red River Métis and their dispersal west and north, is a promising attempt to integrate such recorded materials as parish registers, census returns, land titles, and half-blood scrip applications into one machine-readable data base. As such, it offers new insights into the genealogy of the Red River Métis and the disposal of Manitoba land claims between 1870 and 1882. Sprague and Frye have used evidence from the aforementioned records to indicate that many Métis did not receive their land or scrip entitlements in Manitoba and the North-West Territories.

The mismanagement of the distribution of the half-blood land grant under the Manitoba Act has also been the central theme of other works by D. N. Sprague and a study by Gerhard Ens. In his earlier writings, Sprague argued that it was the deliberate intention of Sir John A. Macdonald and the dominion government, through the unconstitutional amendments to the Manitoba Act, to bring about the relocation of the Métis. This argument is reinforced in a recent article by Sprague and P. R. Maillot entitled "Persistent Settlers: The Dispersal and Resettlement of the Red River Métis, 1870–1885" [62]. Employing the quantitative techniques of family reconstitution to document the dispersal of the half bloods and Métis of Red River to the North West Territories, Sprague and Maillot emphasize the importance of landlessness as the critical factor in causing the migration process.

Gerhard Ens, in acknowledging the excellent work of D. N. Sprague, has examined the largely neglected provincial aspect of the alienation of Métis lands through a study of provincial legislation in "Métis Lands in Manitoba" [21]. While the province of Manitoba was not empowered to formulate policy in the area of administration of Métis lands, it possessed legislative and legal powers to protect the Métis from losing their lands. He suggests that Métis land rights were generally protected until 1878 and subsequently ignored.

A second type of claim concerns those Métis outside the Canadian North-West, whom the federal government refused to recognize as a distinct people with aboriginal title. In Ontario, for example, the federal government's response to Métis claims to aboriginal title was generally to admit half bloods to treaty who were "pursuing the Indian mode of life" or not to deal with them at all. David McNab elaborates on this aspect of Métis claims in "Métis Participation in the Treaty-Making Process in Ontario: A Reconnaissance" [42].

John Long's recent work on the negotiations for Treaty 9 in northern Ontario in 1905–1906 provides an excellent case study on federal government policy towards the Métis. In "Treaty No. 9 and Fur Trade Company Families: Northeastern Ontario's Halfbreeds, Indians, Petitioners, and Métis" [39], he meticulously documents the exclusion of the half bloods of Moose Factory on "grounds that they were not living the Indian mode of life." Petitions concerning Métis land rights were submitted to both levels of government, but settlement of their claims was not forthcoming, nor was the broader question of who was eligible (or ineligible) for treaty status rectified. As Long asserts, "Treaty No. 9 was a tremendously important symbol of nativeness and exclusivity, separating Indians from petitioners, confirming or denying identity by government decree."

A final type of claim that has attracted a considerable amount of research concerns the constitutional position of the Métis and their claims to aboriginal rights. Under the Constitution Act of 1982, Indians, Inuit, and Métis have been identified as distinct groups with a special status in the Canadian state, and their existing aboriginal rights have been recognized and affirmed. These rights nevertheless have not been clearly defined, and many diverse perspectives have been offered regarding their nature and extent. In "Aboriginal Rights and Land Issues: The Métis Perspective" [9], Clem Chartier emphasizes that aboriginal rights are derived by virtue of their descent from Indians and rest upon the same general foundation as those of persons deemed to have Indian status—that is, upon an aboriginal right to territory. That the Métis are Indians for constitutional purposes, he argues, is supported by various legislative enactments which recognized the rights of the aboriginal peoples.

Thomas Flanagan does not share Chartier's views regarding Métis aboriginal rights and maintains that there are difficulties in categorizing the Métis as an aboriginal people. In "Métis Aboriginal Rights: Some Historical and Contemporary Problems" [25], Flanagan contends that there are no historical precedents to support the case for Métis aboriginal rights. The notion that the Métis were a distinct aboriginal people with rights different from those of Euro-Canadians or Indians was accepted by Sir John A. Macdonald for reasons of short-term expediency. According to Flanagan, there is no evidence that Macdonald, who was responsible for the Manitoba Act, recognized the theory of a Métis aboriginal title as inherited from Indian ancestors.

Biographical Studies

In 1978, the University of Alberta received a grant from the Social Sciences and Humanities Research Council of Canada to establish the Louis Riel Project. Its purpose was to publish a critical edition of all writings of Riel still in existence. In 1985, *The Collected Writings of Louis Riel/Les Écrits complets de Louis Riel* [64], under the general editorship of George F. G. Stanley, was released to coincide with the anniversary of the North-West Rebellion and the execution of Riel. Stanley, who first researched Riel some fifty years ago, offered his final comment on the Métis leader in "The Last Word on Louis Riel—The Man of Several Faces" [65] and left any further analysis to others who will have the advantage of ready access to most of Riel's writings in this five-volume study. The first four volumes contain various pieces of Rieliana and are edited by scholars such as Raymond Huel, Gilles Martel, Thomas Flanagan, and Glen Campbell, representing the disciplines of history, sociology, political science, and literature, respectively, and they relate to specific aspects of Riel's career. Each scholar, moreover, presents an overview of his particular field of study and reflects recent trends in that field.

One of the volume editors of the Riel project, Gilles Martel, has introduced new perspectives and modified traditional assumptions regarding certain aspects of Riel's life. His recent book, *Le Messianisme de Louis Riel* [44], which is essentially his doctoral thesis in sociology from the University of Paris (1976), has offered a valuable insight on Riel's career. Unlike those historians such as George F. G. Stanley who viewed Riel within the framework of cultural conflict or

W. L. Morton who adhered to the thesis of a clash of regions, Martel presents a reevaluation of Riel's role. He agrees essentially with the central theme of Thomas Flanagan's pathbreaking biography, *Louis "David" Riel: "Prophet of the New World"* [22], that Riel cannot be understood without analyzing his messianic ideas. In contrast to Flanagan's study, however, which analyzes Riel's religious ideas in the larger context of millenarian movements, Martel traces the evolution of Riel's messianic ideas from a sociological and psychosociological approach.

Social scientists are no longer merely concentrating on Louis Riel and the rebellions but are now branching out and focusing on other Métis personnages, some of whom were not typical of, or identified with, the French and Cree or Saulteau-speaking Roman Catholic buffalo hunters at Red River, who saw themselves as the "New Nation." In gradually overcoming the "Red River myopia," and with the emergence of Métis identities in other communities, social scientists are also now considering Métis figures outside of Red River.

Alexander Kennedy Isbister, whose name is usually associated with opposition to the Hudson's Bay Company, was an English half blood or country-born who also achieved success as a leader in education reform in Great Britain. The latter, less known, aspect of the career of a remarkable "Rupert's Lander" is portrayed by Barry Cooper in "Alexander Kennedy Isbister, A Respectable Victorian" [11]. Isbister was not typical of the mixed-bloods who appeared in the letters of Governor George Simpson and other company officers whose prejudices against mixed-bloods often prevented them from being promoted. He ranked with James Ross in terms of ambition and determination and was able to join the upper middle class as a minor but eminent Victorian within an emerging liberal society. The fact that a half blood was able to reach such heights should lead to a reassessment of some of the more sweeping generalizations about nineteenth-century racism. In this regard, Philip Goldring's useful article, "Governor Simpson's Officers: Elite Recruitment in a British Overseas Enterprise, 1834–1870" [32], should be consulted.

While some mixed-bloods achieved a relatively high level of distinction, in general, limits to their upward mobility were imposed and they experienced the disadvantages common to Natives in colonized places. In "Archdeacon Thomas Vincent of Moosonee and the Handicap of 'Métis' Racial Status," [38] John Long analyzes the career of Thomas Vincent and the policies of the church missionary society in the James Bay region in the second half of the nineteenth century in rejecting men of mixed descent for its highest positions. As Long argues, even the church had a "caste" theory that set upper limits on the career potential of Natives.

That recent historiography on Métis roots has revealed the emergence of separate identities from that of Red River is reflected in the examination of the life and legends of Paulet Paul, a champion of the tripmen in the York boat brigades in the Fort Edmonton region in the post-1820 period. John E. Foster suggests in "Paulet Paul: Métis or 'House Indian' Folk Hero?" [28] that the achievements and bravado of Paulet Paul exemplified the values and practices associated with the Plains Métis of the Athabasca–Peace River region. Yet, as Foster observes, the pattern of Paulet's "household" behavior suggests a style of living not usually associated with the Plains Métis but more with the ways of House Indian bands that chose to make a particular post the focus of their activities.

Métis Culture

The difficulty in defining the term *Métis* in the historical and contemporary context has also created problems in identifying distinct expressions of Métis culture. Problems of identification have increased now that research has revealed the many backgrounds of people who today are referred to as Métis. Responsibility for identifying the varied cultural expressions of the Métis to commemorate the centenary of the North-West Rebellion was assumed by Julia D. Harrison, curator of ethnology at the Glenbow Museum and organizer of the exhibition "Métis." In her article, "Métis: A Glenbow Museum Exhibition" [34], Harrison stated that no museum in Canada, including Glenbow, possessed a real collection of Métis material. In the minds of many Canadians, the Métis died with Louis Riel in 1885, and much of what the Métis produced has been buried in museum collections and often attributed to Indians or pioneers.

The problems of Métis identity and the implications of Métis ethnohistory for the interpretation of "Métis" material in the context of museum exhibits is also the central theme for revealing articles by Trudy Nicks and Ted J. Brasser. In "Mary Ann's Dilemma: The Ethnohistory of an Ambivalent Identity" [47], Nicks argues that some authors have generally employed the term *Métis* for all populations sharing an Indian and European biological heritage and have attributed a Red River ancestry and culture to other groups as well. Consequently, the identification of artifacts for mixed-bloods such as "Mary Anne," who belonged to a population of mixed descent that developed in the western subarctic and had no social or historical connections with the Red River Métis, has posed problems for museum ethnologists. Ted J. Brasser, in his article "In Search of Métis Art" [5], indicates that as a result of recent research, Métis craftwork, which originally was classified under various tribal names, can now be attributed to Métis communities and particularly to their Roman Catholic missions.

Another area of Métis culture which is really in its infancy is the study of Métis linguistics. The reconstruction of the "Michif" language is now being undertaken by scholars in linguistics, and its uniqueness is an important expression of Métis ethnic identity. Some excellent work regarding the reconstruction of the "Michif" language has been provided by John C. Crawford. In "Speaking Michif in Four Métis Communities" [12] he reports the preliminary phases of a research plan to investigate the function of Michif in Belcourt, North Dakota (on the Turtle Mountain Reservation), and in Boggy Creek, Camperville, and Saint Lazare, Manitoba. The question of Métis linguistic distinctiveness at the Turtle Mountain Reservation is the subject of another article by Crawford entitled, "What Is Michif? Language in the Métis Tradition" [13].

Another significant addition to the emerging field of Métis linguistics because of its multidisciplinary approach is *Ethnolinguistic Profile of the Canadian Métis* [18], by Patrick C. Douaud. It examines the mechanisms of cultural and linguistic variations among the Métis of western Canada in general and the Mission Métis community of Lac la Biche in particular.

Métis History Since 1885

Canadian historians have usually ignored the period after the North-West Rebellion, and several aspects of twentieth-century Métis history still need to be researched. Nevertheless, some valuable work on twentieth-century Métis history attempts to rescue the Métis from being prisoners of their historical past and to demonstrate that they did not disappear after the 1885 uprising. Also, in Canada the legal status granted to the Métis by their inclusion in the aboriginal rights provision of the Constitution Act of 1982 and their participation in

first ministers' conferences have prompted some impressive work regarding the constitutional position of the Métis.
Julia D. Harrison's book, *Métis: People Between Two Worlds*
[33], is a general social history of the Métis with four of the five
chapters focusing on twentieth-century issues. In attempting to synthesize existing literature, she treats such subjects as Métis participation in the two world wars, the emergence of Métis political organizations, and the efforts of the Métis in asserting their position in
the Canadian constitution and at the first ministers' conferences.
This centenary publication is not a comprehensive study of the Métis
but offers some new perspectives on some neglected aspects of Métis
history and should open up some avenues to further research.

A significant scholarly contribution to the historiography of Métis
history since 1885 is *Batoche (1870–1910)* [50], by Diane Payment.
In examining the economic, political, religious, and social life of
Batoche before and after the North-West Rebellion, she challenges
the traditional assumptions of writers who contend that the Métis
perished with the 1885 uprising and that it was the ultimate expression of protest and cohesive action by the Métis and left them hu-
miliated and deprived. Extensive documentary research on the Métis
at Batoche and the South Saskatchewan district after 1885 tends to
refute many of these assumptions and suggests new hypotheses to
analyze Métis society in the North-West.

Murray Dobbin has contributed some invaluable work on Métis
organizations. His book, *The One-and-A Half Men: The Story of Jim
Brady and Malcolm Morris, Métis Patriots of the Twentieth Century*
[17], provides a unique perspective on twentieth-century Métis history and indeed was written with the object of recovering twentieth-
century Métis history, which Canadian historians have "ignored and
discounted." Professor Dobbin examines Indian and Métis organizations of the 1930s and 1940s and the roots of contemporary
organizations.

Another perspective regarding the federal government's approach
to Métis and nonstatus Indian groups has been presented by Sally M.
Weaver. In the early 1970s, federal government policy initiatives,
which previously had included only status Indians and Inuit, were
extended to Métis and nonstatus Indians. In "Federal Policy-Making
for Métis and Non-Status Indians in the Context of Native Policy"
[71], Weaver analyzes the futile attempts in the 1960s and 1970s by
the federal government to make policy for the Métis and nonstatus

Indians and to improve socioeconomic conditions. She concludes that the unproductive policy initiatives will continue until the federal government becomes more sensitive and knowledgeable about Métis and nonstatus needs.

Constitutional Issues

More recent questions relating to the identity of the Métis and non-status Indians under the Constitution Act of 1982 now need to be addressed. The full ramifications of the new legal status of the Métis under the Canadian constitution are still unclear. The emphasis has shifted significantly from a concern with mixed ancestry to a concern for identification as a Métis, acceptance by the Métis community, and legal proof of ancestry. Equally complicated is the entrenchment of the principle of self-government. Social scientists now need to consider a recent set of dynamics that is having an affect on Métis identity and should focus more directly on the role of legal definitions and ethnic relationships and the place of the Métis in the modern world. Some impressive work has already been presented, but much still needs to be done.

Joseph Sawchuk deals with the current split between the Métis and nonstatus Indians in "The Métis, Non-Status Indians and the New Aboriginality: Government Influence on Native Political Alliance and Identity" [60] and argues that the recent constitutional entrenchment of aboriginal rights has affected the political alliances of the Métis and nonstatus Indians of the prairie provinces concerning perceptions of ethnicity and group membership. Sawchuk suggests also that the current split between these groups will probably result in the establishment of nonstatus Indian organizations.

The impact of legislated "Indian" status on the Native American population of Canada has been analyzed most effectively by James B. Waldram in "The 'Other Side': Ethnostatus Distinctions in Western Subarctic Native Communities" [70]. He argues that the concept of legal "Indian" status has served to undermine the cultural homogeneity of western subarctic Native communities by creating conflict situations in which cultural considerations are no longer appropriate. Despite references to "Indian" and "Métis" peoples as separate cultural groups, in much of the western subarctic, and indeed in other areas of Canada, there are few discernible cultural differences between the two. The Canadian Constitution of 1982 has compounded the issue and enhanced further ethnostatus distinctions amongst the Native American population.

One of the goals the Métis are seeking under the Canadian constitution is the right to self-government. In "Métis Self-Government in Saskatchewan" [40], Wayne McKenzie, of the Association of Métis and Non-Status Indians of Saskatchewan, elaborates on the concept of Native self-government and the institutions that Saskatchewan Métis feel need to be developed to allow them to share equally in Canada as a self-governing people. Self-government, McKenzie emphasizes, is an inevitable process, and the Canadian public can either support it or continue the trend of the past by impeding it.

Conclusions

Recently, there have been some promising and innovative developments in Métis historiography. There is increasing evidence that Métis research is becoming more interdisciplinary and the field of investigation much wider. Equally promising is the addition of several significant publications to this emerging field of study that have reassessed or revised some of the traditional assumptions regarding certain aspects of Métis history, including Métis roots; the economic, political, and cultural forces that compelled the Métis to express their nationality in various ways; the local emergence of distinct Métis groups that had diverse origins and histories; and the North-West Rebellion. One of the most innovative developments concerns the use of advanced research methodologies to analyze the Red River Settlement. In *The Genealogy of the First Nation* [61] and "Persistent Settlers: The Dispersal and Resettlement of the Red River Métis, 1870–85" [62], the Manitoba Métis Federation has employed quantitative techniques of family reconstitution to document the case for contemporary Métis land claims and the dispersion and relocation of the Métis who left Manitoba after 1870.

Métis historiography has also matured recently in certain areas where previously little research had been undertaken. While several gaps still remain in twentieth-century Métis history, for example, significant progress has been made. Murray Dobbin's work on Métis organizations, Julia Harrison's attempt to synthesize some of the work on twentieth-century Métis history, and the inclusion of several papers on various aspects of twentieth-century Métis history in a recent publication entitled *1885 and After: Native Society in Transition* [2] help fill the void in this area. There has also been significant growth in comparative approach studies [16, 36, 37, 45].

While Métis historiography has matured immensely in recent years, some gaps still remain. We still have much to learn about the process or processes of Métissage. Jennifer S. H. Brown [7] has suggested that the study of women's roles in the critical years before the mid-nineteenth-century ascendancy of settlers requires more attention and will offer us broadened insights of the human backgrounds, contexts, and consequences of Métissage. A more comprehensive social history that not only examines the officer class but also those occupying the lowest rung of "fur trade society" is required. Recently, there have been more studies on Métis settlements other than Red River, but there is a need for more in-depth research. The Native component of Métis history requires more consideration. Little has been revealed about the relations which Indian women and their Métis offspring maintained with their Native kin. Scant attention, moreover, has been paid to how the varied tribal cultural traditions influenced the patterns of Indian-white relationships during the fur trade period. The repercussions of the new legal status imposed upon the Métis in the Canadian Constitution of 1982 and the omission of the nonstatus Indians in the constitutional definition of aboriginality are still unclear and need to be more adequately explored.

The American background of Métis land claims in Canada has never been studied and would make a worthwhile project. Before there was even a land claims issue in the Canadian North-West, the American government had issued land grants and scrip to various Métis groups. This American experience might have influenced Canadian practice, particularly concerning the imitation of American precedents by Canadian authorities.

Other aspects of the history of the American Métis have also been largely neglected. There are positive signs, however, that Jacqueline Peterson's pioneering work on the Great Lakes Métis and the conference on "The Métis in North America" held at the Newberry Library, Chicago, in 1981 have aroused interest in the Métis in the United States. It remains to be seen also if the recognition of the Canadian Métis under the aboriginal rights provisions of the Constitution Act of 1982, will have some impact on ethnic politics in the United States.

References

1. Andrews, Gerry. 1985. *Métis Outpost: Memoirs of the First School-master at the Métis Settlement of Kelly Lake, B.C. 1923–1925*. Victoria, BC.: Pencrest Publications.
2. Barron, F. L., and James B. Waldram, eds. 1986. *1885 and After: Native Society in Transition*. Regina: Canadian Plains Research Centre.
3. Beal, Bob, and Rod Macleod. 1984. *Prairie Fire: The 1885 North-West Rebellion*. Edmonton: Hurtig Publishers.
4. Bieder, Robert E. 1980. "Scientific Attitudes Toward Indian Mixed-Bloods in Early Nineteenth Century America." *Journal of Ethnic Studies* 8:17–30.
5. Brasser, Ted J. 1985. "In Search of Métis Art." In *The New Peoples: Being and Becoming Métis in North America*, ed. Jacqueline Peterson and Jennifer S. H. Brown, pp. 221–29. Winnipeg: University of Manitoba Press.
6. Brown, Jennifer S. H. 1980. *Strangers in Blood: Fur Trade Company Families in Indian Country*. Vancouver: University of British Columbia Press.
7. ———. 1983. "Woman as Centre and Symbol in the Emergence of Métis Communities." *Canadian Journal of Native Studies* 3:39–46.
8. ———. 1985. "Diverging Identities: The Presbyterian Métis of St. Gabriel Street, Montreal." In *The New Peoples: Being and Becoming Métis in North America*, ed. Jacqueline Peterson and Jennifer S. H. Brown, pp. 195–206. Winnipeg: University of Manitoba Press.
9. Chartier, Clem. 1885. "Aboriginal Rights and Land Issues: The Métis Perspective." In *The Quest for Justice: Aboriginal Peoples and Aboriginal Rights*, ed. Menno Boldt and J. Anthony Long, pp. 54–61. Toronto: University of Toronto Press.
10. Coates, K. S., and W. R. Morrison. 1986. "More Than a Matter of Blood: The Federal Government, the Churches and the Mixed Blood Populations of the Yukon and the Mackenzie River Valley, 1890–1950." In *1885 and After: Native Society in Transition*, eds. F. L. Barron and James B. Waldram, pp. 253–77. Regina: Canadian Plains Research Center.
11. Cooper, Barry. 1985. "Alexander Kennedy Isbister: A Respectable Victorian." *Canadian Ethnic Studies* 17:44–63.
12. Crawford, John C. 1983. "Speaking Michif in Four Métis Communities." *Canadian Journal of Native Studies* 3:47–55.
13. ———. 1985. "What is Michif? Language in the Métis Tradition." In *The New Peoples: Being and Becoming Métis in North America*, ed. Jacqueline Peterson and Jennifer S. H. Brown, pp. 231–41. Winnipeg: University of Manitoba Press.
14. Dempsey, Hugh. 1984. *Big Bear: The End of Freedom*. Vancouver and Toronto: Douglas & McIntyre.
15. Dickason, Olive P. 1985. "From 'One Nation' in the Northeast to 'New Nation' in the Northwest: A Look at the Emergence of the Métis." In *New Peoples: Being and Becoming Métis in North America*, ed. Jacque-

line Peterson and Jennifer S. H. Brown, pp. 19–36. Winnipeg: University of Manitoba Press.

16. ———. 1986. "Frontiers in Transition: Nova Scotia 1713–1763 Compared to the North-West 1869–1885." In *1885 and After: Native Society in Transition*, ed. F. L. Barron and James B. Waldram, pp. 23–38. Regina: Canadian Plains Research Centre.

17. Dobbin, Murray J. 1981. *The One-and-A-Half Men: The Story of Jim Brady and Malcolm Norris, Métis Patriots of the 20th Century*. Vancouver: North Star Books.

18. Douaud, Patrick C. 1985. *Ethnolinguistic Profile of the Canadian Métis*. National Museum of Man Mercury Series. Canadian Ethnology Service Paper No. 99. Ottawa: National Museum of Canada.

19. Dusenberry, Verne. 1985. "Waiting for a Day That Never Comes: The Dispossessed Métis of Montana." In *The New Peoples: Being and Becoming Métis in North America*, ed. Jacqueline Peterson and Jennifer S. H. Brown, pp. 119–36. Winnipeg: University of Manitoba Press.

20. Edmunds, R. David. 1985. "'Unacquainted with the Laws of the Civilized World': American Attitudes Toward the Métis Communities in the Old Northwest." In *The New Peoples: Being and Becoming Métis in North America*, ed. Jacqueline Peterson and Jennifer S. H. Brown, pp. 185–93. Winnipeg: University of Manitoba Press.

21. Ens, Gerhard. 1984. "Métis Lands in Manitoba." *Manitoba History* 5:2–11.

22. Flanagan, Thomas. 1979. *Louis 'David' Riel: 'Prophet of the New World.'* Toronto: University of Toronto Press.

23. ———. 1983. *Riel and the Rebellion: 1885 Reconsidered*. Saskatoon: Western Producer Prairie Books.

24. ———. 1985. "Louis Riel and the Dispersion of the American Métis." *Minnesota History* 49:179–90.

25. ———. 1985. "Métis Aboriginal Rights: Some Historical and Contemporary Problems." In *The Quest for Justice: Aboriginal Peoples and Aboriginal Rights*, ed. Meno Boldt and J. Anthony Long, pp. 230–45. Toronto: University of Toronto Press.

26. Foster, John E. 1976. "The Origins of the Mixed Bloods in the Canadian West." In *Essays on Western History, in Honour of Lewis Gwynne Thomas*, ed. Lewis H. Thomas, pp. 71–80. Edmonton: University of Alberta Press.

27. ———. 1978. "The Métis: The People and the Term." *Prairie Forum* 3:79–90.

28. ———. 1985. "Paulet Paul: Métis 'House Indian' Folk-Hero?" *Manitoba History* 9:2–7.

29. ———. 1985. "Some Questions and Perspectives on the Problem of Métis Roots." In *The New Peoples: Being and Becoming Métis in North America*, ed. Jacqueline Peterson and Jennifer S. H. Brown, pp. 73–91. Winnipeg: University of Manitoba Press.

30. ———. 1986. "The Plains Métis." In *Native Peoples: The Canadian Experience*, ed. Bruce Morrison and R. C. Wilson, pp. 375–403. Toronto: McClelland and Stewart.

31. Giraud, Marcel. 1945. *Le Métis Canadien: Son rôle dans l'histoire des Provinces de l'Ouest*. Paris: Travaux et Mémoires de l'Institute d'Ethnologie.
32. Goldring, Philip. 1984. "Governor Simpson's Officers: Elite Recruitment in a British Overseas Enterprise, 1834–1870." *Prairie Forum* 10:251–81.
33. Harrison, Julia D. 1985. *Métis: People Between Two Worlds*. Vancouver and Toronto: Douglas & McIntyre Ltd.
34. ———. 1986. "Métis: A Glenbow Museum Exhibition." *American Indian Art Magazine* 11:54–59.
35. Hildebrandt, Walter. 1985. *The Battle of Batoche: British Small Warfare and the Entrenched Métis*. Ottawa: Parks Canada.
36. Judd, Carol M. 1985. "Moose Factory Was Not Red River: A Comparison of Mixed-Blood Experiences." In *Explorations in Canadian Economic History: Essays in Honour of Irene M. Spry*, ed. Duncan Cameron, pp. 251–68. Ottawa: University of Ottawa Press.
37. Kienetz, Alvin. 1983. "The Rise and Decline of Hybrid (Métis) Societies on the Frontier of Western Canada and Southern Africa." *Canadian Journal of Native Studies* 3:3–21.
38. Long, John. 1983. "Archdeacon Thomas Vincent of Moosonee and the Handicap of Métis Racial Status." *Canadian Journal of Native Studies* 3:95–116.
39. Long, John S. 1985. "Treaty No. 9 and Fur Trade Company Families: Northeastern Ontario's Halfbreeds, Indians, Petitioners, and Métis." In *The New Peoples: Being and Becoming Métis in North America*, ed. Jacqueline Peterson and Jennifer S. H. Brown, pp. 137–62. Winnipeg: University of Manitoba Press.
40. McKenzie, Wayne. 1986. "Métis Self-Government in Saskatchewan." In *1885 and After: Native Society in Transition*, ed. F. L. Barron and James B. Waldram, pp. 297–306. Regina: Canadian Plains Research Centre.
41. McLean, Don. 1985. *1885: Métis Rebellion or Government Conspiracy?* Winnipeg: Pemmican Publications.
42. McNab, David T. 1985. "Métis Participation in the Treaty-Making Process in Ontario: A Reconnaissance." *Native Studies Review* 1:57–79.
43. Madill, Dennis F. K. 1983. *Select Annotated Bibliography on Métis History and Claims*. Ottawa: Research Branch, Corporate Policy, Indian and Northern Affairs Canada.
44. Martel, Gilles. 1984. *Le Messianisme de Louis Riel*. Waterloo, Ontario: Wilfrid Laurier University Press.
45. Mossmann, Manfred. 1985. "The Charismatic Pattern: Canada's Riel Rebellion of 1885." *Prairie Forum* 10:307–325.
46. Murray, Stanley N. 1984. "The Turtle Mountain Chippewa, 1882–1905." *North Dakota History* 51:14–37.
47. Nicks, Trudy. 1985. "Mary Anne's Dilemma: The Ethnohistory of an Ambivalent Identity." *Canadian Ethnic Studies* 17:103–14.
48. ———, and Kenneth Morgan. 1985. "Grande Cache: The Historic De-

velopment of an Indigenous Alberta Métis Population." In *The New Peoples: Being and Becoming Métis in North America*, ed. Jacqueline Peterson and Jennifer S. H. Brown, pp. 163–81. Winnipeg: University of Manitoba Press.

49. Pannekoek, Frits. 1981. "The Historiography of the Red River Settlement, 1830–1868." *Prairie Forum* 6:75–85.
50. Payment, Diane. 1983. *Batoche (1870–1910)*. Saint-Boniface: Les Editions du Blé.
51. ———. 1986. "Batoche After 1885: A Society in Transition." In *1885 and After: Native Society in Transition*, ed. F. L. Barron and James B. Waldram, pp. 178–87. Regina: Canadian Plains Research Centre.
52. Peterson, Jacqueline. 1978. "Prelude to Red River: A Social Portrait of the Great Lakes Métis." *Ethnohistory* 25:41–67.
53. ———. 1981. "The People in Between: Indian-White Marriage and the Genesis of A Métis Society and Culture in the Great Lakes Region, 1680–1830. Ph.D. thesis, University of Chicago. (Ann Arbor: University Microfilms International).
54. ———. 1985. "Many Roads to Red River: Métis Genesis in the Great Lakes Region, 1680–1815." In *The New Peoples: Being and Becoming Métis in North America*, ed. Jacqueline Peterson and Jennifer S. H. Brown, pp. 31–71. Winnipeg: University of Manitoba Press.
55. ———. 1985. "The Indian and the Fur Trade: A Review of Recent Literature." *Manitoba History* 10:10–18.
56. ———, and Jennifer S. H. Brown. 1985. *The New Peoples: Being and Becoming Métis in North America*. Winnipeg: University of Manitoba Press.
57. ———, and John Anfinson. 1984. "The Indian and the Fur Trade: A Review of Recent Literature." In *Scholars and the Indian Experience: Critical Reviews of Recent Writing in the Social Sciences*, ed. W. R. Swagerty, pp. 223–57. Bloomington: Indiana University Press.
58. Pollard, Julliet. 1984. "A Most Remarkable Phenomenon—Growing Up Métis: Fur Traders' Children in the Pacific Northwest." In *An Imperfect Past: Education and Society in Canadian History*, ed. J. Donald Wilson, pp. 120–40. Vancouver: Centre for the Study of Curriculum and Instruction.
59. Ray, Arthur J. 1982. "Reflections on Fur Trade Social History and Métis History in Canada." *American Indian Culture and Research Journal* 6:91–107.
60. Sawchuck, Joe. 1985. "The Métis, Non-Status Indians and the New Aboriginality: Government Influence on Native Political Alliances and Identity." *Canadian Ethnic Studies* 17:135–46.
61. Sprague, D. N., and R. P. Frye. 1983. *The Genealogy of the First Métis Nation*. Winnipeg: Pemmican Publications.
62. ———, and P. R. Mailhot. 1985. "Persistent Settlers: The Dispersal and Resettlement of the Red River Métis, 1870–85." *Canadian Ethnic Studies* 17:1–30.
63. Spry, Irene M. 1985. "The Métis and Mixed-Bloods of Rupert's Land

Before 1870." In *The New Peoples: Being and Becoming Métis in North America*, ed. Jacqueline Peterson and Jennifer S. H. Brown, pp. 95–118. Winnipeg: University of Manitoba Press.

64. Stanley, George F. G., ed. 1985. *The Collected Writings of Louis Riel/ Les Écrits complets de Louis Riel*. Edmonton: University of Alberta Press.

65. ———. 1986. "The Last Word on Louis Riel—The Man of Several Faces." In *1885 and After: Native Society in Transition*, ed. F. L. Barron and James B. Waldram, pp. 3–22. Regina: Canadian Plains Research Centre.

66. Tobias, John L. 1983. "Canada's Subjugation of the Plains Cree, 1879–1885." *Canadian Historical Review* 64:519–48.

67. Van Kirk, Sylvia. 1980. "Fur Trade Social History: Some Recent Trends." In *Old Trails and New Directions: Papers of the Third North American Fur Trade Conference*, ed. Carol M. Judd and Arthur J. Ray, pp. 160–73. Toronto: University of Toronto Press.

68. ———. 1980. *'Many Tender Ties': Women in Fur-trade Society, 1670–1870*. Winnipeg: Watson & Dwyer Publishing Ltd.

69. ———. 1985. "'What if Mama is an Indian?' The Cultural Ambivalence of the Alexander Ross Family." In *The New Peoples: Being and Becoming Métis in North America*, ed. Jacqueline Peterson and Jennifer S. H. Brown, pp. 207–17. Winnipeg: University of Manitoba Press.

70. Waldram, James B. 1986. "The 'Other Side': Ethnostatus Distinctions in Western Subarctic Native Communities." In *1885 and After: Native Society in Transition*, ed. F. L. Barron and James B. Waldram, pp. 279–95. Regina: Canadian Plains Research Centre.

71. Weaver, Sally M. 1985. "Federal Policy-Making for Métis and Non-Status Indians in the Context of Native Policy." *Canadian Ethnic Studies* 17:80–102.

CHAPTER 4

In Search of Multisided Frontiers: Recent Writing on the History of the Southern Plains

WILLARD ROLLINGS

Scholars of Indian history have long recognized that frontiers are two-sided phenomena and that we convey an inaccurate and partial view of historical reality by concentrating exclusively on the Anglo or American side of the frontier. In an area like the Southern Plains, the historical interplay of European, American, and Indian groups is so complex and intricate that a multidimensional approach is necessary. Much recent literature remains tied to outmoded concerns with white initiatives and with military relations and pays little attention to Indian perspectives.

Willard Rollings shows in this chapter that while studies of Spanish policies or Indian wars have a value of their own, they cannot convey the richness and diversity of Southern Plains history if they fail to pursue a cross-cultural approach. Only when the perspectives, policies, and concerns of Comanches, Kiowas, Wichitas, and Osages are integrated with those of the Spanish, French, Mexicans, and Anglo-Americans can a full picture of Southern Plains history be achieved. The abundance of underused material available in French, Spanish, and Mexican archives means that this is a formidable but by no means insurmountable task.

Frontiers are cultural creations. As areas where cultures meet and interact, they are the sites of fascinating events and intricate and complex processes. The Southern Plains have been the scene of cultural contact, conflict, and, ultimately, accommodation. This area, roughly defined for this chapter, is that largely flat and treeless region bounded in the north by the Cimarron River, the east by the

Cross Timbers, the west by the Southern Rockies, and the south by the southern edge of the Edwards Plateau.

Typically frontiers are perceived as specific geographic locations where two cultures meet. Thus, they are conceived as two-sided affairs, and the history of the United States is replete with studies of such dual frontiers. The Southern Plains have produced their share of these frontier studies.

The Spanish, the first Europeans to venture onto the Southern Plains, have received a great deal of study, and an important element of the vast field of Spanish Borderlands history focuses on the Southern Plains frontier. The French, too, were early European explorers and Plains traders. Although the French frontier experience in the Trans-Mississippi has never generated enough interest to create a French Borderlands movement, there are several studies of the French Plains frontier. The Mexican era also has elicited frontier research. But clearly the most extensive historical research of the Southern Plains has been created by historians examining the history of the United States. Most of the history written about the Southern Plains frontier has been written almost entirely from the perspective of United States history.

Some historians have correctly criticized many of these American-framed frontier studies, arguing that frontiers are a two-sided phenomenon and that the history of the region can only be understood if both sides are examined. It is true that Southern Plains history needs to be examined from within the context of United States westward expansion and Hispanic northern expansion. While such studies are valid, scholars should not be so shortsighted as to see the Spanish Borderlands or American Southwest, however one perceives the region, to be merely a two-sided affair. The Southern Plains were the home of indigenous and immigrant Indian peoples and thus contained more than two sides. The dual frontier conceptualization ignores the real dimensions of Southern Plains frontier history. One needs to consider Apache-Wichita frontiers in the same light as Spanish-Comanche frontiers, or realistically Apache-Wichita-Spanish-Comanche frontiers. The Southern Plains was a multisided frontier, and, accordingly, its history is rich and complex. The richness and complexity of the history is lost when such factors and perspectives are ignored.

Unfortunately, despite the abundance of subject material, much of the Indian history of the Southern Plains is conceptually flawed and ethnocentrically biased. Almost all of the history of the region is written in the context of European exploration, conquest, and colonization. In fairness to recent scholars, some work avoids such narrowly conceived conceptualizations, yet much remains to be done if we are to understand the history of this region. Not only must we better understand the Indian perspective, but we must also integrate it with those of the Spanish, French, Mexicans, and Anglo-Americans. Only then will we understand the history of the Southern Plains.

One way to reformulate our view of the region is to redefine the extent of its history. Traditionally historians and archaeologists have worked in separate fields. As a result, much of the archaeological literature consists of narrowly focused site reports written for specialists. Fortunately, there are works that provide regional overviews and summarize current research. These can serve as springboards both for extending our knowledge of Southern Plains history and for better understanding the documents of early contact.

Two surveys of Texas and Oklahoma archaeological research summarize recent work and provide a solid regional synthesis. Robert Bell edited a collection of seventeen articles in *Prehistory of Oklahoma* [5]. Although only a portion of the book deals with the Southern Plains, the essays by David Hughes, Jerry Galm, Jack Hofman, Robert Bell, Christopher Lintz, and Leon Zabavo are particularly helpful in reviewing, analyzing, and summarizing recent Oklahoma Plains prehistory. Bell's comprehensive bibliography is extensive and thorough. It contains over nine hundred items and brings together all the important work on Oklahoma archaeology.

Daniel Fox's *Traces of Texas History* [17] provides a summary of Texas archaeology. Fox's bibliography, although not as lengthy as Bell's, is comprehensive and useful, for it lists many monographs, reports, and studies that otherwise might be overlooked by the nonspecialists. Fox's work is extremely readable and perhaps easier to comprehend than the Oklahoma book, which is clearly written for professionals. Fox's maps, drawings, and photographs are particularly helpful, and the section on eighteenth-century French trading sites is an important contribution. The surveys by Bell and Fox are both successful in presenting the pre-Columbian history of the area and provide access to recent research.

Another important source on Southern Plains archaeology is *Papers in Anthropology* [7, 14, 38, 40], a publication of the Department of Anthropology of the University of Oklahoma. *Papers in Anthropology* has published several recent works about the area's prehistory. Susan Vehik has edited a special issue concentrating on Southern Plains archaeology. The articles contained in the issue are narrowly focused technical reports about bison distribution [14], the relationship of climate and human occupation [7], specialized Caddoan building types [40], and burial goods [38]. Although specialized, the studies are useful.

Archaeological research plays a significant role in Southern Plains history, providing information about tribal locations, migrations, settlement patterns, economic interaction, and environmental exploitation. Archaeologists need to continue working with the historical accounts of Spanish and French explorers to discover village sites that can provide new information about the nature of Southern Plains life and new insights into interaction among ethnic groups in the area. Archaeologists must bring their recent research together and create regional syntheses so that their results can be made available to a broader audience of historians and anthropologists.

For the early contact period, Spanish exploration, conquest, and colonization in the American Southwest has produced an abundance of research. The thrust of this research, however, has always been concerned with the Spanish. Little attention has been given to the Indians of the Spanish Borderlands. Indians, for the most part, merely form part of the backdrop for Spanish activity. Indeed, in many works they appear as little more than additional elements of a harsh landscape. When Indians are included, they often appear either as creatures whose sole concern appears to be war, or as passive drones providing needed labor for Spanish missions. Elements of this inaccurate and incomplete portrayal unfortunately persist.

The early entradas of the Spanish continue to elicit interest. Clearly, the journals of these expeditions provide information essential for the reconstruction of pre- and protohistoric Indian societies. Using exacting research techniques and extensive archival research, scholars have reexamined the early Spanish reports. Some are merely interested in finding the exact routes of the Spanish, while others are trying to decipher and recapture information lost because of gaps in documentation, cultural ignorance, or simply bad translations. The Panhandle Plains Historical Society is sponsoring a project to collect all archival materials concerning the Coronado expedition. Researchers have discovered new material in the Archivo

General de Indias in Seville. The project's focus is primarily collections, but it is also using the new material to create a mapping file to retrace Coronado's exact route. Another element of the project is the creation of a biographical file on all the participants. Although the focus is European, clearly the collected materials can be used by historians interested in adopting a multidimensional approach to early Spanish settlement. Douglas Inglis's "Men of Cibola" [26] provides a summary of this ongoing project.

A preliminary effort at linking early Spanish and Native American histories is Susan Vehik's recent article retracing the route of Oñate's 1601 entrada [47]. She compares villages mentioned in the Oñate accounts to known archaeological sites, and by combining cartographic, archaeological, and historical research with ethnological information she identifies the Indian peoples encountered by Oñate. Vehik demonstrates clearly that, despite the similarities of the various Wichita bands, there were political, social, and economic differences among them.

Research concentrating on Spanish activity in the lower Mississippi Valley often provides important insight into the cross-cultural nature of Southern Plains history. Indians on the Southern Plains were affected by Spanish activities on the Mississippi. Plains Indian captives were often enslaved in Spanish households, and traders based in Spanish Louisiana carried out an extensive trade with the Southern Plains people. M. Carmen Gonzalez Lopez-Briones's study of the Spanish colonization of Arkansas [21] illuminates these relationships. Based on important and little-used Spanish archival materials, her study focuses on the Spanish attempt to use Arkansas as a barrier to foreign economic and political penetration of the west.

Other works that examine the Spanish presence in Arkansas are more narrowly conceived. Gilbert Din's collaborative effort with A. P. Nasatir, *The Imperial Osages* [10], is an excellent study, not of the Osage, but of eighteenth-century Spanish-Indian policy in the Mississippi Valley. Using Nasatir's massive collection of eighteenth-century Spanish documents, Din has produced an impressive study of Spanish-Indian policy. Although ethnocentrically biased, it is nonetheless important as a resource tool for future research in the period and will hopefully stimulate multidimensional studies. Din has also produced a study of "The Spanish Fort on the Arkansas" [9].

Another aspect of Spanish-Indian interaction is treated in an excellent article by Stephen Webre [49]. Webre examines the position of Indian slavery in Louisiana within the Spanish colonial legal framework. His discussion of Indian slaves suing for their freedom in Spanish courts reveals once again the potential for new types of Indian history.

Jack August's [2] study of the Indian policy of Don Fernando de la Concha, governor of New Mexico from 1787 to 1795, demonstrates that studies of government policy can also describe Spanish-Indian relationships. Concha established peace in New Mexico and on the Plains by carefully balancing the interests of the Spanish, Apaches, Comanches, and Utes. August's description of the complex situation and his analysis of Concha's Indian policy is a sound, well-researched, and well-written study of Spanish-Indian diplomacy.

Cheryl Foote's sound study of eighteenth-century Spanish-Plains Indian trade [16] portrays another area of Spanish-Indian interaction. Her description of Spanish policy, trade goods, and prices and the trade fairs at Pecos and Taos clearly demonstrates how extensive and important the trade was to both Spanish and Indians.

In almost all studies of the Spanish colonial period in the Southwest the focus is on Spanish activity. Indians are merely threats to peace or commerce, a people to be conquered, converted, and put to work. There is little attention to Indian life, and seldom is the Indian viewpoint introduced. There is little explanation for their behavior except in the simplest manner, and they remain mysterious, incomplete historical characters for the Spanish to react against. For example, Catherine Price's "The Comanche Threat to Texas and New Mexico in the Eighteenth Century and the Development of Spanish Indian Policy" [39] acknowledges that a comprehension of Comanche and Apache culture is vital to an understanding of the topic, but she fails to incorporate it adequately into the article.

A notable exception is the work of Elizabeth A. H. John. John, the author of *Storms Brewed in Other Men's Worlds* [27], a massive survey of Spanish and Indian relations in the Southwest up to 1795, continues to produce solid historical studies. Relying primarily on the Bexar archives, John provides a better balanced history, which incorporates more of the cultural context of the Southern Plains Indian people. "Nurturing the Peace: Spanish and Comanche Cooperation in the Early Nineteenth Century" [29] is one of her best studies. She demonstrates that the Comanches and the Spanish, despite their different cultural viewpoints and their different political and social institutions, were able to cooperate and achieve peace in the late eighteenth and early nineteenth centuries. John skillfully shows the complexity of the situation and the problems created by the differing perspectives and goals of the Indians and the Spanish. Her use of Spanish archival materials and her careful attention to the historic detail make her description and analysis of Comanche-Spanish diplomacy both understandable and intriguing. Her article is a refreshing contribution to Borderlands history that has for far too long lumped the diverse Indian peoples into simply *Indios barbaros*. John's work is important not only in revealing that the Comanches were people who earnestly sought peace and who often lived in peace with the Spanish, but also in providing an example of what can and should be done in the Spanish colonial period of Southern Plains history.

Elizabeth John is working on a sequel to *Storms Brewed in Other Men's Worlds* that will complete the last years of the Spanish period, and it is hoped she will continue beyond 1821 into the Mexican era, as this period has not been adequately studied. Indeed, the paucity of recent research on the first half of the nineteenth century is regrettable. Few Spanish studies extend into the nineteenth century, and fewer still examine Indian history in the Mexican period. David Weber's *The Mexican Frontier, 1821–1846: The American Southwest Under Mexico* [48] is an exception to that pattern. This study of Mexico's northern frontier is an excellent regional study, but it is primarily concerned with the Mexican aspect of the region's history. Although Weber acknowledges the need to understand the Indian people, he too portrays them primarily as warriors confronting the Mexicans. We can hope that Weber's work combined with Daniel Tyler's recent guide [46] to Mexican-period archival materials will direct more attention to this long-neglected period and stimulate more research into the Indian side of things. New, sophisticated studies about the influence of Mexican independence on the Indian people of the Southern Plains, shifting intertribal relationships, changes in the nature and effect of trade, and the role of Comancheros are needed. We know very little about "Indian life" in the Mexican era, and research in Mexican records can help us better understand life of Southern Plains tribes in the early nineteenth century.

Despite the somewhat ethnocentric bias of most Spanish and Mexican studies, enough basic research has been completed to establish a solid foundation for further study. This unfortunately is not the case for French studies. Although French explorers and traders operating from French outposts along the Arkansas, Red, and Missouri rivers penetrated the Plains in the late seventeenth and eighteenth centuries, this portion of French colonial history has yet to be satisfactorily examined. One of the few scholars working in this area is Mildred Mott Wedel. Wedel has produced several important articles about French exploration and trade in the Central Plains and Southern Plains. Much of her work focuses on the eighteenth-century journeys of La Harpe [50, 55] and DuTisné [51]. Her studies have revealed new information about French-Wichita contact and more precise information about locations of Wichita village sites [52, 53]. Wedel, using French archival material, has shown the shortcomings of the Pierre Margry collections and the danger of relying solely on published translations of French documents. Combining the skills of a paleographer, historian, and anthropologist, she has begun to reconstruct elements of Wichita protohistory. Wedel recently edited some of the work of the noted Jesuit scholar Jean Delanglez [54]. Delanglez's work on French colonial activity in North America is important, for he established rigorous standards. Delanglez discovered "lost" documents and clarified misunderstandings created by incomplete records, bad translations, and fraudulent accounts. His critical studies of French documents are crucial for an understanding of the reliability and nature of early French records. Most of his work was written in the 1940s and published in the Jesuit journal *Mid-America*, unfortunately not a common feature of many libraries. Wedel has resurrected Delanglez's work regarding Indians of the Mississippi Valley from the relative obscurity of *Mid-America* back issues. This collection makes available twelve of Delanglez's articles to a wider audience of scholars.

The pattern of an extensive literature which only partially reveals the complexity of Southern Plains history is evident in studies of Indian-White relations which are unduly concerned with military activity. Paul Hutton's award-winning study of General Phil Sheridan [25] includes portions about campaigns Sheridan directed against Southern Plains tribes, as does William and Shirley Leckie's [31] book about General Benjamin Grierson's activities on the Southern Plains. The Leckies' study of Grierson and his family in Texas is a rare social history of the nineteenth-century military frontier. Both books are excellent studies of military leaders involved in Southern Plains campaigns, but they have little to say about Indians. A closely related book is Thomas Dunlay's *Wolves for the Blue Soldiers* [11], an examination of Indian scouts who worked for the United States

Army in the late nineteenth century. Most of Dunlay's attention is devoted to Apache and Pawnee scouts, and only a small portion deals with the Tonkawa scouts and other Southern Plains participants. It is sound military history, but it is somewhat weak in its treatment of Indian culture. Other examples of this genre include Clayton Williams's encyclopedic study of Fort Stockton, *Texas' Last Frontier* [61], and Leonard Slesick's study of Fort Bascom [42]. The focus is on Indian wars with little or no attempt made to understand any Indian viewpoint.

Two recent dissertations, however, are evidence of new research in nineteenth-century Indian-white relations. William Gannett's "The American Invasion of Texas, 1820–1845; Patterns of Conflict Between Settlers and Indians" [20] is an attempt to reexamine the conflicts while taking into consideration the differing political and cultural organization of the participants. Gannett's examination of the role of environment and Indian subsistence patterns on Indian and White Texas history is a welcome change in nineteenth-century Texas history. Shelly Hatfield's study of "Indians on the United States–Mexico Border During the Porfiriato, 1876–1911" [23] is also significant, for it is perhaps the first that focuses on border-region Indian history in this period.

The growing literature on nineteenth-century trade shows some similar limitations. T. Lindsay Baker and Billy R. Harrison are interested in trade on the Southern Plains, but their emphasis is on a prominent buffalo hunter's trading post on the Canadian River. Their *Adobe Walls: The History and Archeology of the 1874 Trading Post* [3] is a comprehensive historical narrative about the post which includes evidence produced by a recent archaeological investigation. The study is exhaustive, yet it concentrates on white activity in the area and centers on the 1874 battle of Adobe Walls.

Plains Indians were actively engaged in trade with other Indians and white traders. Dan Flores, who previously edited the journals of the Freeman-Custis Red River Expedition [12], has edited the journal of Anthony Glass [13]. Glass, an early Anglo trader on the Southern Plains, kept a journal that reveals important information about the Indian people of the Southern Plains and of the Southern Plains environment. Glass's account provides many details about tribal locations, settlement patterns, social and political organization, intertribal relations, trade, and other information about the Southern Plains in the early nineteenth century. Flores's environmental focus is largely absent from Elizabeth John's editorial work with the Glass journal [28]. John concentrates on the Indian aspects of the journal as Glass describes life among the Wichitas in 1808 and 1809. Both Flores and John have done a fine job of editing this journal, and both reveal a great deal of information on a people, a place, and a time about which we know little.

Some authors have managed to escape the preoccupation with military and economic affairs which so often focuses primarily on whites. Most prominent among these have been the authors of tribal histories. *Kiowa Voices* [8], edited by Maurice Boyd, includes accounts of Kiowa warfare, yet it uses Kiowa sources for such accounts. It is a collection of Kiowa oral history which includes folktales, legends, myths, and personal accounts of events in Kiowa history.

Elizabeth John [30], using Spanish documents, has also written on eighteenth-century Kiowa history. Because of the nature of the sources, the history created deals largely with their interactions with the Spanish, but John has produced a solid historical narrative concerning early Kiowa history and their relationships with other Southern Plains tribes. John's article reveals the Kiowas as a people who sought peace and worked diligently to balance their interests with those of other tribes and Europeans in the region. Once again John reveals the complexity of Kiowa history and provides a new perspective on them.

When the Kiowas and Comanches were finally forced onto reservations in Indian Territory, the federal government actively worked to destroy their culture and replace it with the white culture. Rebecca Herring has examined an element of this forced assimilation [24]. Her study of the missionary field matrons on the Kiowa and Comanche reservations reveals a little-known aspect of Native American reservation history. Although largely descriptive, the work examines the cultural tenacity of the Comanche and Kiowa people.

A lack of twentieth-century studies is a common problem in Native American history generally. It is particularly acute for the Southern Plains tribes. Peter Iverson's collection of twentieth-century Plains Indian history includes essays by Donald Berthrong [6] and Thomas Hagan [22] dealing with problems of Southern Plains people living on reservations in Oklahoma. Berthrong's study of the theft of Cheyenne-Arapaho land after the Dawes Act reveals a familiar story of deceit and treachery. A similar account by Hagan examines the opening of the Kiowa, Comanche, and Kiowa-Apache reservations. Both are careful studies of how Indian people were deprived of their lands in the reservation era.

The reservation era is also examined in Robert Nespor's study of agriculture among the Southern Cheyennes [37]. Nespor shows clearly that the Cheyennes chose certain aspects of white culture, notably agricultural innovation, while rejecting other aspects. Nespar's dissertation examines Native American cultural adaptation and reveals the process whereby Indian people incorporated change without abandoning their culture.

Two other dissertations examine the forced assimilation of Indian people. Henrietta Whiteman [59] uses oral history to provide an Indian perspective in her educational history of Cheyenne-Arapaho education from 1871 to 1982. Sally McBeth's [32] study of ethnic identity within the Indian boarding schools of Oklahoma describes the complex cultural process that occurred at the Indian boarding schools. She concludes that the schools created and fostered a new dynamic pan-Indian identity and ultimately failed to destroy Indian ethnic identity. The process of forced assimilation and acculturation is a complex one worthy of further study.

Another aspect of twentieth-century adaptation and interaction is treated in George Morgan and Omer Stewart's examination of the development of the Texas peyote trade and the nature of the relationship between the Indian peyote user and the largely Hispanic *peyotero* (peyote tráder) [35].

While there remains a need for continued archival research, the critical need for Southern Plains Spanish-era history is new conceptualizations. Scholars need to escape the confines of the Spanish historical and cultural framework and should reexamine Spanish materials with new perspectives and questions. Basic questions about tribal identities, locations, and migration remain unanswered. Information about Indian social, political, and economic life is needed. We lack both description and analysis of Southern Plains cultures and the rate and nature of cultural changes. Questions about Indian religions, leadership, political organization, and environmental interaction need to be answered. Research about the effects of the horse and gun on the Southern Plains peoples, the influence of European trade and disease, inter- and intratribal relationships, and the role of Europeans among Indians as hunters, traders, and tribal members is also needed. The only information available about the early contact period which permits us to reconstruct precontact Indian societies can be found in Spanish and French archival sources. Scholars working in the Spanish period can take advantage of the abundant historical research and archival materials available. The massive work already accomplished by such historians as Hubert Bancroft, Herbert Bolton, John F. Bannon, A. B. Thomas, and others provides a basic foundation and framework for future research. In addition, the holdings of the Archivo General y Público de la Nación (AGN) and the Archivo General de Indias (AGI) contain an abundance of materials containing considerable information about Indian people. Spanish archival materials have been microfilmed and are available in the United States. The Bexar, the Farral, and portions of the Nacogdoches archives have been filmed, as have the "Provincias Internas" and "Historia" *ramos* of the AGN and the "Papeles de Cuba" of the AGI. There are several guides to Spanish archival materials, but the recent research guide of Thomas Barnes, Thomas Naylor, and Charles Polzer [4] is very useful. This comprehensive guide to research in northern New Spain contains information about Spanish archival holdings in Spain, Mexico, and the United States. It also contains a description of the Documentary Relations of the Southwest (DRSW) project, which is collecting, editing, annotating, and cataloging Spanish archival materials. This guide has become a basic tool for research in the Spanish period.

In contrast to the vast amount of research on the Spanish era on the Southern Plains, the French experience has become largely ignored by scholars. Clearly the Spanish presence was more extensive and long-lasting. The French, however, did play a role in Southern Plains history. Scholars interested in the French must use the French archives, specifically the C13A series, which contains letters and reports originating in French Louisiana. There might also be information about events in the West in the C11A series, which contains Canadian-generated materials, and in the Archives de la Marine (AM) and the Archives du Service Hydrographique (ASH). There are calendars available to these series produced by the French archives, but the best guide remains the two-volume calendar prepared by Nancy Miller Surrey [44]. Unfortunately, there are few copies of the archival materials in the United States. The C13A series has been microfilmed, and there are copies at the Library of Congress, the University of Southwestern Louisiana at Lafayette, Loyola University in New Orleans, the Historic New Orleans Collection, Memphis

State University, and the Mississippi Department of Archives and History at Jackson.

French archival material contains reports and accounts of early French explorers who visited and traded with the Southern Plains tribes. We can learn a great deal about the Indians in the French documents. One can look at the work of Richard White [57, 58] and Patricia Galloway [18, 19] on the Choctaws and at Patricia Dillon Wood's study, *French-Indian Relations on the Southern Frontier* [63], to realize the possibilities for research about Indians west of the Mississippi. Another example examining eighteenth-century materials from west of the Mississippi is Willard Rollings's "Prairie Hegemony: An Ethnohistorical Study of the Osage from Early Times to 1840" [41]. Rollings's dissertation focuses on Osage cultural change as the Osages expanded onto the Central Plains and Southern Plains but also includes a description and analysis of French influence on the Osages, the Wichitas, and other Caddoan tribes in the eighteenth century. Robert Wieger's recent dissertation [60] infers Osage culture change from contact and trade with the Caddos and Pawnees. Terry Wilson's *Bibliography of the Osage* [62] provides a valuable guide to the literature on the tribe.

Largely as a result of the limited extent and nature of French exploration and settlement west of the Mississippi, and in part because of the neglect of scholars, there has been little work on the French in the Southwest. With the exception of the earlier work of Henri Folmer and the recent work of Mildred Wedel [50, 51, 52, 53] on La Harpe and DuTisné, little has been done. Scholars have too often depended upon the unreliable Margry collections and have failed to use original French materials. The French traded with the Plains Apache, Comanche, Wichita, and Red and Arkansas river Caddoans. The nature of this trade and its influence on Indian people has been neither adequately described nor analyzed. By examining both French and Spanish records one can better understand the history of the Indian people of the Southern Plains. One cannot truly comprehend Wichita or Comanche history without examining the interaction of these people with one another and with the invading Europeans as revealed in the European record. There is a great potential for individual and comparative studies.

For the later half of the nineteenth century scholars have only to turn to the abundant historical research and archival materials available. As in the Spanish era, scholars can take advantage of previous research and sources and reexamine it with new perspectives. New questions need to be asked about nineteenth-century Indian history. We already know about the plans of General Sheridan and the campaigns of George Custer and Ranald MacKenzie; now we need to focus our attention on the Indian people these men were so intent on destroying. What was the effect of repeated attacks and eventual confinement of Indian people on the reservations? We have a good idea of what happened in the nineteenth century, but we still are unsure of what it all means. There is much to be done in nineteenth-century Southern Plains studies, for our narrow focus on violence and warfare has distorted our vision of Southern Plains history. The reduction of complex activities and processes to single studies of war is a disservice to all the participants.

Native American people shaped and created much of the history of the Southern Plains, yet today we know little about their history. Until we examine and better understand these people and their past, we will never fully grasp what took place there. We must write historical studies of the Southern Plains Indians that take into consideration the cultural context of their actions and incorporate their perspectives. Such studies must be integrated into the histories of the Spanish, French, Mexicans, and Anglo-Americans, for only then can we understand the history of the Southern Plains.

Recent Southern Plains studies are uneven in quality and scope. The region's history is dominated by inordinate emphasis on eighteenth-century Spanish-Indian policy and nineteenth-century military relations. The full cultural and historical context of the Indian inhabitants and their interactions with other groups has been ignored. The one-sided ethnocentric histories have not given way to balanced historical studies. One has only to look at the sophisticated work about the Canadian Cree fur trade or Iroquois diplomacy to realize the potential for Southern Plains Indian studies. Only a multidisciplinary approach in which historians, anthropologists, geographers, sociologists, linguists, and other scholars explore the history of Southern Plains Indians can provide an accurate history of the Indian people and a full understanding of the area's history. This appeal for a new Indian history integrated into the broader context of American history is not original. Scholars have been calling for such history for over fifteen years. Some masterful works have been produced, but much remains to be done.

References

1. Allain, Mathe. 1984. "French Colonial Policy in America and the Establishment of the Louisiana Colony." Ph.D. dissertation, University of Southwestern Louisiana, Lafayette.
2. August, Jack. 1981. "Balance of Power Diplomacy in New Mexico: Governor Fernando de la Concha and the Indian Policy of Conciliation." *New Mexico Historical Review* 56:141–60.
3. Baker, T. Lindsay, and Billy R. Harrison. 1986. *Adobe Walls: The History and Archeology of the 1874 Trading Post.* College Station: Texas A&M University Press.
4. Barnes, Thomas C.; Thomas H. Naylor; and Charles W. Polzer. 1981. *Northern New Spain: A Research Guide.* Tucson: University of Arizona Press.
5. Bell, Robert E., ed. 1984. *Prehistory of Oklahoma.* Orlando, Fla.: Academic Press.
6. Berthrong, Donald D. 1986. "Legacies of the Dawes Act: Bureaucrats and Land Thieves at the Cheyenne-Arapaho Agencies of Oklahoma." In *Plains Indians of the Twentieth Century*, pp. 31–53, ed. Peter Iverson. Norman: University of Oklahoma Press.
7. Bobalik, Sheila J. 1982. "The Relationship of Climatic Change and Late Prehistoric Occupation on the Southern Plains." In "Southern Plains Archaeology," ed. Susan Vehik. *Papers in Anthropology* 23: 37–46.
8. Boyd, Maurice. 1981/1983. *Kiowa Voices.* 2 vols. Fort Worth: Texas Christian University Press.
9. Din, Gilbert C. 1983. "The Spanish Fort on the Arkansas, 1763–1803." *Arkansas Historical Quarterly* 42:271–93.
10. ———, and Abraham P. Nasatir. 1983. *The Imperial Osages: Spanish-Indian Diplomacy· in the Mississippi Valley.* Norman: University of Oklahoma Press.
11. Dunlay, Thomas W. 1982. *Wolves for the Blue Soldiers: Indian Scouts and Auxiliaries with the United States Army, 1860–90.* Lincoln: University of Nebraska Press.
12. Flores, Dan L. ed. 1984. *Jefferson and Southwest Exploration: The Freeman and Custis Accounts of the Red River Expedition of 1806.* Norman: University of Oklahoma Press.
13. ———. 1986. *Journal of an Indian Trader: Anthony Glass and the Texas Trading Frontier, 1790–1810.* College Station: Texas A&M University Press.
14. Flynn, Peggy. 1982. "Distribution of Prehistoric Bison on the Southern Plains: A Test of Dillehay's Model." In "Southern Plains Archaeology," ed. Susan Vehik. *Papers in Anthropology* 23:7–36.
15. Foote, Cheryl L. 1984. "Selected Sources for the Mexican Period (1821–1848) in New Mexico." *New Mexico Historical Review* 59: 81–89.
16. ———. 1985. "Spanish-Indian Trade Along New Mexico's Northern Frontier in the Eighteenth Century." *Journal of the West* 24:22–33.

17. Fox, Daniel. 1983. *Traces of Texas History: Archeological Evidence of the Past 450 Years.* San Antonio: Corona Publishing Co.

18. Galloway, Patricia K. 1982. "The Barthelemy Murders: Bienville's Establishment of *Lex Talonis* as a Principle of Indian Diplomacy." *Proceedings of the French Colonial Historical Society* 8:91–103.

19. ———, ed. 1984. *The Mississippi Provincial Archives: French Dominion*, Vol. 4, 1729–1748; Vol. 5, 1749–1763. Ed. and Trans. Dunbar Rowland and A. G. Sanders. Baton Rouge: Louisiana State University Press.

20. Gannett, William B. 1984. "The American Invasion of Texas, 1820–1845: Patterns of Conflict Between Settlers and Indians." Ph.D. dissertation, Cornell University.

21. Gonzales Lopez-Briones, M. Carmen. 1983. "Spain in the Mississippi Valley: Spanish Arkansas, 1762–1804." Ph.D. dissertation, Purdue University.

22. Hagan, William T. 1986. "Adjusting to the Opening of the Kiowa, Comanche, and Kiowa-Apache Reservations." In *Plains Indians of the Twentieth Century*, pp. 11–30, ed. Peter Iverson. Norman: University of Oklahoma Press.

23. Hatfield, Shelly Ann Bowen. 1983. "Indians on the United States–Mexico Border During the Porfiriato, 1876–1911." Ph.D. dissertation, University of New Mexico.

24. Herring, Rebecca Jane. 1986. "Their Work Was Never Done: Women Missionaries on the Kiowa-Comanche Reservation." *Chronicles of Oklahoma* 64:68–83.

25. Hutton, Paul A. 1985. *Phil Sheridan and His Army.* Lincoln: University of Nebraska Press.

26. Inglis, G. Douglas. 1982. "The Men of Cibola: New Investigations on the Francisco Vásquez de Coronado Expedition." *Panhandle-Plains Historical Review* 55:1–24.

27. John, Elizabeth A. H. 1975. *Storms Brewed in Other Men's Worlds: The Confrontation of Indians, Spanish, and French in the Southwest, 1540–1795.* College Station: Texas A&M University Press.

28. ———. 1982. "Portrait of a Wichita Village, 1808." *Chronicles of Oklahoma* 60:412–37.

29. ———. 1984. "Nurturing the Peace: Spanish and Comanche Cooperation in the Early Nineteenth Century." *New Mexico Historical Review* 59:345–69.

30. ———. 1985. "An Earlier Chapter in Kiowa History." *New Mexico Historical Review* 60:379–97.

31. Leckie, William H., and Shirley A. Leckie. 1984. *Unlikely Warriors: General Benjamin H. Grierson and His Family.* Norman: University of Oklahoma Press.

32. McBeth, Sally J. 1982. "Ethnic Identity and the Boarding School Experience of West Central Oklahoma American Indians." Ph.D. dissertation, Washington State University.

33. Magnaghi, Russell M., trans. and ed. 1984. "Texas As Seen by Gov-

ernor Winthuysen, 1741–1744." *Southwestern Historical Quarterly* 88:167–80.
34. Martin, J. C., and Robert Sidney Martin. 1984. *Maps of Texas and the Southwest, 1513–1900.* Albuquerque: University of New Mexico Press.
35. Morgan, George R., and Omer C. Stewart. 1984. "Peyote Trade in South Texas." *Southwestern Historical Quarterly* 87:269–96.
36. Morris, Richard Brasher. 1984. "Adobe Niche: Ethnohistory and Historical Demography of Pecos and Taos, New Mexico, in the Eighteenth Century." Ph.D. dissertation, Yale University.
37. Nespor, Robert Paschal. 1984. "The Evolution of Agricultural Settlement Patterns of the Southern Cheyenne Indians in Western Oklahoma, 1876–1930." Ph.D. dissertation, University of Oklahoma.
38. Peterson, Dennis A. 1982. "Regression Analyses of Harlan Phase Burial Goods." In "Southern Plains Archaeology," ed. Susan Vehik. *Papers in Anthropology* 23:91–104.
39. Price, Catherine. 1985. "The Comanche Threat to Texas and New Mexico in the Eighteenth Century and the Development of Spanish Indian Policy." *Journal of the West* 24:34–45.
40. Rogers, Daniel J. 1982. "Specialized Buildings in Northern Caddo Prehistory." In "Southern Plains Archaeology," ed. Susan Vehik. *Papers in Anthropology* 23:119–31.
41. Rollings, Willard H. 1983. "Prairie Hegemony: An Ethnohistorical Study of the Osage from Early Times to 1840." Ph.D. dissertation, Texas Tech University.
42. Slesick, Leonard M. 1984. "Fort Bascom: A Military Outpost in Eastern New Mexico." *Panhandle-Plains Historical Review* 61:1–23.
43. Stoddard, Ellwyn R.; Richard L. Nostrand; and Jonathan P. West. 1983. *Borderlands Sourcebook: A Guide to the Literature on Northern Mexico and the American Southwest.* Norman: University of Oklahoma Press.
44. Surrey, N. M. Miller. 1926–28. *Calendar of Manuscripts in Paris Archives and Libraries Relating to the History of the Mississippi Valley to 1803.* 2 vols. Washington, D.C.: Carnegie Institution.
45. Tyler, Daniel. 1982. "The Carrizal Archives: A Source for the Mexican Period." *New Mexico Historical Review* 57:257–67.
46. ———. 1984. *Sources for New Mexico History.* Santa Fe: Museum of New Mexico Press.
47. Vehik, Susan C. 1986. "Oñate's Expedition to the Southern Plains: Routes, Destinations, and Implications for Late Prehistoric Cultural Adaptations." *Plains Anthropologist* 31:13–33.
48. Weber, David. 1982. *The Mexican Frontier, 1821–1846: The American Southwest Under Mexico.* Albuquerque: University of New Mexico Press.
49. Webre, Stephen. 1984. "The Problem of Indian Slavery in Spanish Louisiana History, 1769–1803." *Louisiana History* 25:117–35.
50. Wedel, Mildred Mott. 1971. "J-B Bénard, Sieur De La Harpe: Visitor to the Wichitas in 1719." *Great Plains Journal* 10:37–70.
51. ———. 1972. "Claude-Charles DuTisné: A Review of His 1719 Journeys." *Great Plains Journal* 12:4–25, 146–73.

52. ———. 1981. *The Deer Creek Site, Oklahoma: A Wichita Village Sometimes Called Ferdinandina, An Ethnohistorian's View.* Oklahoma City: Oklahoma Historical Society.
53. ———. 1982. "The Wichita Indians in the Arkansas River Basin." In *Plains Indian Studies: A Collection of Essays in Honor of John C. Ewers and Waldo R. Wedel.* Smithsonian Contributions to Anthropology No. 30. Washington, D.C.: Smithsonian Institution.
54. ———. 1985. *A Jean Delanglez S.J. Anthology: Selections Useful for Mississippi Valley and Trans-Mississippi American Indian Studies.* New York: Garland Publishing.
55. Wedel, Waldo R., and Mildred M. Wedel. 1976. "Wichita Archeology and Ethnohistory." In *Kansas and the West*, pp. 8–20, ed. Forrest R. Blackburn. Topeka: Kansas State Historical Association.
56. Wehrkamp, Tim. 1985. "A Selected Guide to Sources on New Mexico Indians in the Modern Period." *New Mexico Historical Review* 60:435–44.
57. White, Richard. 1981. "Red Shoes: Warrior and Diplomat." In *Struggle and Survival in Colonial America*, pp. 49–68, ed. David Sweet and Gary Nash. Berkeley: University of California Press.
58. ———. 1983. *The Roots of Dependency: Subsistence, Environment and Social Change Among the Choctaws, Pawnees, and Navajos.* Lincoln: University of Nebraska Press.
59. Whiteman, Henrietta. 1982. "Cheyenne-Arapaho Education, 1871–1982." Ph.D. dissertation, University of New Mexico.
60. Wiegers, Robert Paul. 1985. "Osage Culture Change Inferred from Contact and Trade with the Caddo and the Pawnee." Ph.D. dissertation, University of Missouri.
61. Williams, Clayton W. 1982. *Texas' Last Frontier: Fort Stockton and the Trans-Pecos, 1861–1895.* Ed. Ernest Wallace. College Station: Texas A&M University Press.
62. Wilson, Terry P. 1985. *Bibliography of the Osage.* Metuchen, N.J.: Scarecrow Press.
63. Wood, Patricia Dillon. 1980. *French-Indian Relations on the Southern Frontier.* Ann Arbor: UMI Research Press.

CHAPTER 5

Indians and the Law

GEORGE S. GROSSMAN

In an age when Indian communities fight for their rights, lands, and freedoms in courtrooms rather than on battlefields and tribal attorneys are often viewed as a new generation of warriors, it is clear that "law dominates Indian life in a way not duplicated in other segments of American society" (F. Cohen, Handbook of Federal Indian Law *[Washington, D.C.: Government Printing Office, 1982 ed., p. vii]). Historians in other fields may still feel that their professional objectives are incompatible with those of lawyers, but scholars of Indian history must endeavor to keep pace with developments in American Indian law.*

In the past, the major issue in Indian law tended to revolve around federal power over Indian property. Today's conflicts involve preservation of tribal lands; recognition of tribal status; protection and control of water and other natural resources; jurisdiction between tribal, federal, and state governments; and upholding of treaty rights and of the federal trust responsibility as well as securing of basic rights in religious freedom, health, housing, and welfare.

The resulting mass of litigation and legislation of immediate concern to Indian communities has generated a flood of literature which most scholars lack the time, energy, and resources to absorb. George Grossman's initial survey of the literature identified a list of almost three hundred titles published in just three years. In this chapter he selects and reviews the most significant literature in the key areas and provides a bibliographic guide for scholars of Indian history as they enter this massive and multifaceted field.

Following the headline-making protests of the late 1960s and early
1970s—at Alcatraz, the BIA Building, and Wounded Knee—
American Indians were urged to seek reforms "within the system."
Heeding this advice has led to an era of rapid growth in American
Indian law. In one decade an unprecedented thirty-three cases involv-
ing American Indians were decided by the United States Supreme
Court. In Congress, major new legislation involving American In-
dians passed session after session—including the Indian Civil Rights
Act of 1968, the Alaska Native Claims Settlement Act of 1971, the
Indian Education Act of 1972, the Navajo-Hopi Claims Settlement
Act of 1974, the Indian Self-Determination and Educational Assis-
tance Act of 1975, the American Indian Religious Freedom Act of
1978, the Indian Child Welfare Act of 1978, and the Maine Indian
Claims Settlement Act of 1980.

This period was also a vintage era for the bibliography of American Indian law. The *American Indian Law Review* started publication at the University of Oklahoma in 1973. Although it has fallen
behind its publishing schedule, it has become a major outlet for
scholarship in the field. The *Indian Law Reporter*, published by
the American Indian Lawyer Training Program, started in 1974
and has provided the field with its only looseleaf service for current
legislation, court decisions, and administrative material. Two case-
books, *Federal Indian Law*, by David H. Getches and Charles F.
Wilkinson, published by West Publishing Company, and *Law and
the American Indian*, by Monroe E. Price and Robert N. Clinton,
published by the Michie Company (both published in the 1970s and
both in recent second editions), compete for classroom use in the
many law schools now offering Indian law courses, and two paper-
backs provide helpful capsule outlines of the field: William C. Can-
by's *American Indian Law*, published in 1981 as a volume of West
Publishing Company's Nutshell Series, and Stephen L. Pevar's *The
Rights of Indians and Tribes*, published by the American Civil Lib-
erties Union in 1983.

Government publications also played a major role—including the
republication and updating of Charles J. Kappler's classic compilation *Indian Affairs: Laws and Treaties* in the 1970s and the 1977
publications of the American Indian Policy Review Commission. In
1981, the Government Accounting Office also published a useful research tool in the *Guide to Records in the National Archives of the
United States Relating to American Indians.*

Another useful research tool of the era is *American Indian Legal Materials: A Union List*, compiled by Laura N. Gassaway, James L. Hoover, and Dorothy M. Warden and published by Earl M. Coleman in 1980. The *Union List* records the Indian law holdings of twenty-eight law libraries and is now serving as the checklist for the microfilming of all recorded material not under copyright by the Law Library Microfilm Consortium of Honolulu. A collection of Indian tribal codes has also been microfilmed under the editorship of Ralph W. Johnson, in 1981, by the Marian Gould Gallagher Law Library of the University of Washington.

Many new monographs and hundreds of periodical articles round out the bibliographic picture of the era—except for the most significant legal publication of all. The most ambitious scholarly achievement of the era came in 1982 with the publication of a new edition of the *Handbook of Federal Indian Law*, a treatise first published in 1941 by the "Blackstone" of American Indian law, Felix S. Cohen. The new edition features individual chapters written by leading scholars of Indian law prepared under the editorial supervision of Rennard Strickland.

All this adds up to a field which has developed a remarkable set of research resources in a remarkably brief time. Some scholarly tools are missing still: room remains for a "hornbook," halfway between a capsulized paperback and a detailed treatise; the *Handbook of Federal Indian Law* should be periodically updated; and American Indian law still has no comprehensive scholarly bibliography. Nevertheless, the wealth of materials on American Indian law available today is a welcome contrast to the difficulties of doing research in the field a mere fifteen years ago.

At the crest of this bibliographic wave, in 1984, the D'Arcy McNickle Center for the History of the American Indian of the Newberry Library published *Scholars and the Indian Experience*, a collection of bibliographic essays edited by W. R. Swagerty. Although none of the essays focus exclusively on law, essays by W. R. Swagerty, J. Frederick Fausz, Frederick E. Hoxie, and Donald L. Fixico contain many legal references.

This essay takes over where *Scholars and the American Experience* left off—at about mid-1983—but with the focus narrowed to specifically legal sources. As in the 1984 essays, Canadian issues are excluded, as are book reviews, government documents, and newspaper articles. Nevertheless, scholarly output in American Indian law remained so fertile that nearly three hundred citations were located for the three-year period. This essay will cover only highlights from the bibliography.

Despite the volume of output between mid-1983 and mid-1986, the period lacks works comparable to the towering achievements of the preceding fifteen years. This may simply be a result of the fact that the major peaks have been scaled.

Research Guides

The most notable new bibliographic development in American Indian law in the last three years is the appearance of several research guides. Only one—that of Nancy Carol Carter [14]—is specifically directed to legal sources, but general research guides by Marilyn L. Haas [36] and Arlene B. Hirschfelder et al. [41] and a guide to archival material by John A. Fleckner [32] should also be helpful to legal researchers. Another useful research tool is Robert J. Swan's *Grants to Indians, 1972–1983* [83], a list of private-sector funding sources. Included are grants for legal services and "advocacy" projects.

Alaska

The only work of the three-year period which can be called a "treatise" is *Alaska Natives and American Laws*, by David S. Case [15], actually a new edition of *The Special Relationship of Alaska Natives to the Federal Government*, published in 1978, which received limited distribution. This work does for the laws relating to Alaska Natives what Felix S. Cohen did for American Indian law in the 1940s: it defines and brings order to a field—a field which has been considered an anomaly even within the anomalous subject of American Indian law. Like Felix S. Cohen's treatise, *Alaska Natives and American Laws* is not without a normative element. David S. Case takes issue with legal doctrines which deny Alaska Natives benefits available to other Native Americans; he is also supportive of sovereignty for Native groups, calls for participation by Native Alaskans in decisions affecting them, and advocates a trust relationship between Alaska Natives and the United States government even in the wake of the Alaska Native Claims Settlement Act.

The Alaska Native Claims Settlement Act of 1971 (ANCSA) is the most significant federal statute in the legal history of Native Alaskans. Praised at first as the most generous settlement of aboriginal claims ever made (it consigns forty-four million acres and nearly a billion dollars to Alaska Natives as compensation for extinguishment of their claims to the rest of Alaska), the Act has come to be condemned as a "tragic mistake" which "may turn out to be the greatest land steal of all time." The quotes are from the dust jacket of Thomas R. Berger's *Village Journey: A Report of the Alaska Native Review Commission* [7].

A twenty-year period following the enactment of ANCSA has been scheduled to establish "Native corporations" in Alaska on village and regional levels, to issue stock in these corporations to Alaska Natives born before the enactment of ANCSA, and to select and transfer the forty-four million acres of Native land to be controlled by the Native corporations. The intent of ANCSA has been to encourage Native corporations to develop the Native land base profitably.

The Alaska Native Review Commission (ANRC) is a group formed by the Inuit Circumpolar Conference, an Eskimo organization spanning Alaska, Canada, and Greenland. On behalf of ANRC, Thomas R. Berger, a Canadian law professor and former judge, conducted an extensive tour of Alaska to ascertain the opinions of Alaska Natives regarding ANCSA. He found Alaska Natives deeply disenchanted with ANCSA and extremely concerned that its full implementation, scheduled for 1991, may lead to the loss of much of the Natives' land.

Professor Berger's book is a rare event in literature dealing with Indian law. It gives voice to the Natives themselves and is rich in quotations from Native testimony to the ANRC.

The major recommendation to emerge from the ANRC hearings is to have Alaska Native land transferred from Native corporations to Native governments. Native governments should be able to protect the land through their sovereign immunity and their immunity to taxation.

There is, however, considerable "ambivalence" in the law on the governmental status of Alaska's Native villages. A note by Blythe W. Marston [53] is critical of federal courts for using formalistic tests to determine whether Native villages are entitled to the same governmental powers as tribal governments in the "lower 48" states. Marston urges recognition of the governmental status of Alaska Native villages on the basis of their history of self-government. The governmental status of Alaska's Native villages may, of course, be affirmed by Congress. Congress passed some amendments to ANCSA in 1980, and further amendments were proposed in 1985, but a note by John F. Walsh [89] points out that neither provides protection against non-Native takeovers of Alaska Native corporations. Walsh recommends the transfer of Native land to Native governments, which he refers to as "retribalization," and a permanent bar to the sale of shares in Alaska Native corporations to non-Natives. He points out, however, that such a solution can be expected to meet with opposition from Alaska's oil industry, which is anxious to strike a deal with Native corporations for the exploration and development of the Natives' forty-four million acres. The result may be a standoff—while the time bomb of ANCSA keeps ticking toward 1991.

Hopi-Navajo Land "Dispute"

Of even greater immediacy than the dilemmas of Alaska's Natives created by Congress through ANCSA is the situation created by Congress through its legislated "solution" to what it considered a land dispute between the Hopi and Navajo tribes. The "dispute" may not be a dispute at all, but "a problem manufactured in Washington," according to an article by Hollis A. Whitson [92].

The 1974 Navajo-Hopi Claims Settlement Act established July 1986 as the deadline for the removal of six thousand Navajos living on land Congress assigned to the Hopis. Although the deadline has been extended, the pressure remains, and the Navajos who have been persuaded to move by a combination of government threats and enticements continue to suffer from having their lives uprooted.

The major book on this topic, *The Second Long Walk: The Navajo-Hopi Land Dispute*, by Jerry Kammer, was published in 1980. Hollis A. Whitson's article has given the issue a new airing and has advanced some urgent recommendations for Congressional action. Despite facts connecting the Peabody Coal Company to the Navajo removal legislation, Whitson cautions against the conclusion that the Navajo removals were instigated by an energy-industry "conspiracy." Rather, he finds the relocations objectionable because of the failure of the relocation program and because whenever non-Indians have encroached on Indian lands removal has been considered unthinkable. Only when one tribe is alleged to have encroached on the land of another tribe has Congress sought a "solution" in massive relocations. Congress acted in the belief that relocations would cost little ($28 million was estimated) and attractive alternatives could be offered to the relocated Navajos. Experience has now been sufficient to raise the relocation cost estimates to over $500 million and to document that, even at that cost, relocation has "a devastating effect on the Navajo relocatees."

Whitson sees the best hope for a solution in negotiation between the Hopi and the Navajo tribal governments. He alleges that such negotiations have been deliberately derailed by lawyers who stand to profit from a continuation of the "dispute." Whitson also recommends a number of interim steps designed to prevent deterioration of conditions for those waiting for relocation and those already relocated.

Land Claims

The usual method for dealing with Indian land claims, when the claims are against non-Indians, can be seen in the work of the Indian Claims Commission (ICC). The ICC was established in 1946 amid rhetoric that it would give Indians their "day in court" and "wipe the slate clean" of past injustices. Before 1946, Indian tribes were allowed to sue for unjust land takings by the United States only when Congress enacted specific jurisdictional statutes.

The ICC was hedged about by restrictions. The ICC had no power to return land to Indian tribes; it could award only money. And the money the ICC could award was drastically circumscribed. Monetary damages were limited to the value of property at the time the property was taken, with no additional sum for interest, inflation, or trespass damages. Moreover, expenditures which the United States made "gratuitously" for the benefit of a tribe could be offset against a money award to that tribe.

Nevertheless, nearly six hundred claims were filed with the ICC by 1951, the deadline for filing claims. To handle the unexpected number of claims, the ICC was kept alive until 1978, when its remaining load of sixty-eight claims was transferred to the Court of Claims.

Following the demise of the ICC, several scholars evaluated its work in a collection of essays, *Irredeemable America: The Indians' Estate and Land Claims*, edited by Imre Sutton [82]. In a brief history of the ICC, Harvey D. Rosenthal points out that Indians themselves were little involved in the work of the ICC. The ICC process was carried on by tribal attorneys (appointed subject to Interior Department approval), government attorneys, a variety of expert witnesses, and the ICC commissioners. In the concluding essay, Nancy Oestreich Lurie points out that the commissioners, with one exception, were generally inexperienced and poorly informed about Indian affairs. The one exception was former senator Arthur V. Watkins of Utah, who headed the ICC from 1960 to 1967—one of the leading crusaders against Indian interests of the postwar era.

Lurie also laments that the ICC was established as an adversarial body, which was contrary to the intent of Congress. In the act establishing the ICC, Congress provided for an "investigation division" to enable the ICC to gather its own expert evidence. The ICC never established the division. In an essay on the role of expert witnesses, anthropologist Ralph L. Beals sees a threat to scientific objectivity in adversarial proceedings and advises that the "ideal role of the expert witness should be above the conflict theater" as a "friend of the court."

The extraordinary complexity of litigating Indian land claims is set out in essays by Michael J. Kaplan, Leonard A. Carlson, and Imre Sutton and in "case studies" by Omer C. Stewart and David J. Wishart which explain the difficulties of establishing titles, values, and boundaries and cite "fraud, duress or unconscionable" dealing by the United States.

Rosenthal's historical essay cites the growing disillusionment with the ICC by the 1960s, particularly among Indians, many of whom came to look upon the ICC as just another method to extinguish their titles to land. Some tribes have refused to accept ICC awards, and Rosenthal evaluates the ICC's record as "generally dismal." However, in the opening essay of the collection, Wilcomb E. Washburn has high praise for the United States for the "extraordinary recognition accorded to the now-powerless Indian tribes."

The second part of *Irredeemable America* contains essays looking "Beyond the Commission." Included is an essay by John C. Christie, Jr., which pleads for the "innocent" non-Indian landholder who may have a land title clouded by Indian claims. Christie advises legislative settlements of Indian land claims rather than litigation, which may endanger private non-Indian landholders. Christie's advice has been well heeded by policy makers. As Michael J. Kaplan's essay points out, every major Indian land claim which has been settled has been settled with government funds. Never have non-Indians had to face the fate of the Navajos being removed from Hopi land. Whenever Indians have received land, it was public land or unoccupied private land purchased for market value.

An essay by Imre Sutton reviews a number of instances in which Indian tribes succeeded in having legislation enacted for the restoration of some lost lands. He attributes the success largely to political factors and warns of the difficulty of future restorations because of the "backlash" of the western "Sagebrush Rebellion." Roxanne Dunbar Ortiz's essay recommends that Indians turn to international organizations to seek protection for Indian rights. (She has expanded her thesis in a book [62] covering South and Central America as well as the United States and Canada.)

Concluding "case studies" by John F. Martin, David H. Getches, and Jack Campisi discuss successes in having Indian lands restored. Martin deals with the Havasupai tribe's success in having 180,000 acres added to its reservation even after an ICC award for its land claim; Getches describes the Alaska Native Claims Settlement Act and compares it to the situation of Hawaii natives, who have not received any settlement yet for their lost lands; and Campisi describes the success of the eastern tribes in obtaining settlements of land claims which included not only monetary compensation but also some lands.

The land claims of the eastern tribes are also the subject of an entertaining book (originally published as a series of articles in the *New Yorker*) by Paul Brodeur entitled *Restitution: The Land Claims of the Mashpee, Passamaquoddy, and Penobscot Indians of New England* [8]. The Mashpees, Passamaquoddys, and Penobscots were deprived of lands at the end of the eighteenth century, not by the United States government but by individual states. The actions of the states violated the federal Indian Trade and Intercourse Act of 1790, which prohibited the acquisition of any Indian land by non-Indians without the express approval of Congress. Thus, the Mashpees, Passamaquoddys, and Penobscots did not bring their claims to the Indian Claims Commission, but filed in federal court in the 1970s to establish title to their lost lands. The Mashpee suit failed, as the jury concluded in a highly questionable finding that the Mashpees no longer constitute a "tribe" as legally defined. (The problem of not being "recognized" is shared by many other tribes and bands. The problem is discussed by Frank W. Porter III [68], and a note by Michael C. Walch [87] points out that forty-four tribes "terminated" in the 1950s remain without federal recognition although the termination policy has long since been thoroughly repudiated.)

The claims of the Passamaquoddys and Penobscots included about two-thirds of the state of Maine—12.5 million acres. When land title companies became hesitant to insure Maine land titles, the lawsuit made headlines around the nation.

The initial question to be settled in the Passamaquoddy and Penobscot lawsuit was the applicability of the Indian Trade and Intercourse Act to the eastern states. As this issue was decided in favor of the Indian claimants, Brodeur describes the rise of anti-Indian sentiment among Maine's politicians and populace. Both state politicians and Maine's congressional delegation, including Senator Edmund Muskie, then a presidential hopeful, dropped all pretense of principles and simply advocated Congress's exercise of its power to extinguish Indian claims. With the intervention of President Carter, a settlement was negotiated and embodied in the Maine Indian Claims Settlement Act of 1980. The act provided for a cash payment of just over eighty million dollars from which the tribes were entitled to buy three hundred thousand acres of land. Brodeur presents this case as a major Indian victory. He acknowledges that some Passamaquoddy and Penobscot tribal members opposed the settlement, but he appears to accept the premise that by pressing for more, the tribes would have gotten less—or nothing.

Brodeur's prediction can be supported by a polemical article, by Robert T. Coulter and Steven M. Tullberg [19], which charges that United States courts and political institutions are virtually unrestrained by legal principles when dealing with Indian lands. The authors trace the "unchecked federal power" over Indian lands to misinterpretation of classic nineteenth-century Supreme Court cases on Indian rights.

From an opposite perspective, an article by Daniel M. Crane [20] also tends to bear out Brodeur's pessimistic prognosis. Crane's article is critical of the courts dealing with eastern Indian land claims cases for too readily accepting jurisdiction under the Indian Trade and Intercourse Act. Crane warns: "A court that recognizes remedies under the Trade and Intercourse Act for both return of the land and money damages should realize that this may mean millions of acres, billions of dollars, and incredible social and economic disruption." Crane's contention that the Indian Trade and Intercourse Act did not confer the necessary jurisdiction on federal courts to hear the eastern Indian land claims is supported in a comment by John Eduard Barry [3], but Barry contends that nonstatutory, "federal common law" right of action should be available to the eastern tribes.

The land claims issue remains alive and may gain new momentum. Perhaps the most potent Indian land claim case will be one which will recognize a legal right of action for the breakup of Indian reservations between the 1880s and the 1930s under the General Allotment Act of 1887. Although the General Allotment Act prohibited the sale or taxation of individual Indian allotments for twenty-five years, many Indians were given "forced fees" to allow them to sell without meeting the legislative criteria.

An article by LeeAnn Larson LaFave asks the question, "South Dakota's Forced Fees Indian Land Claims: Will Landowners be Liable for Government's Wrongdoing?" [46]. The author estimates that 1.5 to 2.0 million acres are subject to potential challenge for having been sold after their Indian owners received "forced fees," and she pleads for non-Indian "innocent landowners," recommending federal legislation to pay compensation to the heirs of former Indian owners and, perhaps, to turn over some "idle public lands" to Indian use.

In another article [64], Edward Michael Peterson, Jr., estimates that title to about nine thousand acres of the White Earth Indian Reservation in Minnesota is clouded by forced fees, unauthorized sales or tax foreclosures, condemnation proceedings, probate proceedings, and other unauthorized state actions.

An article by H. Barry Holt [43] points out that off-reservation Indian rights to hunt, fish, or use certain natural resources may also be increasingly asserted in future litigation.

Freedom of Religion

One of the reasons Indian tribes seek the return of specific parcels of land is the location of sacred sites on the parcels. The return of Blue Lake to the Taos Pueblo Indians during the presidency of Richard Nixon was the greatest success story of any Indian tribe seeking the return of sacred sites, but success is extremely rare. Consequently, many tribes seek merely access to sacred sites now on public lands and prevention of land development which would desecrate sacred sites.

In 1978, Congress passed the American Indian Religious Freedom Act (AIRFA). Among its provisions, the act directs federal agencies to review their regulations and procedures to remove unnecessary impediments to Indian access to sacred sites.

AIRFA has led to considerable litigation—and has given rise to a sizeable literature—but the consensus has emerged that AIRFA has accomplished little for Indians. As a note by Sarah B. Gordon [34] points out, Indian challenges to federal agency actions denying access to sacred sites have generally been decided in favor of the agencies, because the courts consider access to sacred sites to be an insubstantial religious issue. Gordon recommends that, instead of considering the substantiality of the religious practice, the courts should consider the substantiality of the government's interest in denying access to sacred sites.

The negative evaluation of the effect of AIRFA is shared by every writer on the subject. Rarely can such unanimity be found in the literature. The best overview of the issues is by Robert Michaelsen [56], who sees AIRFA as a "time bomb" which will gain its potential impact as non-Indian society comes to understand Indian religions. Dean B. Suagee [81] recommends strategies likely to be more effective than litigation under AIRFA. He sees the greatest hope in early involvement by tribes in federal agency decision making in alliance with archaeologists, environmentalists, and others interested in historic preservation.

Suagee recognizes that Indian religious interests may at times conflict with the position of archaeologists, environmentalists, and other potential allies. An article by C. Dean Higginbotham [40] and a comment by H. Barry Holt [42] cover areas of potential conflict between Indians and archeologists, and an article by Kenneth P. Pitt, "Eagles and Indians: The Law and the Survival of a Species" [67], provides an example of an environmentalist attack on Indian religious practices. Pitt's position in turn is debated in a note by Jana L. Walker [88]. An article by Walter R. Echo-Hawk [29] also points to potential conflicts between museums and Indians and contains constructive suggestions to museum administrators.

History

Recent years have seen increased attention to American Indian policy in the twentieth century, and works by Francis Paul Prucha, Frederick E. Hoxie, and others cited in chapter 6 of this volume contain significant considerations of legal issues. This chapter concerns only selected books and articles dealing specifically with the legal aspects of Indian-white relations focused on three eras: the colonial era (Spanish and English), the late nineteenth century, and the New Deal.

In an impressive mix of historical and theological scholarship [95], Robert A. Williams, Jr., traces current legal attitudes toward Indians to the Crusades, when Europeans were driven by the religious certainty that "one way of life existed for all mankind"; through the Renaissance, when notions of individualism reduced that certainty; to sixteenth-century Spanish theologian Francisco de Vitoria, who provided a secular justification for subjugating non-Christian peoples and at the same time recognized some basic rights for all.

The current relevance of ancient Spanish law is brought home by a lively history of a single tract of land, *Four Leagues of Pecos: A Legal History of the Pecos Grant, 1800–1933*, by G. Emlen Hall [38]. Although the original Pueblo Indian owners are off the land by chapter 3 of his book, Hall keeps their rights in focus as he traces court challenges based on initial Indian possession and presents, without polemic, damning evidence against Congress, the courts, bureaucrats, speculators, and the legal profession.

A major work in colonial legal history came off the press in the fall of 1986. The work is Yasuhide Kawashima's *Puritan Justice and the Indian* [44], based on surviving court records from the Massachusetts Colony. This is the first book-length study of the legal treatment of Indians in early colonial New England. Kawashima credits Puritan beliefs for a legal system which, though "strict," was not "harsh" in its initial application to Indians. Nevertheless, population decline among the Indians, the effect of the fur trade, and increased factionalism in Indian government caused by Puritan meddling led to a "clash of legal cultures" which culminated in King Philip's War of 1675. Kawashima sees the increasing use of English law as an instrumentality of "imperialism and social control" following the Indian defeat,

James Warren Springer [79] also examined New England court records. He found that "Indian rights to unimproved lands were generally recognized" by Puritans, contrary to the assertions of "polemicists" and contrary to some of the general assertions of Puritan spokesmen themselves.

The greatest stimulant to scholarly production on historical issues of legal interest in the past three years appears to have been anniversaries with large round numbers. Sharing the limelight during this period with the Statue of Liberty was the centennial of the Indian Rights Association and the golden anniversary of the Indian Reorganization Act of 1934.

William T. Hagan's study of the Indian Rights Association [37] details the activities of the leading group of reformers from their initial success with the General Allotment Act to the early twentieth century, when the influence of the association was in decline.

The fiftieth anniversary of the Indian Reorganization Act is marked in two volumes. Vine Deloria, Jr., and Clifford M. Lytle have written *The Nations Within* [27] as a general history of Indian "self-government," but the heart of the book is a detailed, blow-by-blow legislative history of the Indian Reorganization Act; and *Indian Self Rule*, edited by Kenneth R. Philp [66], is based on the proceedings of a commemorative conference which included some of the major participants in the application and interpretation of the act. In both books the act is both praised for putting an end to the allotment era and condemned for imposing a new "indirect rule" over reservations. Elsewhere, Laurence M. Hauptman concludes that "recent assessments condemn more than they praise" the Indian Reorganization Act.

Hauptman's essay appears in a collection of essays by Sandra L. Cadwalader and Vine Deloria, Jr., reviewing the past century in Indian-white relations in commemoration of the centennial of the Indian Rights Association [12]. In other essays, Deloria topically surveys a century of federal Indian statutes; Alvin J. Ziontz reviews the decisions of the Supreme Court dealing with tribal sovereignty, and James E. Officer provides a chronological survey of the Bureau of Indian Affairs. Another essay by Ann Laquer Estin examines the case of *Lone Wolf* v. *Hitchcock* which was brought with the support of the Indian Rights Association in 1903 to stop allotments of Indian lands without tribal consent. As Estin puts it, the case turned out to be a "trap." Not only did the Supreme Court fail to apply the constitutional protection against the "taking" of property without just compensation to the General Allotment Act, but in broad language the Court held that Congress has "plenary power" in Indian affairs. In the words of the Indian Rights Association, the Supreme Court's decision established the principle that "Congress has a right to do as it pleases" in Indian policy.

Plenary Power

Echoes of the historical scholarship can be discerned in the pages of the law reviews. A central concern of legal scholars has been the lingering effects of the "plenary power" doctrine first enunciated in *Lone Wolf* v. *Hitchcock*. In the best law review article on Indian law published in the past three years, Nell Jessup Newton [60] reviews the history of the plenary power doctrine and finds the doctrine based on several "misinterpretations" which have made Indians "constitutional castaways." Newton explores the possibility of "constructing a constitutional framework that will protect tribal rights." She finds "analytically appealing" a proposal identified with Robert N. Clinton to limit Congress's power to legislate in derogation of tribal rights to areas coming directly under the Constitution's Commerce Clause (which grants Congress the power to legislate in Indian affairs). Such a proposal would prevent Congress from adversely interfering in internal tribal affairs, but Newton does not believe the Supreme Court would accept such a limit. Instead, Newton proposes a thoughtful plan to apply constitutional property rights, due process of laws, and equal protection of laws to Indian tribes. She admits, however, that the Supreme Court may not be ready to endorse these proposals, either.

Robert N. Clinton's proposed limitation of Congress receives support in a note by Irene K. Harvey [39]. Harvey also traces the explicitly racist reasoning of the Supreme Court through the decisions which formed the basis of the plenary power doctrine from 1903 to the 1950s, and she points out that courts continue to cite these decisions with approval.

Susan D. Campbell's note [13] urges an attack on the plenary power doctrine through allotment statutes passed under it. She reasons that, since the allotment statutes were enacted to destroy Indian culture and reduce Indian lands, they should be treated as unconstitutional "bills of attainder."

E. P. Krauss [45] despairs of seeking any effective limitation on the plenary power doctrine through the courts. Since the plenary power doctrine leaves Indian tribes with "no protection of law" and is a potential tool for "cultural genocide," Krauss hints that the solution for Indian tribes lies in "political action."

Krauss's pessimism is echoed in a popularized account of administrative abuses in Indian affairs by Russel Lawrence Barsh [6]. Barsh states: "No federal Indian enactment *has ever* failed for overbreadth, vagueness, or lack of standards under the Fifth Amendment or for exceeding Congress' enumerated powers." Elsewhere, Barsh [4] argues that the plenary power of Congress over Indians constitutes a violation of international law norms on the treatment of indigenous populations and is "a fairly candid description of a state of colonialism." A note in *Harvard Law Review* [69] states: "There exists today no theory of federal obligation to Indians that can adequately guide judges and lawyers to morally acceptable conclusions."

The Supreme Court

What courts do in the absence of guiding principles can be seen in the recent Indian law decisions of the Supreme Court. The drama can be followed in the *Annual Survey of American Law*, published by New York University, which contains a section on Indian cases. Elsewhere, Russel Lawrence Barsh [5] published a review of the Supreme Court's 1982 term, the busiest ever for Indian decisions, and found a "disintegration of principled decision making." Predictability, according to Barsh, has vanished, as the Court could come up with "almost any result" depending only "on the facts of each case." An article by Robert Laurence [49] traces the opinions of one justice, Thurgood Marshall, as he tried to apply general principles to the confusing array of Supreme Court cases on Indian law. (Wilkinson [94], published as this book went to press, provides a treatment of the Supreme Court's Indian decisions since 1959.)

Mounting an attack on the plenary power doctrine may be the top legal priority for Indian tribes today. A victory over the doctrine may become the "*Brown* v. *Board of Education*" of Indian rights. However, the major recent setbacks in Indian rights have come not from Congress, but from judicial decisions reducing the scope of tribal powers. In an article by Robert S. Pelcyger [63], the Supreme Court is criticized not for deference to the plenary power of Congress, but, echoing Barsh, for "ad hoc" decision making which arrogates to the Court the legislative functions of Congress. Pelcyger is particularly critical of a Supreme Court decision requiring Indian businesses on tribal lands to collect state cigarette taxes on sales to non-Indians. The tension between state and tribal jurisdictions in this and other cases is at the heart of the current legal threats to Indian self-determination.

Jurisdiction

Philip Lee Fetzer [31] notes that in the Supreme Court, between 1959 and 1973, Indian tribes won five consecutive jurisdictional cases, but between 1975 and 1980, Indian tribes lost five consecutive jurisdictional cases. He finds "no logical explanation" for this turnaround and thus attributes it to "external factors" such as population shifts and a backlash against the occupation of Wounded Knee. Fetzer's article is unusual in applying social science data to explain a legal phenomenon.

Stephen M. Feldman [30] recommends that the Supreme Court avoid inconsistencies in its decision on state vs. tribal jurisdiction on Indian lands by looking to the constitutional roots of the jurisdiction issue. According to Feldman, the Court should first consider whether Congress "preempted" state jurisdiction. If congressional preemption can be found, federal or tribal jurisdiction should be given absolute deference under the Constitution's "supremacy" clause. Only if Congress has not preempted state jurisdiction should the Court be free to "balance" state interests against tribal interests in determining jurisdiction.

A research project by Steven B. Anderson [2] identifies a trend by the Burger Court to extend a "balancing" test to nearly all jurisdictional issues. Laurie Reynolds [70] also discerns the Court's use of "balancing" and urges "a presumption of tribal preemption of state regulation" which a state could overcome only by showing a "well-defined regulatory need," an off-reservation "nexus," and the use of the "least intrusive" regulation available. Reynolds is especially critical of a Supreme Court decision restricting tribal regulation of hunting and fishing on reservation lands owned by non-Indians.

Jane E. Scott [74] also recognizes "vacillations" in Supreme Court jurisdictional decisions, but she finds an explanation in the Supreme Court's protection of non-Indians from possibly discriminatory tribal laws. She is critical of tribes for enacting laws which may have discriminatory application. Nondiscriminatory tribal regulations such as zoning laws and mineral severance taxes have been upheld by the Court, although David B. Wiles [93] notes that state concurrent jurisdiction may continue to exist in some circumstances. Robert N. Clinton [16] joins in criticizing some tribes for pressing "unrealistic claims." He advances the provocative, but problematic, thesis that courts should take into account the context of each reservation—particularly land ownership patterns and demographics—in deciding jurisdictional cases. He recognizes that such "contextualism" can lead to increased "ad hoc" decisions, but he appears to accept that cost with the response: "Where the line should be drawn . . . must be worked out in practice."

The "jursdictional maze" caused by overlapping federal, state, and tribal jurisdictions on reservations has caused difficulties in several legal areas. An article by Antonia Vaznelis [86] describes the "maze" in the probating of estates and proposes vesting all jurisdiction over persons and property on reservations in the tribes. If non-Indians object, Vaznelis suggests they sell their lands to the tribes. She also recommends consideration of a uniform tribal probate code.

A legislative solution is also proposed to the growing tensions caused by bingo on Indian reservations. A comment by Stefanie A. Lorbiecki [51] rejects state regulations of bingo in favor of the proposed federal Indian Gambling Control Act.

Blake A. Watson [90] points out another jurisdictional problem. The eminent domain powers of states over allotted reservation land are unclear in existing federal legislation. Watson suggests one way to protect allotted land from the state condemnation is to deed allotted land to the United States in trust for a tribe.

Robert Laurence [48] explores the even less clear question of how state courts can get personal jurisdiction over Indians on reservations and how state court judgments can be enforced on reservations for cases arising off-reservation. Laurence finds the cases dealing with the issue "split and . . . unenlightening" and suggests cooperative agreements between tribes and states to clarify the situations.

Glenn A. Phelps [65] also recommends intergovernmental agreements to solve a problem which reverses the age-old charge of non-Indian discrimination against Indians. In some areas of the Southwest, some counties now have a majority of Indian voters and, consequently, Indians now control some county governments. Since Indian reservation property is tax-exempt, taxes imposed by Indian-controlled county governments fall unevenly on Indian and non-Indian inhabitants of the counties. This fact has caused some to call for disenfranchisement of Indians, creation of all-Indian counties, termination of Indian reservations, or debt ceilings for county governments. Phelps suggests instead agreements by tribal governments to "in-lieu payments."

Indian Civil Rights Act

One of the major objections to tribal court jurisdiction has been the lack of full constitutional safeguards in tribal courts. Although the Indian Civil Rights Act of 1968 mandates that tribal governments must provide most of the individual rights contained in the United States Constitution, some rights available in state and federal courts, such as the right of indigents to defense counsel at government expense, are not included in the act, and the Supreme Court has ruled that the included rights can be enforced by appeals to the federal courts only in cases involving incarceration (that is, *habeas corpus*). As a note by Tiane L. Sommer [78] points out, even appeals for *habeas corpus* must first be made through all available means within the tribal government.

A note by Stephen Lafferty [47] suggests that tribal governments may become subject to injunctions and awards of damages if they fail to provide due process of laws to all, and a note by Gordon K. Wright [97] suggests that, in order for tribal courts' decisions to receive "full faith and credit" in state and federal courts, tribal courts should be reformed and a "Court of Indian Appeals" should be established (a court once proposed as part of the Indian Reorganization Act, but cut from the act).

An article by Kevin Gover and Robert Laurence [35] warns that federal courts are increasingly finding ways to review tribal courts' compliance with the Indian Civil Rights Act despite the Supreme Court's limitation on such reviews to *habeas corpus* cases. They criticize such federal courts for "result-oriented jurisprudence" but suggest a legislated compromise which would give federal courts the power of limited oversight over tribal courts and, in exchange, extend tribal court civil and criminal jurisdiction over non-Indians.

Water Rights

In addition to jurisdictional issues, the major source of tensions between tribes and their surrounding non-Indian communities has been water rights. Since 1908, when the Supreme Court recognized "reserved" Indian rights which cannot be extinguished by non-Indian water users, Indian water rights have been a growing source of tension in the water-scarce western states. Here, too, tribal-state negotiations have been proposed to avoid legal confrontation. Claudia Marseille [52] reviews such negotiation in Montana, Utah, and Arizona and sounds a note of optimism, even though no tribal-state water compact has yet resulted from the negotiations.

A study prepared for the Western Governors' Association by the Western States Water Council [91] also cites federal efforts at negotiation of Indian water rights. The study estimates "potential claims" by Indian tribes state-by-state throughout the western states and provides a brief review of litigation and legislation relating to Indian water rights. It acknowledges that most tribes oppose a "quantification" which would place a limit on their future water rights but also states that non-Indians may find it difficult to accept continuing uncertainty in the quantity of water "reserved" for Indian reservations.

Richard B. Collins [17] suggests that Indian tribes opposing "quantifications" are "mistaken." He believes that setting specific figures on tribal water rights would help water conservation as well as the leasability and transferability of Indian water rights. He sees an "instability" in the present uncertainties and indicates that the quantification of Indian water rights should be based not only on irrigation needs but also on needs for stock watering, electrical power, fisheries, and other uses.

Contrary to Collins's suggestions, the "practicably irrigable acreage" of reservations is the only basis for quantifying Indian reserved water rights firmly recognized by the courts. Elsewhere, Collins [18] and Margaret Crow [22] indicate that even this basis may not be recognized for allotted Indian lands. Charles T. DuMars, Marilyn O'Leary, and Albert E. Utton's book on *Pueblo Indian Water Rights* [28] favors a more flexible quantification standard based on Spanish law, which may result in considerably less water for Pueblos than quantification based on "practicably irrigable acreage."

David S. Brookshire, James L. Merrill, and Gary L. Watts [9], see a movement by courts away from the "practicably irrigable acreage" standard to consider the "primary purpose" and "minimal needs" of reservations. They point to reservation population, "economic feasibility" of irrigation, and non-Indian water needs as factors courts should consider in quantifying Indian water rights. On the other hand, H. S. Burness and his coauthors [10] argue that the quantification of Indian water rights should be based not only on strict economic analysis, but also on the ethics and fairness of considering the evolving needs of the tribes living on reservations.

An unsympathetic trend in the treatment of Indian water rights by courts can also be discerned in the Supreme Court's refusal to reconsider the quantification of Indian water rights in one case in which it was admitted by all sides that the federal government failed to adequately present the Indians' claims. A note by William C. Scott [75] criticizes the Supreme Court's decision for leaving Indians with an inadequate water supply, while Roger Florio [33] defends the Supreme Court because of the value of "finality" in water adjudications.

Stephen J. Shupe [76] suggests that the only way for Indian tribes to truly protect their water rights is to put them to use. He details possible tribal water management strategies and urges federal financial support and state cooperation to help implement the strategies.

Contests over water resources have also led to jurisdictional issues as state courts have tried to assume jurisdiction over the adjudication of Indian water rights. The claim for state jurisdiction is based on federal legislation giving states jurisdiction to adjudicate water rights on federal lands. The legislation is silent on whether Indian lands are included in the definition of "federal lands." Moreover, most western state constitutions contain specific disclaimers of state jurisdiction over Indian lands. Nevertheless, a comment by William P. Schwartz [73] contends that states should be able to assume jurisdiction over Indian water rights cases; but a note by Michael Lieder [50] counters that federal and state courts should simultaneously adjudicate Indian and non-Indian water rights in the same stream. The debate has been rendered moot for general stream adjudication, as the Supreme Court has sided with Schwartz in a decision with potentially ominous consequences for Indian water rights.

The Supreme Court's decision on general stream adjudication is an example of the Court's abandonment of a rule of statutory interpretation which required statutory uncertainties to be resolved in favor of Indians. A note by Jill De La Hunt [25] cites other examples and recommends that the rule of interpretation favoring Indians be enacted as a statute by Congress.

Environment

Margaret Seelye Treuer [85] recommends that litigation over Indian water rights be broadened from quantification to "expanding the reserved rights doctrine to protect water quality." Allen H. Sanders [71] considers the impact of Indian fishing rights on a conservation program linked to hydroelectric power development in the Northwest. The two articles illustrate the images of Indians as both upholders of environmentalist ideals and threats to the environment. A special issue of the *Environmental Review* on "American Indian Environmental History" [1] examines the two images to correct the excesses of each.

Natural Resources

The drive toward tribal sovereignty in the 1970s and 1980s has had as one of its focal points the assertion of tribal control over reservation resources. Louis R. Moore [59] reviews the Indian successes of the era in an article aimed at the mining industry and makes suggestions on how contracts with tribes can protect non-Indians from such powers of tribal government as sovereign immunity, taxation, and land use regulations.

The major issue of natural resources management to surface in the legal literature of the last three years is the scandal surrounding the reported undervaluation of resources extracted by non-Indian lessees from Indian lands. Peter C. Maxfield [54] estimates that hundreds of millions of dollars in royalties have been lost by Indian tribes through underreporting by mining, oil, and gas companies operating on Indian lands. Maxfield examines the current law and proposed regulations and finds them insufficient to protect Indian tribes. He recommends, instead, that tribes take charge of regulating by getting tribal officials appointed as Department of the Interior inspectors and getting a tribal right to inspect the books of lessees operating on tribal lands. Articles by Russell Davis, James E. Wilen, and Rosemarie

Jergovic [23, 24] disagree on the extent of the actual losses to Indian tribes and claim they constitute probably less than 2 percent of their royalty entitlements, while supervision to eliminate losses may cost more than the losses. Donald T. Sant, Abraham E. Haspel, and Robert E. Boldt [72] directly respond with the opposite estimate. They consider the costs of supervision minimal in comparison to the loss of Indian royalties.

Other writings on Indian natural resources include a note by Andrew S. Montgomery [58] on gas pipeline rights-of-way and an article by Charlene L. Smith and Howard J. Vogel [77] on wild rice cultivation in Minnesota. Other studies deal with reservation economic development in general—including an article by Robert A. Williams, Jr., proposing legislation to authorize tribes to issue industrial development bonds [96] and a note by Maureen M. Crough [21] cautioning that Indian resource and industrial development should be accompanied by the extension of the Occupational Safety and Health Act to reservations.

Traditional Law

Traditional Indian legal practices have received relatively little attention in the literature of the past three years. Ken Traisman [84] has written the only article purely devoted to traditional law. The article examines historic law enforcement practices among the Cherokee, Great Plains, Central Prairie, and Woodland Indians. Among the interesting points made in the article are the use of "police" by the Great Plains tribes to direct their migration and hunts and the eventual use of a written code by the Shawnees.

James W. Zion has published two articles [98, 99] on the use of traditional Indian legal concepts by modern Indian tribal courts. In one, he urges tribal courts to use traditional holy men and ethnologists to help develop an Indian "common law" of torts; in the other, he reviews an experimental procedure set up by the Navajo in 1982 for the voluntary submission of legal disputes to traditional modes of settlement.

Children

The gaps between traditional and modern Indian communities have become evident in the area of child custody. The Indian Child Welfare Act of 1978 was passed to protect Indian communities from non-Indian courts, which were removing children from Indian families at an inordinate rate for unjustifiable reasons. The act gives tribal courts precedence in Indian child custody matters and gives tribal governments a right to be heard in custody cases involving Indian children in non-Indian courts. Although a note by Therese Buthod [11] accuses state courts of trying to narrow or ignore the act, the act has largely been well received. A note by Robert F. Mills [57] calls for extension of the act's protections to Indian groups not legally recognized as tribes. Another note, by David Null [61], however, deplores the application of the act to urban, "nominal" Indians, who have little or no tribal contacts, since the act makes it more difficult to remove Indian children from abusive Indian homes than to remove the children of other races.

The Future

Jim Messerschmidt's account of the trial of Leonard Peltier [55] tends to lead to the conclusion that the legal system is largely a conspiracy hostile to Indians. Navajo removals and the potential for "the greatest land steal of all time" in Alaska threaten to provide new evidence to support that thesis.

In a collection of essays on *American Indian Policy in the Twentieth Century* [26], edited by Vine Deloria, Jr., the authors give further cause for a pessimistic view of the future, based on the record of the recent past. Joyotpaul Chandhuri dwells on the "ambivalence, confusing intent, and self-contradictory premises" of Indian law; Sharon O'Brien finds continuing violations of international standards in the treatment of unrecognized and terminated Indian communities and in the assertion of plenary power by Congress over Indian affairs; Fred L. Ragsdale, Jr., reviews three key cases on tribal self-determination to illustrate that a legal "victory" for Indian tribes can constitute a "risk" when tribal leaders do not exercise their powers with understanding; Michael G. Lacy views government reforms of the past as efforts at "cooptation" of Indians to assure continuing government control; Tom Holm sees a "crisis" in tribal government largely because of the splits between "traditional" Indians and tribal governments; David L. Vinje traces the effects of the splits on issues of reservation economic development; Robert A. Nelson and Joseph F. Sheley accuse the BIA of frustrating tribal self-

determination through two decades of criminal justice planning;
Mary Wallace examines the Supreme Court's expansion of the powers of states in the determination of reserved Indian water rights; and
John Petoskey finds insufficient recognition of Indian rights to the
free exercise of traditional religions. Nevertheless, the editor, Vine
Deloria, Jr., sees cause for optimism in the very lack of major current initiatives in Indian policy. Rather than grand policy schemes,
Deloria sees promise in "small models" which may treat the "Indians' problem" as a "social problem area . . . [to] be resolved as
other such problems are resolved." For American Indians, this
should provide hope for continuing to "work within the system." For
legal scholars, it should point to Rennard Strickland's [80] admoni-
tion that "law alone is not enough," that we need a "new analytical
look at Indian law and Indian policy" which is "renewed, systematic
[and] policy-oriented."

References

1. "American Indian Environmental History." 1985. *Environmental Re-
    view* special issue 9:101–92.
2. Anderson, Steven B. 1985. "Native American Indian Law and the
    Burger Court: A Shift in Judicial Methods." *Hamline Law Review*
    8:671–712.
3. Barry, John Eduard. 1984. "*Oneida Indian Nation* v. *County of Oneida*:
    Tribal Rights of Action and the Indian Trade and Intercourse Act." *Co-
    lumbia Law Review* 84:1852–80.
4. Barsh, Russel Lawrence. 1983. "Indigenous North America and Con-
    temporary International Law." *Oregon Law Review* 62:73–125.
5. ———. 1984. "Is There Any Indian 'Law' Left? A Review of the Su-
    preme Court's 1982 Term." *Washington Law Review* 59:863–93.
6. ———. 1984. "The Red Man in the American Wonderland." *Human
    Rights* 11(4):14.
7. Berger, Thomas R. 1985. *Village Journey: The Report of the Alaska
    Native Review Commission.* New York: Hill and Wang.
8. Brodeur, Paul. 1985. *Restitution: The Land Claims of the Mashpee,
    Passamaquoddy, and Penobscot Indians of New England.* Boston:
    Northeastern University Press.
9. Brookshire, David S.; James L. Merrill; and Gary L. Watts. 1983.
    "Economics and the Determination of Indian Reserved Water Rights."
    Natural Resources Journal 23:749–65.
10. Burness, H. S.; R. G. Cummings; W. D. Gorman; and R. R. Lansford.
    1983. "Practicably Irrigable Acreage and Economic Feasibility: The
    Role of Time, Ethics, and Discounting." *Natural Resources Journal*
    23:289–303.

11. Buthod, Therese. 1982. "Children: An Analysis of Cases Decided Pursuant to the Indian Child Welfare Act of 1978." *American Indian Law Review* 10:311–31.
12. Cadwalader, Sandra L., and Vine Deloria, Jr., eds. *The Aggressions of Civilization: Federal Indian Policy Since the 1880s.* Philadelphia: Temple University Press.
13. Campbell, Susan D. 1984. "Reservations: The Surplus Lands Acts and the Question of Reservation Disestablishment." *American Indian Law Review* 12:57–99.
14. Carter, Nancy Carol. 1985. *American Indian Law: Research and Sources.* New York: Haworth Press.
15. Case, David S. 1984. *Alaska Natives and American Laws.* Fairbanks: University of Alaska Press.
16. Clinton, Robert N. 1985. "Reservation Specificity and Indian Adjudication: An Essay on the Importance of Limited Contextualism in Indian Law." *Hamline Law Review* 8:493–543.
17. Collins, Richard B. 1985. "The Future Course of the Winters Doctrine." *University of Colorado Law Review* 56:481–94.
18. ———. 1985. "Indian Allotment Water Rights." *Land and Water Law Review* 20:421–57.
19. Coulter, Robert T., and Steven M. Tullberg. 1985. "Indian Land Rights." *Antioch Law Journal* 3:153–82.
20. Crane, Daniel M. 1983. "Congressional Intent or Good Intentions: The Inference of Private Rights of Action Under the Indian Trade and Intercourse Act." *Boston University Law Review* 63:853–915.
21. Crough, Maureen M. 1985. "A Proposal for Extension of the Occupational Safety and Health Act to Indian-Owned Businesses on Reservations." *University of Michigan Journal of Law Reform* 18:473–502.
22. Crow, Margaret. 1985. "Water, Water Everywhere: *U.S.* v. *Adair* Keeps Indian Rights in Federal Court." *Golden Gate University Law Review* 15:151–69.
23. Davis, Russell; James E. Wilen; and Rosemarie Jergovic. 1983. "Oil and Gas Royalty Recovery Policy on Federal and Indian Lands." *Natural Resources Journal* 23:391–416.
24. ———. 1983. "Royalty Management in the New Minerals Management Service: A Reply to Sant, Haspel and Boldt." *Natural Resources Journal* 23:435–39.
25. De La Hunt, Jill. 1984. "The Canons of Indian Treaty and Statutory Construction: A Proposal for Codification." *University of Michigan Journal of Law Reform* 17:681–712.
26. Deloria, Vine, Jr., ed. 1985. *American Indian Policy in the Twentieth Century.* Norman: University of Oklahoma Press.
27. ———, and Clifford M. Lytle. 1984. *The Nations Within: The Past and Future of American Indian Sovereignty.* New York: Pantheon Books.
28. DuMars, Charles T.; Marilyn O'Leary; and Albert E. Utton. 1984. *Pueblo Indian Water Rights: Struggle for a Precious Resource.* Tucson: University of Arizona Press.
29. Echo-Hawk, Walter R. 1986. "Museum Rights vs. Indian Rights: Guide-

lines for Assessing Competing Legal Interests in Native Cultural Resources." *New York University Review of Law & Social Change* 14:437–53.
30. Feldman, Stephen M. 1986. "Preemption and the Dormant Commerce Clause: Implications for Federal Indian Law." *Oregon Law Review* 64:667–700.
31. Fetzer, Philip Lee. 1981. "Jurisdictional Decisions in Indian Law: The Importance of Extralegal Factors in Judicial Decision Making." *American Indian Law Review* 9:253–72.
32. Fleckner, John A. 1984. *Native American Archives: An Introduction.* Chicago: Society of American Archivists.
33. Florio, Roger. 1984. "Finality As a Water Management Tool." *Catholic University Law Review* 33:457–77.
34. Gordon, Sarah B. 1985. "Indian Religious Freedom and Government Development of Public Lands." *Yale Law Journal* 94:1447–71.
35. Gover, Kevin, and Robert Laurence. 1985. "Avoiding *Santa Clara Pueblo* v. *Martinez*: The Litigation in Federal Court of Civil Actions Under the Indian Civil Rights Act." *Hamline Law Review* 8:497–542.
36. Haas, Marilyn L. 1983. *Indians of North America: Methods and Sources for Library Research.* Hamden, Conn.: Library Professional Publications.
37. Hagan, William T. 1985. *The Indian Rights Association: The Herbert Welsh Years, 1882–1904.* Tucson: University of Arizona Press.
38. Hall, G. Emlen. 1984. *Four Leagues of Pecos: A Legal History of the Pecos Grant, 1800–1933.* Albuquerque: University of New Mexico Press.
39. Harvey, Irene K. 1982. "Constitutional Law: Congressional Plenary Power Over Indian Affairs—a Doctrine Rooted in Prejudice." *American Indian Law Review* 10:117–50.
40. Higginbotham, C. Dean. 1982. "Native Americans Versus Archaeologists: The Legal Issues." *American Indian Law Review* 10:91–115.
41. Hirschfelder, Arlene B.; Mary Gloyne Byler; and Michael A. Dorris. 1983. *Guide to Research on North American Indians.* Chicago: American Library Association.
42. Holt, H. Barry. 1985. "Archaeological Preservation on Indian Lands: Conflicts and Dilemmas in Applying the National Historic Preservation Act." *Environmental Law* 15:413–53.
43. ———. 1986. "Can Indians Hunt in National Parks? Determinable Indian Treaty Rights and *United States* v. *Hicks.*" *Environmental Law* 16:207–54.
44. Kawashima, Yasuhide. 1986. *Puritan Justice and the Indian: White Man's Law in Massachusetts, 1630–1763.* Middletown, Conn.: Wesleyan University Press.
45. Krauss, E. P. 1983. "The Irony of Native American 'Rights.' " *Oklahoma City University Law Review* 8:409–49.
46. LaFave, LeeAnn Larson. 1984. "South Dakota's Forced Fees Indian Land Claims: Will Landowners Be Liable for Government's Wrongdoing?" *South Dakota Law Review* 30:59–102.

47. Lafferty, Stephen. 1981. "Sovereignty: Tribal Sovereign Immunity and the Claims of NonIndians Under the Indian Civil Rights Act." *American Indian Law Review* 9:289–308.
48. Laurence, Robert. 1982. "Service of Process and Execution of Judgment on Indian Reservations." *American Indian Law Review* 10:257–85.
49. ———. 1984. "Thurgood Marshall's Indian Law Opinions." *Howard Law Journal* 27:3–89.
50. Lieder, Michael. 1983. "Adjudication of Indian Water Rights Under the McCarren Amendment: Two Courts Are Better than One." *Georgetown Law Journal* 71:1023–61.
51. Lorbiecki, Stefanie A. 1985. "Indian Sovereignty Versus Oklahoma's Gambling Laws." *Tulsa Law Journal* 20:605–33.
52. Marseille, Claudia. 1983. *Conflict Management: Negotiating Indian Water Rights*. Cambridge, Mass.: Lincoln Institute of Land Policy.
53. Marston, Blythe W. 1984. "Alaska Native Sovereignty: The Limits of the Tribe-Indian Country Test." *Cornell International Law Journal* 17:375–405.
54. Maxfield, Peter C. 1983. "Tribal Control of Indian Mineral Development." *Oregon Law Review* 62:49–72.
55. Messerschmidt, Jim. 1983. *The Trial of Leonard Peltier*. Boston: South End Press.
56. Michaelson, Robert S. 1984. "The Significance of the American Indian Religious Freedom Act of 1978." *Journal of the American Academy of Religion* 52:93, 104–109.
57. Mills, Robert F. 1984. "The Indian Child Welfare Act of 1978: The Massachusetts Dilemma." *Boston College Third World Law Journal* 4:205–19.
58. Montgomery, Andrew S. 1985. "Tribal Sovereignty and Congressional Dominion: Rights-of-Way for Gas Pipelines on Indian Reservations." *Stanford Law Review* 38:195–225.
59. Moore, Louis R. 1983. "Mineral Development on Indian Lands—Cooperation and Conflict." *Rocky Mountain Mineral Law Institute* 28:1–77.
60. Newton, Nell Jessup. 1984. "Federal Power over Indians: Its Sources, Scope, and Limitations." *University of Pennsylvania Law Review* 132:195–288.
61. Null, David. 1984. "*In Re Junious M.*: The California Application of the Indian Child Welfare Act." *Journal of Juvenile Law* 8:74–86.
62. Ortiz, Roxanne Dunbar. 1984. *Indians of the Americas: Human Rights and Self-Determination*. New York: Praeger Publishers.
63. Pelcyger, Robert S. 1983. "Justices and Indians: Back to Basics." *Oregon Law Review* 62:29–47.
64. Peterson, Edward Michael, Jr. 1983. "That So-Called Warranty Deed: Clouded Land Titles on the White Earth Indian Reservation in Minnesota." *North Dakota Law Review* 59:159–81.
65. Phelps, Glenn A. 1985. "Representation Without Taxation: Citizen-

ship and Suffrage in Indian Country." *American Indian Quarterly* 9:135–48.

66. Philp, Kenneth R. 1985. *Indian Self-Rule: First Hand Accounts of Indian-White Relations from Roosevelt to Reagan.* Salt Lake City: Howe Bros.

67. Pitt, Kenneth P. 1984. "Eagles and Indians: The Law and the Survival of a Species." *Public Land Law Review* 5:100–109.

68. Porter, Frank W. III. 1983. *Nonrecognized American Indian Tribes: An Historical and Legal Perspective.* Chicago: Newberry Library.

69. "Rethinking the Trust Doctrine in Federal Indian Law." 1984. *Harvard Law Review* 98:422–40.

70. Reynolds, Laurie. 1984. "Indian Hunting and Fishing Rights: The Role of Tribal Sovereignty and Preemption." *North Carolina Law Review* 62:743–93.

71. Sanders, Allen H. 1983. "The Northeast Power Act and Reserved Tribal Rights." *Washington Law Review* 58:357–86.

72. Sant, David; Abraham E. Haspel; and Robert E. Boldt. 1983. "Oil and Gas Royalty Recovery Policy on Federal and Indian Lands: A Response." *Natural Resources Journal* 23:417–33.

73. Schwartz, William P. 1983. "State Disclaimers of Jurisdiction over Indians: A Bar to the McCarran Amendment?" *Land & Water Law Review* 18:175–99.

74. Scott, Jane E. 1982. "Zoning: Controlling Land Use on the Checkerboard: The Zoning Powers of Indian Tribes After *Montana v. United States.*" *American Indian Law Review* 10:187–209.

75. Scott, William C. 1984. "The Continuing Saga of Pyramid Lake: *Nevada v. United States.*" *Natural Resources Journal* 24:1067–82.

76. Shupe, Steven J. 1986. "Water in Indian Country: From Paper Rights to a Managed Resource." *University of Colorado Law Review* 57:561–92.

77. Smith, Charlene L., and Howard J. Vogel. 1984. "The Wild Rice Mystique: Resource Management and American Indians' Rights as a Problem of Law and Culture." *William Mitchell Law Review* 10:743–804.

78. Sommer, Tiane L. 1983. "Exhaustion of Tribal Rememdies Required for Habeas Corpus Review Under the Indian Civil Rights Act." *American Indian Law Review* 11:57–76.

79. Springer, James Warren. 1986. "American Indians and the Law of Real Property in Colonial New England." *American Journal of Legal History* 30:25–58.

80. Strickland, Rennard. 1983. "The Puppet Princess: The Case for a Policy-Oriented Framework for Understanding and Shaping American Indian Law." *Oregon Law Review* 62:11–28.

81. Suagee, Dean B. 1982. "American Indian Religious Freedom and Cultural Resources Management: Protecting Mother Earth's Caretakers." *American Indian Law Review* 10:1–58.

82. Sutton, Imre, ed. 1985. *Irredeemable America: The Indians' Estate and Land Claims.* Albuquerque: University of New Mexico Press.

83. Swan, Robert J. 1984. *Grants to Indians, 1972–1983.* Broken Arrow, Okla.: DCA Publishers.
84. Traisman, Ken. 1981. "Native Laws: Law and Order Among Eighteenth-Century Cherokee, Great Plains, Central Prairie, and Woodland Indians." *American Indian Law Review* 9:273–87.
85. Treuer, Margaret Seelye. 1984. "An Indian Right to Water Undiminished in Quality." *Hamline Law Review* 7:347–68.
86. Vaznelis, Antonina. 1984. "Probating Indian Estates: Conqueror's Court Versus Decedent Intent." *American Indian Law Review* 10:287–309.
87. Walch, Michael C. 1983. "Terminating the Indian Termination Policy." *Stanford Law Review* 35:1181–1215.
88. Walker, Jana L. 1986. "On-Reservation Treaty Hunting Rights: Abrogation v. Regulation by Federal Conservation Statutes—What Standard?" *Natural Resources Journal* 26:187–96.
89. Walsh, John F. 1985. "Settling the Alaska Native Claims Settlement Act." *Stanford Law Review* 38:227–63.
90. Watson, Blake A. 1982. "State Acquisition of Interests in Indian Land: An Overview." *American Indian Law Review* 10:219–56.
91. Western States Water Council. 1984. *Indian Water Rights in the West: A Study.* Denver: Western Governors' Association.
92. Whitson, Hollis A. 1985. "A Policy Review of the Federal Government's Relocation of Navajo Indians Under P.L. 93–531 and P.L. 96–305." *Arizona Law Review* 27:371–414.
93. Wiles, David B. 1982. "Taxation: Tribal Taxation, Secretarial Approval and State Taxation—*Merrion* and Beyond." *American Indian Law Review* 10:167–85.
94. Wilkinson, Charles F. 1987. *American Indians, Time, and the Law: Native Societies in a Modern Constitutional Democracy.* New Haven: Yale University Press.
95. Williams, Robert A., Jr. 1983. "The Medieval and Renaissance Origins of the Status of the American Indian in Western Legal Thought." *Southern California Law Review* 57:1–99.
96. ———. 1985. "Small Steps on the Long Road to Self-Sufficiency for Indian Nations: The Indian Tribal Governmental Tax Status Act of 1982." *Harvard Journal on Legislation* 22:335–97.
97. Wright, Gordon K. 1985. "Recognition of Tribal Decisions in State Courts." *Stanford Law Review* 37:1397–1424.
98. Zion, James W. 1984. "Harmony Among the People: Torts and Indian Courts." *Montana Law Review* 45:265–79.
99. ———. 1983. "The Navajo Peacemaker Court: Deference to the Old and Accommodation to the New." *American Indian Law Review* 11:89–109.

CHAPTER 6

Scholars and Twentieth-Century Indians: Reassessing the Recent Past

JAMES RIDING IN

When so much has been written about American Indians, the paucity of literature for the twentieth century is surprising. Historians and the general public alike seem to have been comfortable with the notion that Indian history ended in 1890 with Wounded Knee and the official closing of the frontier. Exceptions to the pattern have focused primarily on federal policy, to the extent that one might be forgiven for believing that Indians arranged their lives according to historical periods scheduled by Washington. Agendas that seemed important in Washington might in fact loom very small in the minds of Indian people at White Earth and Wind River or in Minneapolis and Los Angeles.

Of course, federal policy, the Bureau of Indian Affairs, and the prevailing philosophy of the administration in power produced, and continue to produce, tremendous reverberations in Indian communities. All too often, though, historians have concentrated on policy making and neglected the effect of those policies on the daily lives of Indian people. In this survey of recent literature on the twentieth century, a young Indian author acknowledges the progress made in this field but finds that "grass roots" studies of Indian communities and how they have responded to federal initiatives are still few in number.

Until fairly recently library shelves have contained a dearth of literature on twentieth-century American Indians. Published works generally pertained more to the formation of federal Indian policy and white reformers than to the Indians themselves. A survey of the lit-

erature written since 1983 indicates that scholars have begun to focus
their attention more directly on Indian experiences in the twentieth
century. It also indicates that, though their numbers are compara-
tively low, more Indians than ever before are writing scholarly works
on Indian history. These writings of Indians and non-Indians cover a
wide variety of topics, ranging from biographies to tribal histories
and from federal Indian policy to Indian resistance to colonialism.
Much of this work has been revisionary.

The recent outpouring of literature shows that interest in contemporary Indian issues is becoming increasingly popular not only
among historians, but also among scholars from other disciplines as
well. Essays on Indian history are found scattered throughout libraries in a wide variety of scholarly journals focusing on law, ethnic
studies, labor, history, religion, and anthropology. Trying to keep
abreast of new publications is a difficult task.

The literature on twentieth-century Indians published before 1983
has been discussed in other essays. An excellent historiographical
essay that summarizes the development of scholarship on Indians in
the present century is Robert C. Carriker's "The American Indian
from the Civil War to the Present" [7]. Carriker points out that before the 1940s white historians routinely stressed the alleged warlike
and savage character of Indians in a narrative style. Scholars took
the first step towards maturity during the 1940s, according to Carriker, when "documentary history was questioned as being only the
history of Indians as they affected whites" (p. 190). The testimony
of anthropologists during the proceedings before the Indian Claims
Commission in the 1950s provided historians with the impetus for
merging the study of history with that of culture as a new method for
achieving a more comprehensive understanding of the Indians' past,
and by the late 1970s this ethnohistorical approach had contributed
to the enrichment and diversification of studies on Indian history.

Carriker views the emergence of American Indian scholars with
mixed emotions. On the one hand, he unduly criticizes the writings
of Vine Deloria, Jr., perhaps the most influential and brilliant Indian
scholar of our time, for being more political than historical. He also
rebukes a Nez Perce tribal historian for eliminating footnotes and
condemning non-Indian scholars whose writings have defamed his
people. "Such attitudes," Carriker charges, "contribute little to the
growth of Indian scholarship" (p. 193). On the other hand, he notes
that "accomplished [Indian] scholars like R. David Edmunds, along

with Veronica Tiller, Terry Paul Wilson, and Clifford Trafzer are quietly making an impact on the writing of Indian history that will soon exceed the protest of Vine Deloria, Jr." (p. 194).

Four bibliographical essays in *Scholars and the Indian Experience* survey the literature on twentieth-century Indian topics written from 1975 to the early 1980s [48]. Donald Fixico, himself an Indian, in "Twentieth Century Federal Indian Policy" gives an overview of works dealing with Indian water rights, sovereignty, legislation, education, assimilation, law, and health issues. In "Contemporary American Indians," Russell Thornton, a Cherokee sociologist, concentrates on the writings covering the issues of urbanization, family life, education, health, criminal justice, economic development, and federal policy. Peter Iverson's "Indian Tribal Histories" covers books and articles on tribal experiences, while Richard White's contribution, "Native Americans and the Environment," examines works on cultural ecology.

Several bibliographies produced in the past few years have helped categorize the literature on contemporary Indian subjects. Terry P. Wilson, who is of Potawatomi ancestry, has compiled the sixth volume of the Native American Bibliography Series, *Bibliography of the Osage* [57]. Another, on Indian leadership in the twentieth century, has been published by Velma S. Salabiye and James R. Young [44], both of whom are Indians. Cherokee Rayna Green's bibliography on Indian women is a valuable addition to the field [13].

Since most literature on twentieth-century Indian history published before 1983 has already been placed in its historiographical context, this essay will focus on books and articles appearing in print after 1983 which deal with federal Indian policy, biographies, cultural survival, and resistance. This study will ignore works which are primarily legal in character, since chapter 5 in this volume treats the relationship between Indians and the law. Studies of Indian women in the twentieth century are included in chapter 2.

That much recent literature on twentieth-century Indian history pertains to federal Indian policy is not surprising. Federal legislation has probably affected Indian people, for better or worse, more than any other group of people in the United States. In addition, scholars generally have easy access to records of congressional hearings and investigations as well as a host of other federal documents concerning Indian policy. Federal archives, state historical societies, and university libraries contain hundreds of thousands of primary sources on federal Indian policy in the twentieth century. In fact, the availability of these written sources may encourage many scholars to remain within the confines of their ivory towers where they can research and write history on subjects about which they have virtually no firsthand knowledge. Even scholars who employ multidisciplinary techniques frequently rely too heavily on secondary anthropological sources to obtain an "Indian perspective." Familiarity with a topic or people does not necessarily mean that good history will be written, but field research among Indian people on reservations, where the influence of federal policy is more keenly felt, may give the researcher a perspective not found in traditional documented sources.

Nevertheless, a growing number of important books, monographs, and articles on federal Indian policy have enhanced our understanding of the twentieth century. Perhaps symbolic of the proliferating interest in Indians of this century is the recent work of Francis Paul Prucha, a historian who had previously produced studies on eighteenth- and nineteenth-century federal-Indian relations. In his article "American Indian Policy in the Twentieth Century" [39], Prucha lists ten characteristics which he believes distinguish nineteenth-century Indian history from that of the twentieth century. The first five have been the shift in emphasis of federal policy from the tribes to individuals, the urbanization of Amerian Indians, the dispersing of responsibility for dealing with Indians from the Bureau of Indian Affairs to other government departments as well as state agencies, and the rise of influential pan-Indian organizations and factionalism. The sixth is that tribal leaders have become more effective in dealing with the federal government. Next, Indian tribes have acquired the ability to successfully meet contemporary legal challenges by employing astute attorneys, many of whom, it should be noted, are themselves Indians. The eighth characteristic concerns attempts by tribal officials to attain self-sufficiency through economic development.

Prucha finds his ninth and tenth features—increased emphasis on both Indian self-determination and the federal government's responsibility, respectively—to be contradictory principles. While Indian leaders are demanding more autonomy over tribal affairs, they are also asking the federal government to expand its trust obligations to protect tribal interests. Espousing a very narrow interpretation of the trust relationship, Prucha argues that the trust responsibility of the federal government to Indian tribes is "similar to that of a bank that acts as a trustee for one of its clients." "It is impossible," he asserts, "to expand trust responsibility without expanding paternalism, however devoutly the Indians and their spokesmen in government wish it were not so" (p. 18). Readers should be aware, however, that a broader definition of the trust relationship stresses that the federal government has a solemn moral and legal obligation to protect Indian property and right of self-government as well as to promote the best interests of Indian tribes. In this later view, tribal self-determination and the federal trust obligation are complementary rather than contradictory concepts.

Paternalism is a pervasive theme of Prucha's work. The second volume of *The Great Father: The United States Government and the American Indians* [40], a study of federal Indian policy from the founding of the American republic to 1980, deals with the twentieth century. Despite congressional attempts to end federal supervision over Indians through allotments, self-determination, and termination, Prucha argues that paternalism has increased. The allotment policy, 1887 to 1934, failed to suspend federal control over Indians because benevolent, well-intentioned, but somewhat misguided policy makers failed to consider the cultural differences between the two races. Prucha states that Indian New Deal legislation of the 1930s inadvertently expanded federal paternalism by imposing European concepts of government and economic development upon Indians and rendering tribal policy making prerogatives subject to federal approval. Then, too, Indian Commissioner John Collier precluded Indian participation in the planning of New Deal policies. The termination policy of the 1950s and 1960s, Prucha argues, represented a temporary departure from the movement towards self-determination set in motion by Collier's policies. Increased federal spending on reservations during the 1970s gave tribes more control over local programs but administrative regulations and guidelines accompanying the federal funds subjected tribal governments to more federal restrictions. Prucha's other recent work, *The Indians in American Society: From the Revolutionary War to the Present* [41], is a collection of several of his essays and lectures which discuss his concept of paternalism and dependency in more depth.

Since Prucha focuses primarily on the formulation and implementation of federal policy at the national level, one can acquire neither an understanding of nor an appreciation for Indian responses to federal Indian policy. If Prucha can fault Collier for not seeking Indian perspectives on policy matters, then we can criticize Prucha for not including Indian viewpoints on historical issues.

Fortunately, Vine Deloria, Jr., and Clifford Lytle have written a valuable study from an Indian perspective that analyzes the impact of federal policy on the status of Indian sovereignty at the federal, tribal, and state levels. In *The Nations Within: The Past and Future of American Indian Sovereignty* [12], Deloria and Lytle point out a major weakness of previous works on Indian sovereignty. "The old scholarship that treated political and economic activities as separate from the rest of human experience," they write, "can no longer describe political and economic developments in tribes without reference to the profound cultural and emotional energies that are influencing Indians today" (p. 264). By skillfully blending cultural, spiritual, and psychological dimensions of tribal life with historical and legal methodology, they have discerned factors that have influenced the thinking of Indians about tribal government. The authors find that the proposed adoption of the Indian Reorganization Act (IRA) governments during the Collier era created a divisive political climate on many reservations between traditional and assimilated Indians. The traditionalists preferred living under their own customary, informal types of government which functioned largely independent of outside interference and in accordance with their interpretation of nineteenth-century treaties. These traditional people feared quite correctly that political change would enable assimilated Indians to dominate tribal politics. To the authors, the confrontation in 1973 between traditional Indians and supporters of the IRA tribal government on the Pine Ridge reservation in South Dakota symbolized the ongoing political struggle occurring throughout Indian country.

Much of the recent literature on the Indian New Deal has been highly critical of John Collier and his policies, but Deloria and Lytle demonstrate that the Collier formula of tribal self-government and economic livelihood has enhanced the political status of tribal governments. Referring to the importance of Collier's plan of government to Indian tribes in the future, they predict that it has "prepared the ground for an entirely new expression of Indian communal and corporate existence. We are just beginning to recognize the nature of this expression." Another study by Deloria and Lytle is *American Indians, American Justice* [11]. This work finds that the modern political and legal rights of Indian nations have evolved because of court decisions, federal legislation, and administrative policies.

Along the same line, Deloria and Sandra L. Cadwalader have co-edited a collection of essays, *The Aggressions of Civilization: Federal Indian Policy Since the 1880s* [5], which analyze the motivations behind the development and implementation of federal Indian policy and show how these policies helped transform Indian life. Essays by Deloria, Laurence Hauptman, Ann Laquer Estin, Wilcomb E. Washburn, and others demonstrate that Indian culture, sovereignty, and rights have survived the advances of white society, but in a form of expression more compatible with non-Indian values. Deloria also has edited a collection of essays, *American Indian Policy in the Twentieth Century* [10] in which the authors discuss historical problems and current issues confronting Indian communities. Topics include Indian voting, the crisis in tribal government, cultural values and economic development on reservations, the influence of the BIA on Indian self-determination, the Supreme Court and Indian water rights, Indians and the First Amendment, and overviews of federal Indian policy.

An excellent textbook on federal Indian policy in the current century is James S. Olson and Raymond Wilson's *Native Americans in the Twentieth Century* [33]. Writing from the perspective that cultural plurality is a desirable aspect of American life, they state that shifting public attitudes between acceptance and rejection of ethnic pluralism have precipitated the periodic reversals in Indian policy. These policies have affected Indian peoples unevenly. While some groups have managed to retain their culture, language, and land base, others have lost practically everything.

In addition to overviews of federal Indian policy, a number of books and articles have focused on specific aspects of the Indian–federal government relationship. The allotment era has attracted the attention of several scholars, all of whom emphasize how forces in the larger American society influenced the shaping of federal Indian policy. Frederick E. Hoxie's *A Final Promise: The Campaign to Assimilate the Indians, 1880–1920* [17] shows how shifting political, social, intellectual, and economic forces influenced the development and transformation of the allotment policy. To Hoxie, theories on culture and race advanced by ethnocentric social scientists played a pivotal role in shaping public opinion and federal Indian policy. When Congress enacted the Dawes Act in 1887, reformers, social scientists, policy makers, and the general public believed that Indians and other minorities could be rapidly assimilated into mainstream society with full rights of citizenship. Taking a controversial view, Hoxie insists that federal officials implemented the allotment process in a slow, cautious manner. Yet he states that about 1900 the intellectual and political climate in the United States began to change. Social scientists helped alter public perceptions on assimilation by developing new theories on race which stressed that Indians and other "backward people" lacked the mental capacity to duplicate white culture. Many whites, including Indian Service personnel and policy makers, reasoned that since Indians could not be assimilated into white society, they would have no need for land and education. About the same time, western politicians with no sympathy for Indians and a strong desire to open reservation lands for white settlement gained control of congressional subcommittees on Indian affairs and pushed for alteration of the allotment policy. Responding to such pressure, Congress passed a series of laws in the early 1900s which authorized the removal of trust restrictions from millions of acres of allotted land. At the same time, federal officials allowed Indian schools to lower their academic standards. The irony in such actions, Hoxie concludes, is that relaxing assimilation goals helped perpetuate Indian culture.

By contrast, Leonard A. Carlson finds that economic considerations rather than intellectual forces induced Congress to loosen restrictions on allotted lands. In an article, "Federal Policy and Indian Land: Economic Interests and the Sale of Indian Allotments, 1900–1934" [6], Carlson uses statistical models to explain the behavior of Indian Office personnel. Carlson disagrees with Prucha's contention that the upper echelon of the Indian bureaucracy was staffed with honest and moralistic administrators. He finds that federal officials compromised their role as guardians of Indian lands by tailoring their land policies more to the economic interests of whites than Indians. The Indian Office sharply increased the issuance of patents-in-fee from 1917 to 1920 while agricultural prices soared, and decreased the issuance of patents in the 1920s as crop prices fell.

Another essay on the allotment period is David Beaulieu's "Curly Hair and Big Feet: Physical Anthropology and the Implementation of Land Allotment on the White Earth Chippewa Reservation" [2]. Using an interdisciplinary approach, Beaulieu gives an impressive analysis of the role social scientists played in legitimizing the loss of thousands of acres of allotted land which had been taken fraudulently from a number of Chippewa allottees by lumber companies and land developers. Under federal law, full-blood Chippewas were deemed incompetent and, therefore, could not sell their allotments, as could their mixed-blood kindred. When local non-Indian businessmen produced documents which indicated that a large number of Chippewas, many of whom were apparently full-bloods, had sold their 160-acre parcels, federal agents filed suit to stop the transactions involving full-bloods. They hired two physical anthropologists to distinguish the mixed-bloods from the full-bloods. Ignoring tribal terminology which defined the difference between mixed- and full-bloods, the anthropologists devised several "scientific" tests, including physical observation, chest scratching, and hair measurement, that determined the vast majority of the Chippewas in question were mixed-bloods. As a result, the White Earth people lost a considerable amount of land.

One recent study discusses the growing opposition to the allotment policy during the 1920s. Benay Blend's essay, "The Indian Rights Association, the Allotment Policy, and the Five Civilized Tribes, 1923–36" [4], shows that the Indian Rights Association, a staunch pro-assimilation organization, gradually reversed its support of the allotment policy after gathering evidence that Indians were rapidly becoming a landless people. Still advocating assimilation, many members eventually supported the Indian Reorganization Act as a means of halting the allotment process.

In recent years, scholars have begun to reappraise John Collier and his Indian policies. Lawrence C. Kelly's, *The Assault on Assimilation: John Collier and the Origins of Indian Policy Reform* [22], a biography of Collier's life until about 1930, exemplifies this revisionism. Dismissing the notion that Collier was a kind, compassionate man, Kelly gives us another, albeit controversial, view of Collier's personality. Cast in the mold of a self-righteous crusader, Collier emerges as a ruthless, uncompromising propagandist who attacked his political opponents unmercifully and alienated his supporters. Despite his outwardly aggressive behavior, Collier was troubled by self-doubts stemming from personal and financial problems. The introduction of this book, written by John Collier, Jr., however, provides a more balanced picture of Collier. Kelly's methodical research covers virtually every base except one: he fails to include firsthand perspectives of Indians who were acquainted with Collier and his policies.

Kelly and other scholars have assumed that Collier developed the

ideological foundation of his Indian policy while working with ethnic minorities in New York City. Frederick J. Stefon's two-part
article, "The Indians' Zarathustra: An Investigation into the Philosophical Roots of John Collier's New Deal Educational and Administrative Policies" [47], revises that assumption. Stefon postulates
that Collier studied radical social theories while attending graduate
classes at Columbia University. These theories profoundly influenced his thinking about cultural pluralism, self-government, and
economic self-sufficiency even before his involvement in the New
York social movement. Stefon also suggests that Collier championed
Indian rights because he had become disillusioned by the excessive
amount of individualism, greed, and materialism among white
Americans.

   Most studies on the Indian New Deal have stressed that Collier
fought indefatigably to protect Indian rights from white encroachments. Although this assessment may hold true for the Pueblo and
other southwest tribes, Donald L. Parman suggests that Collier neglected the rights of some Indians. In his essay, "Inconstant Advocacy: The Erosion of Indian Fishing Rights in the Pacific Northwest,
1933–1956" [34], Parman reveals that Collier did not actively support Indian tribes of Washington and Oregon in their intense struggle
with state authorities over fishing rights, which had been guaranteed
to the Indians by several nineteenth-century treaties. Collier's failure
to support Indian fishing rights not only enabled those states to extend their jurisdiction over customary Indian fishing sites in waters
located beyond reservation boundaries, but also caused a precipitous
decline in local tribal economies.

   Alison Bernstein's essay, "A Mixed Record: The Political Enfranchisement of American Women During the Indian New Deal" [3],
tests John Collier's commitment to advancing the political and economic standing of Indian women and finds mixed results. Tribal constitutions written during the Indian New Deal granted Indian women
voting rights in tribal elections. This paved the way for women to
participate in tribal government and in national Indian organizations.
New Deal programs for Indians, such as the Civilian Conservation
Corps, employed Indian women in clerical positions. Despite the
existence of a number of qualified candidates, Bernstein finds that
Collier excluded Indian women and men from upper-level positions
in the government. Thus the gains Indian women made during the
New Deal era paralleled those of their counterparts in white society.

A book which focuses on a component of Collier's Indian policy is Robert Fay Schrader's *The Indian Arts and Crafts Board: An Aspect of New Deal Indian Policy* [45]. Writing an institutional history, Schrader traces the steps leading to the founding of the Indian Arts and Crafts Board and its subsequent activities. Collier advocated the formation of the board because he viewed the production of traditional arts and crafts items, including rugs, pottery, baskets, and turquoise jewelry, as a means for Indians to achieve self-sufficiency and to preserve their cultures. Schrader finds that the board succeeded in increasing the volume of sales of Indian craftwork, but growing opposition to New Deal policies and cultural pluralism following World War II caused the board's role in Indian affairs to diminish. Although Schrader focuses primarily on Rene d'Harnoncourt and other board members, all of whom were non-Indians, the study enhances our knowledge of a major Indian New Deal program.

Two revisionist articles have appeared within the past three years which suggest that Indian opposition to New Deal policies may have added momentum to the push for termination—that is, the policy of withdrawing federal services and programs provided to Indians—which arose in the 1950s during a period of widespread opposition to ethnic pluralism. Laurence M. Hauptman's "The American Indian Federation and the Indian New Deal: A Reinterpretation" [14] emphasizes the campaign initiated by the American Indian Federation (AIF) in 1934 to remove Collier from office, abolish the Bureau of Indian Affairs, and repeal the Indian Reorganization Act. Finding that most AIF members were not extremists, Nazi sympathizers, or racists, as previous studies have stated, Hauptman points out that the vast majority of the membership, including traditional, conservative, and assimilated Indians, expressed valid concerns about Collier's program of reform. In "Termination: A Legacy of the Indian New Deal" [36], Kenneth R. Philp makes a similar statement. "Tired of broken pledges and weary of continued bureaucratic control," he writes, "many Indians joined with federal officials and legislators in looking toward termination for a measure of self-rule" (p. 180). Philp has also edited *Indian Self-Rule: First-Hand Accounts of Indian-White Relations from Roosevelt to Reagan* [38], in which Indian participants, government officials, lawyers, and scholars review the fifty years of Indian history after the passage of the Indian Reorganizaton Act.

According to Steven C. Schulte, historians have been more preoccupied with finding the source of the termination movement than discovering motives for it. In an essay entitled "Removing the Yoke of Government: E. Y. Berry and the Origins of Indian Termination Policy [46]," Schulte declares that E. Y. Berry, a congressman from the state of South Dakota, and other western conservative politicians "were held captive by an inability to move intellectually beyond their own backgrounds—to overcome the modified strains of frontier prejudice and ethnocentric belief in the superiority of Anglo-Saxon values . . ." (p. 67). In addition to this prejudicial attitude, those western conservatives supported termination as a means of freeing Indians from restrictive federal supervision and of reducing the federal budget. Although Berry played an instrumental role in pushing termination legislation through Congress in the early 1950s, he later toned down his rhetoric on termination out of fear that the large Sioux electorate in South Dakota would vote him out of office. The essays by Schulte, Philp, and Hauptman indicate that Indians have been active participants in the historical process during the twentieth century. Essays by Peter Iverson [18] and Kenneth Philp [37] show how Indians managed to emerge from the eras of termination and relocation with new strength and new direction.

An impressive number of articles and books contain discussions of the era of Indian self-determination, basically the 1970s. Scholars disagree on whether Indians have benefitted from self-determination policies. Most scholars, including Deloria and Prucha, agree that the era was an extension of Collier's New Deal policies and that it occurred during a period of public concern for poverty, the Vietnam War, and cultural pluralism. During the 1970s Congress enacted a number of laws designed, among other things, to strengthen tribal governments, to protect Indian religious practices, and to promote Indian education. For the first time, a number of social and economic programs became available for reservation Indians. Edmund J. Danziger, Jr., in "A New Beginning or the Last Hurrah: American Indian Response to Reform Legislation of the 1970s" [9], gives a favorable appraisal of the era. In spite of complicated federal regulations and guidelines for receiving grants under general and special legislation, Danziger argues that tribal officials managed to overcome these obstacles and enhance the social, political, and economic standing of Indian communities.

Other scholars challenge the efficacy of the federal Indian policy during the era of self-determination. Three articles emphasize the failure of federal initiatives to make lasting improvements in the quality of Indian life. A Chippewa sociologist, Duane Champagne, contends that the national trend of allowing local self-government to minority groups had little effect on the status of tribal autonomy. In "Organizational Change and Conflict: A Case Study of the Bureau of Indian Affairs" [8], Champagne argues that by the 1970s the dominance of the Bureau of Indian Affairs (BIA) over Indian tribes had become so entrenched that BIA officials managed to thwart several attempts by the administrative and legislative branches of government to reorganize the BIA. These victories enabled the BIA to exert more control over tribal governments.

"The Structure of Federal Aid for Indian Programs in the Decade of Prosperity, 1970–1980" [1], by coauthors Russel Lawrence Barsh and K. Diaz-Knauf, examines federal fiscal policies as they pertained to Indian reservations. Barsh and Diaz-Knauf acknowledge that federal allocations provided jobs and improved health care and expanded tribal operations, but they state that the long-term benefits of federal programs were minimal. Referring to the effect of cuts in federal spending initiated by the conservative administration of Ronald Reagan in the 1980s, they write: "When the subsidy air is released from the fiscal balloon, many tribal governments, like the Crow Tribe in Montana, simply collapsed" (p. 1). Another scholar who believes that federal programs during the 1970s have not improved the economic standing of Indians in South Dakota is the historian Herbert T. Hoover. In "Arikara, Sioux and Government Farmers: Three American Indian Agricultural Legacies" [16], Hoover suggests that South Dakota Indians can achieve self-sufficiency by combining traditional gardening techniques with farming and stock production.

Several recent essays center on the issue of Indian religious freedom during the 1970s. Steve Talbot, in "Desecration and American Indian Religious Freedom" [49], and John Petoskey, in "Indians and the First Amendment" [35], agree that the suppression of Indian religious practices by the federal government has posed an ideological contradiction to the First Amendment guarantee of religious freedom. According to Talbot, the rallying of public support by Indians persuaded Congress to pass the American Indian Religious Freedom Act in 1978. Lawmakers intended for the law to protect traditional religious practices by granting tribal access to religious sites on all public lands, permitting possession and use of sacred objects and guaranteeing freedom of worship. Both scholars concur that the act has largely failed to protect Indian religion because it provided no penalty for noncompliance. Robert S. Michaelsen has also written several articles on the subject of Indian religious freedom in which he takes a similar viewpoint [28, 29, 30].

While most works in recent years have concentrated on federal Indian policy, tribal histories and biographies, as well as studies on Indian leadership and resistance, have also appeared. These writings are significant because they stress aspects of Indian life at the grassroots level. The genre of tribal history is important to Indian people who are anxious to learn about the past experiences of their tribes. Many Indians realize that there is an urgent need for them to document their own stories from a tribal perspective, because with the death of each tribal elder another part of history is lost. But relatively few tribal members have taken up this endeavor. As a result, most tribal histories reflect non-Indian values, perspectives, and world views. A critical evaluation of why so few Indians, especially full-bloods, have become professional historians would make an interesting study.

Since 1983, at least one Indian scholar, Veronica E. Velarde Tiller, has written a history of her own people. Tiller advises readers not to view her book, *The Jicarilla Apache Tribe: A History, 1846–1970* [50], as being representative of an Indian viewpoint, since non-Indians produced most of her primary and secondary sources. This caution, however, is unwarranted. Her blending of written documents with oral traditions and her Jicarilla perspective give us an insightful and sensitive interpretation of a tribal experience. Tiller focuses on the relationship between the Jicarilla people and the federal government. Not surprisingly, she finds that the Dawes Act had disastrous consequences for the Jicarillas. Attempts by federal agents to force them to adopt subsistence farming on unfertile land and in a harsh climate caused rampant poverty, social problems, and disease on the reservation. Those problems, along with mismanagement of tribal trust funds by federal authorities, prolonged the guardian relationship with the federal government that the Dawes Act had intended to sever. Unlike revisionists who stress the failures and weaknesses of Indian New Deal programs, Indian scholars such as Tiller and Deloria hold a positive view of Collier's accomplishments. Tiller argues that the formation of a tribal government under the Indian Reorganization Act and revenues from oil production on the reservation provided a foundation on which the Jicarillas could begin moving towards regaining control over their own destinies. With a stable economy and an effective political system, they have successfully met the challenges of changing times. According to Tiller, the Jicarillas achieved self-determination long before the term gained popularity in the 1970s.

Using an approach similar to that employed by Tiller, Terry P. Wilson has also written a valuable, but somewhat less sensitive, history of the Osage Indians. In *The Underground Reservation: Osage Oil* [58], Wilson details the experiences of an atypical, oil-rich Oklahoma tribe in the twentieth century. While poverty caused hardships for most twentieth-century Indians, royalties from oil production created problems for the Osages between the 1910s and the Great Depression. Many Osages developed a disdain for work and abused alcohol and drugs. Political friction grew between those who received royalty payments and those who, for whatever reason, had been omitted from the tribal rolls. Meanwhile, local parasitic whites, who viewed Indians as objects for exploitation, robbed, defrauded, married, and even murdered Osages to obtain a share of the oil money. Fearing that a strong tribal government would interfere with their money-making schemes, a group of these non-Indians lobbied Congress and managed to have the Osages exempted from inclusion in the Oklahoma Indian Welfare Act, a measure that extended IRA provisions to tribes of that state. During the 1930s, many Osages became impoverished because of declining oil prices. Cultural retention, outward migrations, and movements to enfranchise Osages not included on the tribal roll and to bring women into tribal politics characterized the Osage experience since World War II.

Another study that uses a tribal case-study approach is Richard White's *The Roots of Dependency: Subsistence, Environment and Social Change Among the Choctaw, Pawnee, and Navajo* [53]. White analyzes the interaction of environmental, economic, political, and cultural factors which caused the decline of three tribes of Indian people. His aim is to show how and why the eighteenth-century Choctaws, nineteenth-century Pawnees, and twentieth-century Navajos lost the ability to feed and clothe themselves. Navajo dependency on the market began in the 1930s after the Bureau of Indian Affairs implemented a stock-reduction program that destroyed the Navajos' economic base. This misguided policy, White argues, was implemented because federal officials believed that the overgrazing of sheep, goats, and horses by Navajo herdsmen caused topsoil erosion that deposited silt behind Hoover Dam. White skillfully draws information from a wide variety of sources, including federal documents and minutes from Navajo council meetings as well as a host of published materials, to make his point. Despite his exhaustive archival research, White has failed to elicit the views of contemporary Navajos who carry a repository of first-hand knowledge of many events discussed in his work.

In recent years scholars have begun to produce more writings on the lives of Indian men and women who have been influential during the twentieth century. A collection of biographical essays, *Indian Lives: Essays on Nineteenth and Twentieth Century American Indian Leaders* [32], edited by L. G. Moses and Raymond Wilson, discusses the lives of twentieth-century Indians from a new perspective. Instead of viewing contemporary Indians as hanging in limbo trapped between an Indian world and a white world, as others have done, the editors suggest that "American Indians live in a complex world of multiple loyalties" (p. 4). Using the multiple-loyalties theme, the contributors provide biographical sketches of eight prominent Indians, including Susan LaFlesche Picotte, Henry Chee Dodge, Luther Standing Bear, and Peterson Zah. In *Ohiyesa: Charles Eastman, Santee Sioux* [56], a biography of an Indian man who was raised to be a warrior in Sioux culture but who later became a physician, reformer, and lecturer in mainstream society, Wilson attempts to use the multiple-loyalties theme. Yet Raymond Wilson implies that towards the end of Eastman's long life, he had indeed become suspended between two worlds. "He [Eastman] could no longer live the expectations of others in the white world," Wilson states, and "he could no longer return to the deep woods" (p. 189).

Another volume of essays containing biographical accounts of important twentieth-century Indians is *Indian Leadership*, edited by Walter Williams [55]. These essays, some of which are discussed elsewhere in this study, by Terry P. Wilson, Frederick Hoxie, Melissa Meyer, W. Dale Mason, Loretta Fowler, and William Willard, among others, show that the pressure of allotments, racial discrimination, and termination has precipitated the rise of Indian leaders. A typical essay is that by William Willard, a Cherokee anthropologist, on Gertrude Bonnin's campaign for Indian policy reform from 1911 to 1938 [54]. Bonnin, an author, lecturer, and reformer from the Yankton Sioux reservation, became a harsh critic of BIA officials and Congress for their abuses of trust responsibilities. According to Willard, Bonnin became an influential figure in several Indian organizations, including one that she herself founded. "Her role demonstrates," he writes, "the importance of educated individuals who rose, by their own commitment to their people's welfare, to a position of national leadership" (p. 75).

Non-Indians who have been influential in Indian affairs have also been the subject of several biographies. In addition to the study of John Collier discussed above, a book has been written on James Mooney's academic work among Indians. In *The Indian Man: A Biography of James Mooney* [31], L. G. Moses argues that Mooney, a self-taught ethnologist with the American Bureau of Ethnology, has not received the recognition he deserves for his contribution to the development of American anthropology. According to Moses, Mooney differed from his colleagues in that he rejected the theory that cultures evolved through stages. Mooney also rid himself of an attitude of racial superiority after establishing close friendships with the Indians he studied. While his colleagues continued to stress false notions of Indian savagery in their writings, Mooney came to emphasize the humanity of Indian culture. As with other recent works, a weakness of this study is that Moses apparently did not attempt to obtain a viewpoint on Mooney from the Sioux, Kiowas, and eastern Cherokees, the people about whom Mooney wrote.

A number of recent works deal with the issue of Indian cultural survival and identity. Most studies published before 1983 assume that the policy of removing Indian children from their homes and placing them in federal boarding schools caused social and mental problems for many students as well as a steady deterioration of tribal languages and cultures. In "Indian Boarding Schools and Ethnic Identity: An Example from the Southern Plains Tribes of Oklahoma," Sally J. McBeth offers another view [25]. On the basis of interviews with former students of several Indian schools, she found that many of them had fond memories of their boarding school experiences. "The very segregationist and assimilationist beginnings of the Oklahoma boarding schools," she writes, "effectively, if inadvertently, seem to have fostered the formation of an Indian identity" (p. 120).

James J. Rawls's *Indians of California: The Changing Image* [42] discusses Indian survival in terms of white attitudes. He finds that since the nineteenth century, when many white Californians used negative imagery to justify the removal and extermination of local tribal people, white racial attitudes have become less belligerent, a change which assures the cultural survival of Native Californians. The final section of another book, *Red & White: Indian Views of the White Man, 1492–1982* [43], by Annette Rosenstiel, contains excerpts from the writings and speeches of Carlos Montezuma, Plenty Coups, Luther Standing Bear, Ruth Muskrat, and Russell Means in addition to a few other prominent twentieth-century Indians. These people discuss Indian attitudes toward non-Indians as well as Indian survival, identity, and pride. A short collection of essays, all by Indian authors and edited by Clifford E. Trafzer, also focuses on the theme of American Indian identity [51]. In addition, Peter Iverson's anthology *The Plains Indians of the Twentieth Century* [19] emphasizes the ability of Plains Indians to change and adapt and still maintain tribal identity in the face of tremendous pressures on their lands and cultures, and Laurence M. Hauptman examines *The Iroquois Struggle for Survival* from World War II to the Red Power movement [15].

The literature on the Indian resistance (usually referred to as "Red Power") to political oppression, racism, cultural genocide, and economic exploitation has also been increasing in the past few years. Virtually all of these studies deal with struggles at the grass-roots level and attempt to present the story from an Indian perspective. A voluminous study of the case involving Leonard Peltier, an Ojibwa who allegedly participated in the slaying of two federal agents during a shoot-out on the Pine Ridge reservation in South Dakota in 1975, is Peter Matthiessen's *In the Spirit of Crazy Horse* [26]. "The ruthless persecution of Leonard Peltier," Matthiessen asserts, "had less to do with his own actions than with underlying issues of history, racism, and economics, in particular Indian sovereignty claims and growing opposition to massive energy development on treaty lands and the dwindling reservation" (p. xx). Matthiessen charges that agents of the Federal Bureau of Investigation framed Peltier in an attempt to undermine the influence of those on the reservation who opposed the tribal government, which had been created under the Indian Reorganization Act. Jim Messerschmidt investigated the court records of the Peltier case and offered a similar conclusion in *The Trial of Leonard Peltier* [27].

Now that the Buffalo's Gone: A Study of Today's American Indians [21], by Alvin M. Josephy, Jr., shows how Indian individuals, organizations, and nations have struggled against overwhelming odds to maintain their ethnic heritage, to eradicate negative racial stereotypes, and to preserve the essence of their spirituality. Josephy also discusses the battles which have occurred in legal and political arenas over land retention, hunting and fishing rights, water rights, and sovereignty. Although Indians did not win every confrontation, he stresses that the determination to end the policies of abuse, discrimination, and exploitation has improved the status of Indians.

Matthiessen and Josephy portray the leaders of the American Indian Movement (AIM), including Russell Means, Dennis Banks, and Vernon Bellecourt, as having a deep-seated commitment to Indian people. On the other hand, Gerald Vizenor, in "Dennis of Wounded Knee" [52], depicts Dennis Banks, a cofounder of AIM, as being an opportunistic "word warrior" who enriched himself with cash contributions given to AIM by church organizations, the federal government, and individuals. The case against Banks seems considerably overstated, but nevertheless it reflects an attitude held by some Indians and non-Indians alike.

Indian opposition to the mining of uranium and coal resources lying beneath reservation lands is a prominent theme in the work of Winona LaDuke, an Anishinabe. She views the development of mineral resources on reservations as colonial exploitation. In "Native America: The Economics of Radioactive Colonization" [24], LaDuke indicates that uranium mining on the Navajo and Laguna reservations has created a state of tribal dependency on multinational mining companies. Radioactive debris from mining operations, she argues, has contaminated the earth, causing severe health and environmental hazards for local Indians and non-Indians alike. "To Indian people," LaDuke states, "this is the final act of genocide, we are in no position to 'evacuate' our land base" (p. 19). In "The Morality of Wealth: Native America and the Frontier Mentality" [23], LaDuke argues that the ruthless exploitation of mineral resources by the multinationals as well as coercive federal policies have undermined the traditional way of life on the Navajo reservation.

The research of one historian, Joseph G. Jorgensen, indicates that Indians have found a few unlikely allies in the struggle against mining companies and the federal government. In "Land is Cultural, So is a Commodity: The Locus of Differences among Indians, Cowboys, Sodbusters, and Environmentalists" [20], he compares the diverse attitudes of Indians, ranchers, farmers, entrepreneurs, and environmentalists toward land. Focusing on the Northern Cheyennes of Montana and the Achomawi tribelets of northeastern California, Jorgensen notes that many Indian people still define their relationship with the land in nonmonetary values. On the other hand, whites have traditionally viewed land as a commodity, something to be bought and sold for profit. According to the author, white ranchers have adopted Indianlike nonmonetary standards for determining the value of land and have come to view the development of mineral resources as a threat to their way of life.

This survey of recent literature on twentieth-century Indian history demonstrates that the field has been enriched by a growing number of important books and articles, many of them revisionist. Yet the field remains top-heavy—that is, there are far more studies on federal policy at the national level than on the implementation of that policy at the reservation level. Studies on individuals, both men and women, tribes, cultural survival, and resistance are being written with increasing regularity and are expanding the breadth of our knowledge on twentieth-century Indians. Moreover, these studies on grass-roots people more often than not reflect Indian viewpoints, ideas, values, and cultures.

Despite these gains, there are still many aspects of twentieth century Indian life which deserve attention. There need to be more analyses of how federal policy has affected the daily lives of reservation people. For example, the operation of tribal governments and programs during the 1970s should be studied more systematically to help determine the effect of self-determination policies on reservation economics. Perhaps the researching and writing of history at the grass-roots level of Indian life will become the next challenge for scholars.

References

1. Barsh, Russel Lawrence, and Katherine Diaz-Knauf. 1984. "The Structure of Federal Aid for Indian Programs in the Decade of Prosperity, 1970–1980." *American Indian Quarterly* 8:1–35.
2. Beaulieu, David, 1984. "Curly Hair and Big Feet: Physical Anthropology and the Implementation of Land Allotment on the White Earth Chippewa Reservation." *American Indian Quarterly* 8:281–314.
3. Bernstein, Alison. 1984. "A Mixed Record: The Political Enfranchisement of American Indian Women During the Indian New Deal." In *Indian Leadership*, ed. Walter Williams, pp. 13–20. Manhattan, Kans.: Sunflower University Press.

4. Blend, Benay. 1983. "The Indian Rights Association, the Allotment Policy, and the Five Civilized Tribes, 1923–1936." *American Indian Quarterly* 7:67–80.
5. Cadwalader, Sandra L., and Vine Deloria, Jr., eds. 1984. *The Aggressions of Civilization: Federal Indian Policy Since the 1880s.* Philadelphia: Temple University Press.
6. Carlson, Leonard A. 1983. "Federal Policy and Indian Land: Economic Interests and the Sale of Indian Allotments, 1900–1934." *Agricultural History* 17:33–45.
7. Carriker, Robert C. 1983. "The American Indian from the Civil War to the Present," in *Historians and the American West*, ed. Michael P. Malone, pp. 177–208. Lincoln and London: University of Nebraska Press.
8. Champagne, Duane. 1983. "Organizational Change and Conflict: A Case Study of the Bureau of Indian Affairs." *American Indian Culture and Research Journal* 7:3–26.
9. Danziger, Edmund J., Jr. 1983. "A New Beginning or the Last Hurrah: American Indian Response to Reform Legislation of the 1970s." *American Indian Culture and Research Journal* 7:69–82.
10. Deloria, Vine, Jr., ed. 1985. *American Indian Policy in the Twentieth Century.* Norman: University of Oklahoma Press.
11. ———, and Clifford M. Lytle. 1983. *American Indians, American Justice.* Austin: University of Texas Press.
12. ———. 1984. *The Nations Within: The Past and Future of American Indian Sovereignty.* New York: Pantheon Books.
13. Green, Rayna. 1983. *Native American Women: A Contextual Bibliography.* Bloomington: Indiana University Press.
14. Hauptman, Laurence M. 1983. "The American Indian Federation and the Indian New Deal: A Reinterpretation." *Pacific Historical Review* 52:378–402.
15. ———. 1985. *The Iroquois Struggle for Survival: World War II to Red Power.* Syracuse: Syracuse University Press.
16. Hoover, Herbert T. 1983. "Arikara, Sioux, and Government Farmers: Three American Indian Agricultural Legacies." *South Dakota History* 13:22–48.
17. Hoxie, Frederick E. 1984. *A Final Promise: The Campaign to Assimilate the Indians, 1880–1920.* Lincoln: University of Nebraska Press.
18. Iverson, Peter. 1985. "Building Toward Self-Determination: Plains and Southwestern Indians in the 1940s and 1950s." *Western Historical Quarterly* 16:163–73.
19. ———, ed. 1985. *The Plains Indians of the Twentieth Century.* Norman: University of Oklahoma Press.
20. Jorgensen, Joseph G. 1984. "Land Is Cultural, So Is a Commodity: The Locus of Differences Among Indians, Cowboys, Sodbusters, and Environmentalists." *Journal of Ethnic Studies* 12:1–21.
21. Josephy, Alvin M., Jr. 1984. *Now that the Buffalo's Gone: A Study of Today's American Indians.* Norman: University of Oklahoma Press.
22. Kelly, Lawrence C. 1983. *The Assault on Assimilation: John Collier*

and the Origins of Indian Policy Reform. Albuquerque: University of New Mexico Press.

23. LaDuke, Winona. 1983. "The Morality of Wealth: Native America and the Frontier Mentality." *Radical America* 17:69–79.

24. ⸺. 1983. "Native America: The Economics of Radioactive Colonization." *Review of Radical Political Economy* 15:9–19.

25. McBeth, Sally J. 1983. "Indian Boarding Schools and Ethnic Identity: An Example from the Southern Plains Tribes of Oklahoma." *Plains Anthropologist* 28:119–28.

26. Matthiessen, Peter. 1983. *In the Spirit of Crazy Horse.* New York: The Viking Press.

27. Messerschmidt, Jim, 1983. *The Trial of Leonard Peltier.* Boston: South End Press.

28. Michaelsen, Robert S. 1983. "Red Man's Religion/White Man's Religious History." *Journal of the American Academy of Religion* 51: 667–84.

29. ⸺. 1983. "The Significance of the American Indian Religious Freedom Act of 1978." *Journal of the American Academy of Religion* 52:93–115.

30. ⸺. 1983. "'We Also Have a Religion': The Free Exercise of Religion Among Native Americans." *American Indian Quarterly* 7: 111–25.

31. Moses, L. G. 1984. *The Indian Man: A Biography of James Mooney.* Urbana and Chicago: University of Illinois Press.

32. ⸺, and Raymond Wilson. 1985. *Indian Lives: Essays on Nineteenth- and Twentieth-Century Native American Leaders.* Albuquerque: University of New Mexico Press.

33. Olson, James S., and Raymond Wilson. 1984. *Native Americans in the Twentieth Century.* Provo: Brigham Young University Press.

34. Parman, Donald L. 1983. "Inconsistant Advocacy: The Erosion of Indian Fishing Rights in the Pacific Northwest." *Pacific Historical Review* 53:163–89.

35. Petoskey, John. 1985. "Indians and the First Amendment." In *Amerian Indian Policy in the Twentieth Century*, ed. Vine Deloria, Jr., pp. 221–38. Norman: University of Oklahoma Press.

36. Philp, Kenneth R. 1984. "Termination: A Legacy of the Indian New Deal." *Western Historical Quarterly* 14:165–80.

37. ⸺. 1985. "Stride Toward Freedom: The Relocation of Indians to Cities, 1952–1960." *Western Historical Quarterly* 16:175–90.

38. ⸺. 1986. *Indian Self-Rule: First-Hand Accounts of Indian-White Relations from Roosevelt to Reagan.* Salt Lake City: Howe Brothers.

39. Prucha, Francis Paul. 1984. "American Indian Policy in the Twentieth Century." *Western Historical Society* 15:5–18.

40. ⸺. 1984. *The Great Father: The United States Government and the American Indians.* 2 vols. Lincoln and London: University of Nebraska Press.

41. ———. 1985. *The Indians in American Society: From the Revolutionary War to the Present.* Berkeley: University of California Press.
42. Rawls, James J. 1984. *Indians of California: The Changing Image.* Norman: University of Oklahoma Press.
43. Rosenstiel, Annette. 1983. *Red & White: Indian Views of the White Man, 1492–1982.* New York: Universe Books.
44. Salabiye, Velma S., and James R. Young. 1984. "American Indian Leaders and Leadership of the Twentieth Century: A Bibliographical Essay." In *Indian Leadership*, ed. Walter Williams, pp. 85–91. Manhattan, Kans.: Sunflower University Press.
45. Schrader, Robert Fay. 1983. *The Indian Arts and Craft Board: An Aspect of the New Deal Indian Policy.* Albuquerque: University of New Mexico Press.
46. Schulte, Steven C. 1984. "Removing the Yoke of Government: E. Y. Berry and the Origins of Indian Termination Policy." *South Dakota History* 14:49–67.
47. Stefon, Frederick J. 1983/1984. "The Indians' Zarathustra: An Investigation into the Philosophical Roots of John Collier's New Deal Educational and Administrative Policies." *Journal of Ethnic Studies* 11:1–45.
48. Swagerty, William, ed. 1983. *Scholars and the Indian Experience.* Bloomington: Indiana University Press.
49. Talbot, Steve. 1985. "Desecration and American Indian Religious Freedom." *Journal of Ethnic Studies* 12:1–18.
50. Tiller, Veronica E. Velarde. 1983. *The Jicarilla Apache Tribe: A History, 1846–1970.* Lincoln: University of Nebraska Press.
51. Trafzer, Clifford E., ed. 1985. *American Indian Identity: Today's Changing Perspectives.* San Diego: San Diego State University.
52. Vizenor, Gerald. 1983. "Dennis of Wounded Knee." *American Indian Quarterly* 7:51–65.
53. White, Richard. 1983. *The Roots of Dependency: Subsistence, Environment, and Social Change Among the Choctaws, Pawnees, and Navajos.* Lincoln and London: University of Nebraska Press.
54. Willard, William. 1984. "Gertrude Bonnin and Indian Policy Reform, 1911–1938." In *Indian Leadership*, ed. Walter Williams, pp. 70–75. Manhattan, Kans.: Sunflower University Press.
55. Williams, Walter, ed. 1984. *Indian Leadership.* Manhattan, Kans.: Sunflower University Press.
56. Wilson, Raymond. 1983. *Ohiyesa: Charles Eastman, Santee Sioux.* Urbana: University of Illinois Press.
57. Wilson, Terry P. 1985. *Bibliography of the Osage.* Metuchen, N.J., and London: The Scarecrow Press.
58. ———. 1985. *The Underground Reservation: Osage Oil.* Lincoln and London: University of Nebraska Press.

PART TWO

Emerging Fields

Despite the steady expansion of the published literature in American Indian history, many areas of scholarship remain untouched. Even as students of Native American life congratulate themselves on the growth of their field, they need to avoid getting caught in intellectual ruts, repeating old errors or ignoring new fields of inquiry. The following three chapters are intended to counteract disciplinary arteriosclerosis by sketching out three areas where work in Indian history has been either lacking or undeveloped. While there may be considerable scholarship in each area—linguistics, economics, and religion—there has been little attention paid to native histories with a focus on these topics. One hopes that the three chapters, each written by a scholar who is working to correct past oversights, will help other students define new approaches to our subject.

CHAPTER 7

The Importance of Language Study for the Writing of Plains Indian History

DOUGLAS R. PARKS

Most historians recognize the importance of language as a fundamental attribute of Indian culture and identity. Yet few who write Indian history do so with any serious attention to the languages spoken by Indian peoples or with any real appreciation of the insights to be gained from familiarity with those languages. Scholars who call for a multidisciplinary approach to the writing of Indian history have made little headway in integrating the study of linguistics into their work.

Focusing on the writing of Plains Indian history, Douglas R. Parks links a survey of recent literature with the work of scholars in the past, explains the difficulties inherent in the study of linguistics, and highlights some of the pitfalls. Historians who venture to employ Indian names and words all too often do so in a casual, inconsistent, and indiscriminate manner. Parks's chapter points the way toward an effective integration of the study of language in the writing of Indian history.

With little exception all sound anthropologic investigation of culture must have a firm foundation in language. Customs, laws, governments, institutions, mythologies, religions, and even arts can not be properly understood without a fundamental knowledge of the languages which express the ideas and thoughts embodied therein.
— J. W. Powell

Well over a century ago, John Wesley Powell proclaimed the fundamental importance of language for the study of the American Indian thereby giving direction to the American Indian research undertaken by members of the newly formed Bureau of Ethnology of the Smithsonian Institution [58]. Three decades later, Franz Boas, who came to be the dominant figure in the development of academic anthropology after the turn of the century, rearticulated the necessity of native language study when he wrote:

"Our needs become particularly apparent when we compare the methods that we expect from any investigator of cultures of the Old World with those of the ethnologist who is studying primitive tribes. Nobody would expect authoritative accounts of the civilization of China or Japan from a man who does not speak the languages readily, and who has not mastered their literatures. The student of antiquity is expected to have a thorough mastery of the ancient languages. A student of Mohammedan life in Arabia or Turkey would hardly be considered a serious investigator if all his knowledge had to be derived from second-hand accounts. The ethnologist, on the other hand, undertakes in the majority of cases to elucidate the innermost thoughts and feelings of a people without so much as a smattering of knowledge of the language. [9]

Both Powell and Boas exerted strong formative influence on early anthropology and made linguistics an essential part of the ethnological endeavor in the United States. Early bureau staff, beginning with J. Owen Dorsey and Albert Gatschet, engaged in salvage linguistic studies, publishing collections of native language texts and dictionaries, while Boas's students in ethnology were required, in addition to their primary concerns, to record and analyze linguistic data ample enough to provide descriptions of the languages spoken by the peoples they studied. Boas, in particular, but no less importantly his equally influential students Alfred L. Kroeber and Edward Sapir, shaped the subsequent development of the discipline so intrinsically that most of the finest cultural studies of the American Indian have continued to this day to be based in part upon a knowledge of the people's language, even if the compilation of dictionaries long ago ceased being a primary goal of anthropology.

The historical study of the American Indian contrasts markedly with the cultural approach in the extent to which knowledge of native languages has been considered integral to the undertaking. Bureau ethnologists like James Mooney and John R. Swanton were the only anthropologists during the first half of this century to appreciate the value of historical documents for the writing of American Indian culture history. [72] The *Handbook of American Indians* was a systematic—indeed the first—compendium of Indian history to be based partially on documentary sources and to provide synonymies of tribal names coming from those documents as well as from field investigations. [29] Although later bureau ethnologists such as William N. Fenton and their archaeological colleagues such as Waldo R. Wedel continued this historical tradition at the Smithsonian Institution, academic anthropologists followed the lead of Boas, eschewing written documents as valuable sources of information for the reconstruction of culture history, and relied instead solely on observed behavior and the material they collected in the field from living informants.

Because early anthropologists disdained to study historical documents, while at the same time professional historians almost totally neglected the American Indian, most Indian history during this century has been written by amateurs. Nowhere is this more poignantly illustrated than on the Plains, where the most prominent tribal chroniclers once were Doane Robinson [63], Stanley Vestal [77], and George Hyde [32] and where even today tribal histories are written by individuals for whom writing is an avocation. These writers, of course, have no linguistic training and do not know the languages of the peoples about whom they write, with the obvious result that their studies either omit linguistic material altogether or only occasionally cite Indian words, generally personal or place names, which vary radically in their transparency. Sometimes, however, such writers attempt to analyze Indian names to bolster a historical argument or interpretation, but these are almost invariably incorrect and misleading.

Since midcentury a small number of professional historians has established an emergent identity as students of American Indian history. [79] These include Arrell Gibson [18] and Donald Berthrong [7], who began writing narrative history at the University of Oklahoma, and Robert Berkhofer [6], who has taken a problem-oriented approach. In spite of this new scholarly attention, the treatment of native language material has suffered a consistent fate among historians: benign neglect. In contrast to their confreres in other geographical areas, American Indian historians do not ordinarily study the language of the people they chronicle, nor do they master linguistics sufficiently to handle language data competently and insightfully.

Ironically, the disregard of language characterizing the work of historians has become progressively more common among anthropologists who are interested in historical study. Coincidentally with the rise of autonomous linguistics in many universities, most anthropology departments no longer insist that their students have minimal competence in descriptive linguistics, and since knowledge of a group's language is neither a practical necessity for doing historical work nor a requirement for professional certification, students all too frequently forego the difficulties of language learning or mastery of the techniques of linguistic analysis.

The results for Indian history are twofold: standards of scholarship lag behind those in other historical specialties, maintaining a situation no different from the one decried by Boas in 1911, and many fundamental insights to historical problems are lost. This chapter will discuss and illustrate some of the ways in which language can contribute to the historical study of the American Indian and why knowledge of an Indian language is essential to historical scholarship. Because there is no extensive or well-defined recent literature on the uses of linguistics in history, the paper will take a broad sweep through time, and focus on the Plains as a sample geographical region.

Orthographies

Nowhere is the inattention to native languages more glaring than in the historical citation of words, particularly names. Contemporary authors uncritically copy older writers, many of whom knew little or nothing of their subjects' language and almost certainly nothing about phonetics. Sometimes these early renderings can be unmistakably recognized, especially when the sounds of the Indian language are not radically different from the recorder's own or when the word is a simple one, but just as frequently they are not readily transparent, and sometimes they are hopelessly obscure.

Pawnee, a Caddoan language characterized by an unusually simple phonetics but complex morphology, so that words are often exceptionally long, offers abundant examples of words originally recorded incorrectly which, through repetition by subsequent writers, have become established in the literature. For example, Richard White cites the Pawnee forms of several names of chiefs as they appear in records from the mid-nineteenth century [83]. Two are close approximations: Likitaweelashar ("Captain Chief") and Petalesharo (no translation given, but meaning "Man Chief"), which phonemically transcribed are *rihkitawi reesaaru'* and *piita ree-*

saaru', respectively. A third name, Lalahwahlerasharo, would be more problematic were it not for an accompanying translation, "Sky Chief"; its correct form is *tiraawaahat reesaaru'* and is more accurately translated as "Heavens Chief" (see, for example, [81]). In another publication White cites Man Chief's name differently, as Peta-la-sharo, creating an unexplained and confusing inconsistency [82]. Similarly, Clyde Milner cites Pawnee names from nineteenth century records [46]. Le-cuts-lasharo ("Eagle Chief"), for example, omits one entire syllable and is properly *riitahkacteesaaru'*. La-ruchuck-are-shar, translated as "Sun Chief," is *raruhcakureesaaru'* and actually means "His Chiefly Sun." The translation given in Milner's source is particularly misleading, since there are two other Pawnee names that translate more precisely as "Sun Chief": *sakuuru' reesaaru'* and *sakuuru' rareesaaru*, the latter name meaning literally "His Being a Chiefly Sun."

Milner and White, moreover, like many contemporary historians, perpetuate a misleading tradition common among nineteenth-century writers when they cite Indian words with dashes to separate syllables. Some early recorders apparently used this convention merely as a notational device to aid English readers pronounce exotic words, but many were undoubtedly influenced by the characterization of American Indian languages as polysynthetic, a trait first claimed for them by the French scholar Peter S. Duponceau in his translation of Zeisberger's Delaware grammar in 1827 and later elaborated in an essay published in 1838. Duponceau and contemporary early-nineteenth-century American philologists like John Pickering [57], Albert Gallatin [16], and Henry Schoolcraft [69] observed that these languages formed individual words by combining large numbers of meaningful elements into integrated units and that such formations required several words for translation into European languages. Since the meaningful elements—what linguists now call morphemes—frequently consisted of a single syllable, the notion that each syllable composing a word had its individual meaning became prevalent, graphically represented by the separation of syllables in writing Indian words.

Illustrative of this conception of the structure of American Indian languages is John Dunbar's sketch of the Pawnee language. There he states that verbs could be reduced to monosyllabic roots from which verbal forms were constructed by means of inflectional and terminal, or euphonic, syllables [14]. Although Pawnee is a polysynthetic language, and many morphemes do have a monosyllabic shape, many more consist of either a single consonant—less than a syllable—or two or more syllables that combine into forms more complex than Dunbar or his contemporaries realized. Thus there is no basis in the Pawnee language for the hypothetical form Peta-la-sharo cited by White, since it consists of two nouns, *piita,* "man" (unanalyzable), and *reesaaru',* "chief" (composed of the descriptive verbal stem *reesaar* plus the nominal suffix -*u'*). In the name Eagle Chief given by Milner, Le-cuts-la-sharo, the dashes likewise fail utterly to correspond to the constituent morphemes, which are *reetahkac,* "eagle," and *reesaaru',* "chief." The name Sun Chief, given as La-ru-chuck-are-shar, has an even remoter relationship to its formative elements, which in uncontracted form are *ra + a + ri + ur + sakuur + reesaar + u.* The citation of Pawnee words as strings of meaningful syllables thus has no linguistic validity whatsoever and merely perpetuates an erroneous nineteenth-century conception of its structure.

Types of Orthographies

To assess the value of transcriptions of Indian words and other linguistic materials in both historical and contemporary sources, it is necessary to distinguish among the types of orthographies that are encountered and to be cognizant of their characteristics. Based on the relationship of the written symbols to the sound system of a language, there are four varieties that are typically found: a phonetic rendition; a phonemic transcription; a practical, or native, orthography; and an idiosyncratic recording.

Phonetic Rendition. The type of transcription least often found in sources on the American Indian is the phonetic, which is an exact recording of each sound in an utterance. Such a recording, usually made by a trained investigator who may or may not be familiar with the language being recorded, is not based upon the phonological *system* of a given language and its individual sound units, but instead is one by which the recorder seeks to reduce to written symbols all the details of the physical production of sounds as they are perceived. A phonetic transcription, which uses the International Phonetic Alphabet or some similar notational system, is thus an accurate recording of a word or utterance. However, it generally contains more articulatory detail than is required for representing words in a writing system to be used either by native speakers of the language or by scholars studying it, since much phonetic detail (especially in narrow transcriptions) is predictable and therefore redundant. It is this redundancy that in large part distinguishes the phonetic rendition from the phonemic.

Phonemic Transcription. A writing system that represents each of the significant sound units of a language—the sounds of the underlying system—is a phonemic one. In part, this means that phonetic variation and redundancy are eliminated in representing individual sounds. In Pawnee, for example, there is a phoneme *r*, which is generally an apico-alveolar flap like the *r* of Spanish (for example, *pero* "but"), but among some speakers it varies between *n* and *l* sounds as well as *r*. This fluctuation is not significant but is merely the range of phonetic variation that the phoneme *r* allows. Hence in writing Pawnee there is no need to write *n* and *l* when they occur because their incidence is limited to certain individuals and is in free variation with *r*. Likewise, in the Teton dialect of Sioux there is an aspirated series of voiceless stops (*p'*, *t'*, and *k'*), each of which varies freely between two readily perceived varieties of sounds: one, the stop with a strong aspiration following it, and the other, the stop with a strong velar fricative off-glide (like the *ch* sound of German) following its release. The difference between these two varieties of the same phoneme is obvious even to a phonetically untrained listener but in fact it has no significance beyond individual style or habit.

A related characteristic of phonemes is the tendency of some sounds to have phonetic variants that are conditioned by their environment; that is, the position of one sound relative to other sounds may affect its form. A simple example of this environmental conditioning is provided by the Pawnee phoneme *c*. When it occurs before a consonant, it is an alveolar affricate, pronounced *ts* (as in English cen*ts*), but when it precedes a vowel it is a lenis palatal affricate *č*, pronounced as an unaspirated *č* as in English chur*ch*). These two phonetic variants, *ts* and *č*, are said to be in complementary distribution since they occur in mutually exclusive environments (one before vowels, the other before consonants). Because the two phonetic sounds are similar and because the occurrence of one or the other variant is predictable based upon context, it is unnecessary to write the two sounds with separate symbols (that is, as distinct entities) in a phonemic rendition [50].

Mandan and Hidatsa, two Siouan languages of the Northern

Plains, offer another example. In both languages there are *m* and *w* sounds that are nearly identical phonetically to the sounds written as *m* and *w* in English. In both languages they are also variants of a single phoneme written as *w*, but the contexts determining each variant are different in the two languages. In Hidatsa *w* occurs in all contexts except after a pause, where it is pronounced as *m*. For example, when the word for "woman" is uttered with a pause preceding it, it is pronounced *mia*, but when it occurs after another element, as in a compound, it is pronounced *wia* as in *cakaakawia*, "Bird Woman," the Shoshone guide of Lewis and Clark. Similarly in Hidatsa there is a contextually determined variation between *r* and *n*, the latter (also a nasal sound like *m*) occurring only before a pause. The morpheme *raaka* "young of anything," is, as an illustration, pronounced *naaka* after a pause and *raaka* in compounds like *cakaakaraaka* "chick," "egg" [36]. In Mandan, in contrast, the nasal variant *m* occurs before a nasalized vowel but is *w* everywhere else; for example, $ma^nná^nte'š$, "I stand up," but *wáratokaxi*, "old man." The phoneme *r* likewise becomes *n* phonetically before a nasalized vowel but is *r* elsewhere; thus, $rá^nku$, "road," is phonetically $ná^nku$, while *srut*, "to slide," is phonetically *sirut* [30].

Conceptually, the important point is that a limited set of phonemes exists in every language that composes its phonological (or sound) system and functions to make the distinctions necessary for differentiating meaning among morphemes or words. Because each language has its unique inventory of phonemes, it is crucial that in writing a language previously lacking a literary tradition, a scientifically accurate orthography be composed to represent each phoneme with a single symbol. That is, a language must be represented in terms of its own phonemes, not those of another language, if the written form is to convey adequately the semantic and grammatical distinctions of that language. This is not to say that the same orthographical conventions, frequently representing the same or very similar sounds, are not to be used for different languages, but rather that the phonemic distinctions peculiar to each language must be made accurately. Failure to do so results in confusion.

The radical differences among phonemic inventories found in Plains languages can be illustrated by comparing the class of *stop* consonants in Pawnee and Sioux. Pawnee has a single series consisting of three stops, *p*, *t*, and *k*, which are voiceless and unaspirated

[50]. Sioux, in contrast, has four series: one consisting of the voiceless, unaspirated stops *p*, *t*, and *k*; one consisting of their aspirated counterparts, *p'*, *t'*, and *k'*; another consisting of their glottalized counterparts, *p'*, *t'*, and *k'*; and finally one made up of two voiced equivalents, *b* and *g*. Thus in Teton Sioux (Lakota), semantic distinctions commonly hinge on unaspirated/aspirated contrasts (for example, *paha*, "hill," and *p'aha*, "head hair"; *ka*, "there yonder" and *k'a*, "to mean, signify"), on nonglottalized/glottalized differences (for example, *p'e*, "sharp, pointed," and *p'e*, "elm tree"; *ku*, "to be coming home," and *k'u*, "to give to someone"), and less frequently on voiceless/voiced differences (for example, *bu*, "to make a beating sound," and *p'u*, "I am coming") [10].

Practical, or Native, Orthography. Practical orthographies have been devised at one time or another for many Plains Indian languages, generally with the goal of promoting literacy in the native language. Most nineteenth-century efforts were made by missionaries who sought to promote education and establish Christianity. On the Plains the first orthographies generally appeared in primers, the earliest of which were published in the 1830s for Osage [47], Oto [45], Dakota [71], and Pawnee [14]. In some cases missionaries went on to compile extensive linguistic records, including grammars and dictionaries as well as hymnals and translations of the Scriptures. These activities reached their climax in the late nineteenth century but continued into the early twentieth.

Endeavors to achieve literacy for most tribes were short-lived; for the Pawnees, in fact, the pioneering efforts of the Reverend Dunbar went for nought. But for the Sioux, who represented the largest and most widely distributed speech community on the Northern Plains, there was such success that by the late nineteenth century a relatively large portion of the people could read and write their language. Underpinning this flourishing literacy movement was, of course, a vast amount of published material in Sioux: primers and dictionaries for teaching; hymnals and translations of the Scriptures; and three newspapers, the *Iapi Oaye*, or *Word Carrier*, (1871–1939), *Anpao Kin*, or *The Daybreak* (1878–1937), and *Sina Sapa Wocekiye Taeyanpaha*, or Catholic Sioux Herald (1893–1935). The newspapers in particular, each published under the auspices of a different religious denomination and featuring articles as well as letters from readers, were influential in spreading and sustaining literacy, since they served as a primary source of intercommunity news throughout the Dakotas, Minnesota, Nebraska, eastern Montana, and parts of Manitoba, Saskatchewan, and Alberta. Although the newspapers ceased publication before World War II and the primers long ago fell into disuse in education, the hymnals and the dictionaries continue in use today, and the translations of the Scriptures are still read by the elderly. But the viability of the missionary literacy movement began to wane early in the twentieth century, and while today many elderly people can read and write their language, few people born after the Great Depression period carry on the tradition.

Many of the linguistic descriptions compiled by missionaries are monumental reference works, rich in data carefully amassed over years of painstaking labor and rarely equaled even today in scope and detail. Among the most remarkable are the dictionaries of Santee Sioux compiled by Stephen R. Riggs and his associates [61]; of Teton Sioux compiled by Eugene Buechel, S.J., and edited posthumously [10]; and of Cheyenne compiled by Rodolphe Petter [56]. Rich as these dictionaries are, however, their orthographies suffer from varying technical limitations which pose problems for nonspeakers—although they may not necessarily be critical for native speakers.

Illustrating these deficiencies, the Riggs dictionary, for example, fails to distinguish aspirated stops from unaspirated ones, so one must know whether a stop is aspirated or not. Although this does not normally pose a problem for a native speaker, in some cases it does result in ambiguity. The Buechel dictionary makes this distinction unsystematically. The Cheyenne orthography in the Petter dictionary is more problematic, however, undoubtedly in part because Cheyenne is a more complex language phonologically and morphologically, especially for a speaker of a European language. Petter, for example, failed to write glottal stops and stress (both of which are phonemic), omitted voiceless vowels, and either omitted preaspiration (a breathy h before another consonant) or confused it with x (velar spirant) preceding another consonant. Moreover, he overdifferentiated vowels in Cheyenne, recognizing five (a, e, i, o, and u) when in fact there are only three (a, e, and o) [48].

Immediately preceding World War II, the Bureau of Indian Affairs initiated a literacy program for the Sioux, Hopis and Navajos and prepared a number of bilingual readers for use in Indian schools (for example, Clark [12]). The orthography used in the Sioux readers was a phonemic one prepared by the anthropologist Edward Kennard, but few teachers were trained to use the books. In the 1950s, educational philosophy changed, and use of the bilingual readers was discontinued; consequently, the orthography failed to gain currency.

Beginning in the early 1970s, primarily with funding from the U.S. Department of Education (Office of Indian Education and Office of Bilingual Education), many schools in Indian communities throughout the Plains region developed bilingual education programs, most of which have sought to revive native languages by teaching them to children who in most instances know little or nothing of their traditional languages. Although it remains to be seen whether any of these programs will have a sustained influence on their communities, each program has generally developed its own orthography for writing its language. Some of these writing systems are based on older ones, but frequently they are newly constructed. Many have been devised by or with the assistance of linguists, who have insured that all the phonemic distinctions in the language are represented, while others have been less systematically created, often with the avowed intention of making the writing system "simple" for the learner and ignoring crucial phonological distinctions. Among the many separate programs in Sioux communities there is as well the problem of competing orthographies: each program has adopted its own slightly different alphabet, and attempts to reach an agreement on a standard orthography have to date been unsuccessful.

Idiosyncratic Recordings. In contrast to the preceding types of writing systems, which conform to some established linguistic or social criteria, are the idiosyncratic alphabets of a wide array of people—travelers, army officers, Indian agents, journalists, indeed anyone who has recorded linguistic material for personal or official purposes using an alphabet that is neither linguistically based nor employed by a community of speakers. Most American Indian language data in historical documents are recorded in such idiosyncratic alphabets. They present the greatest number of problems for interpretation since they require identification and often reconciliation with many variant, sometimes baffling transcriptions.

What distinguishes idiosyncratic recordings as a group is the characteristic that they are written from the perspective of the recorder's own language. Having no other reference point—unless he knew more than one language—the recorder perceived the alien language in terms of the familiar sounds of his native language, using the writing system of his own language to represent unfamiliar sounds with the nearest perceived equivalent, or perhaps with some combination of letters that seem to approximate it.

In a Spanish Texas document from 1795, for example, a group of Skiri Pawnees provided officials in San Antonio with a list of thirty-three Indian "nations" with whom their tribe had friendly relations [76]. In the recorded list are several names that in Pawnee have a *w* sound (a bilabial glide just like English *w*). Contemporary Spanish, however, did not have an identical equivalent, the nearest sounds being the bilabial spirant written as a *b* and the labialized velar spirant written as *gu*. Hence we find Pawnee *cawii'i*, "Chawi," written as "Chagui"; *awaahiri'* written as "Aguajere"; *ka'iwa*, "Kiowa," written as "Chaibao"; and *tuhkiwaku'*, written as "Tuquibacu." Similarly, Spanish did not have a phoneme identical to Pawnee *c* (pronounced *ts* before a consonant); hence, the Spanish recorder used the nearest perceived equivalent, *s*, when he wrote Pawnee *actarahi* as "Astaray" and *piitakicahaaru'* as "Pitaquisagaru." Examples such as these illustrate that the interpretation of early transcriptions of Indian words must begin from a knowledge of the *recorder's* language, its phonology, and the phonetic values of its graphemes in order to determine as closely as possible the approximate phonetic form of the recording. (For a classic discussion of how alien sounds are perceived and recorded, see the essay by Boas [8]).

While cognizance of the recorder's native language is essential in transcriptional interpretation, there are two other critical factors determining the quality of recordings and thus their identity: the recorder's sensitivity to alien languages and his "ear" or ability to deal with new sounds. Some individuals are simply more sensitive to languages than others and have a greater facility for coping with (and learning) new forms of speech, and consequently recordings made by such people tend to be more transparent or amenable to confident interpretation than are those of the person who either lacks any linguistic skills or who gives little attention to his subjects' speech. Consider, for example, the recordings of the names of three divisions of the Sioux made by Lewis and Clark [74] and those made by a contemporary French fur trader, Pierre Antoine Tabeau [1], compared with their actual phonemic forms:

Lewis and Clark	Tabeau	Phonemic
Hoin de borto		
Hone-ta-par-teen	Hont-patines	$hu^nkpat'ina$
Wau pa ton		
Wah-pa-tone	Warhpetons	$waxpet'u^nwa^n$
Sou si toon		
Sis-sa-tone	Seisiton	$sisit'u^nwa^n$

In each instance the form given by Tabeau is closer to the Sioux phonemic form. The Lewis and Clark forms, moreover, illustrate another problem in old sources: variant forms given by the same recorder that frequently do not agree in sounds. The two renderings they give for $Hu^nkpat'ina$, for example, require careful examination to perceive that they represent the same word.

Other early transcribers like Prince Maximilian, in contrast, compiled word lists that are remarkable for their attention to phonetic detail and consistency [75]. Thus Maximilian, unlike any other Plains traveler, consistently indicated long vowels in Arikara (which are phonemic) by writing an *h* after the vowel; for example, *uhchu* for *uúxu'*, "hair"; *kahchu* for *kaáxu'*, "leg"; in contrast to *nix* for *níkUs*, "bird"; *hiachti* for *hi'axti'*, "my father." Maximilian also provided phonetic notes with many of his transcriptions that enable the modern student to determine the presence of various features characterizing modern Arikara speech.

No matter what the quality of the transcription may be, however, there are many forms in older records that absolutely defy identification today. Lewis and Clark, for example, give two Arikara names for tribal (or band) groups, Noo-tar-wau and Au ner-hoo, which have the appearance of Arikara words, but both their phonemic forms and the peoples they designate remain enigmas. Languages change,,and words become obsolete; therefore, some historically recorded forms will undoubtedly always remain problematic.

Modern Citations

How names and other words in Indian languages should be cited in contemporary works—whether in phonemic, practical, or idiosyncratic form—is an issue that historians seem to have skirted. For anthropologists, who in the past have worked with living people and eschewed historical documents, there was no problem: one presented words in phonemic form, either as written by a linguist or the anthropologist, or one worked out a practical orthography that would serve for the moment. But now that many anthropologists work with peoples who no longer speak their native language, or engage in historical study, frequently without the benefit of association with native speakers, the question of what form to use becomes as appropriate for them as for historians.

In citing Indian language material the overriding criterion should be concern for linguistic accuracy—for a transcription that is true to the original language. Indian language forms, then, should be presented phonemically, or at least in a close approximation, rather than preserving the historical recorder's naive misperception of unfamiliar sounds. Certainly, forms must be quoted at the outset as they occur in historical documents, but then their phonemic forms should be identified there and used subsequently to avoid ambiguity.

Not infrequently, there are personal names, toponyms, and other Indian language designations that recur often enough to warrant an anglicization, in which the phonemic form of the original language is recast into one composed of its nearest equivalents in English. In a discussion of Pawnee religion, for example, the term for the supreme deity, *tiraawaahat* ("The Heavens"), occurs so often that after the first citation in phonemic form, subsequent references in an anglicized form, Tirawahat, seem appropriate, doing no injustice to the original and making its constant citation easier by bringing it into English. The Sioux word for the supreme power, *wak'a^nt'a^nka* ("Great Holy"), likewise can be anglicized as Wakantanka, as is frequently done.

In forming and using anglicizations, the criterion of fidelity to the original is of paramount importance, making it imperative that the form adapted reflect as closely as possible the original phonemic form. Thus in the case of the name of the Pawnee chief *piita reesaaru'* ("Man Chief," cited above), the most fitting anglicization would be Pitaresaru rather than Petalesharo or one of the more deviant variants so frequently given.

The names of two Hidatsa villages, *awaxaawi* and *awatixaa*, provide another instructive example. The first has been cited variously as Amahami, Awaxawi, and Awahawi; the latter as Amatiha, Awatixa, and Awatiha. The forms containing *m* for phonemic *w* are easily explained: when a Hidatsa speaker syllabifies a word, as he would do for a nonspeaker struggling to write it, he pauses before each syllable, articulating a phonetic *m* for underlying *w* after the pause—a sound that would be *w* when the word is spoken at normal tempo. Hence these anglicizations for the village names are clearly inappropriate. The more difficult question is whether to write *h* or *x* for what is phonemically an *x* (velar spirant). Since English does not have a velar spirant and *h* has another phonetic value, it seems that *x* is perhaps the better choice—although in English it, too, has other values, *ks* as in *exodus* and *gs* as in *exam*. Thus it seems that the choice here must be arbitrary.

A criterion that is as important in forming and using anglicizations as fidelity to the original is consistency of usage. Too many anglicized variants exist for many Indian names, and contemporary authors seem to choose indiscriminately, or at least without clearly articulated criteria, among the various historical possibilities. Tribal and band names provide abundant illustrations, among which are the variants of the Hidatsa village names noted above. For the Pawnee band names there certainly is no systematic usage, so one continually encounters competing forms: Skiri and Skidi; Chawi and Chaui; Pitahawirata, Pitahawirat, and Pitihauerat; and Kitkehahki, Kitkahahki, and Kitkehaxki. (Here the forms Skiri, Chawi, Pitahawirata, and Kitkahahki conform best to the native Pawnee names.)

Another example—one that has occasioned much controversy and misunderstanding in the literature—is the name of Lewis and Clark's Shoshone guide, which has been written as Sacajawea, Sacagawea, and Sakakawea. Although some historians have argued that the name is a Shoshone word, linguists insist that it is quite clearly a name in Hidatsa, *cakaakawia*, "Bird Woman," which is the translation that Lewis and Clark gave for it. But in addition to its linguistic provenience, scholars have also debated the way the name should be spelled, based on historical evidence and poor linguistic source material. Although both Irving Anderson [2] and James Ronda [64] argue for Sacagawea, it is clear that Sakakawia would be an anglicization more in accord with the Hidatsa form of the name.

Most importantly, these illustrative spelling variants point to the need for linguistically informed standardization among the most commonly cited Plains names so that each writer is not set adrift when confronting them and their many variants.

Still another problem in the citation of native language words is the form that cannot be adequately identified. As one goes farther back in time, the number of names that can no longer be recognized by contemporary speakers of a language increases, since many have fallen into disuse and are not known any more. Some names, too, were undoubtedly written down so incompetently as to defy recognition even when the form may in fact be known to individuals today. Whatever the reason, such names remain unrecognizable. All one can do is to cite them as they are found in the historical sources.

There is, finally, the ultimate issue at point when attempting to cite Indian linguistic forms: the inability, and frequent unwillingness, of publishers—and university presses in particular—to accommodate language material requiring special symbols. When type was set by hand, the inclusion of diacritical marks and nonstandard symbols was less of a problem than it is today when computers and word processors are employed to prepare printed copy. Because publishers have not yet found a simple, inexpensive solution to what is frequently deemed a negligible problem, they have opted for either eliminating phonemic citations altogether or omitting diacritics and other nonstandard symbols. Both options restrict the quality of American Indian scholarship—the former to preclude non English text, and the latter to eliminate crucial phonemic distinctions. In books dealing with the Sioux, for example, omission of diacritics has been commonplace, thereby neutralizing such phonemic distinctions as those between aspirated and unaspirated stops and others like s and $š$. A word like *wašicu*, "white man," for example, is printed as *wasicu* and becomes a nonword, creating confusion over its actual form for someone who does not know the language. Often, too, this practice yields quite unintended results, as when White writes of the Pawnees [83, p. 175]: "When in council, members were addressed as *a-ti'-us* (fathers). . . ." Dunbar, White's source for this form, wrote a breve mark over the vowel u (that is, $ŭ$) to symbolize the vowel sound in the English word *but*; Dunbar distinguished $ŭ$ from u (written without a breve) to represent the vowel sound in the English word *toot*. Thus the form that White gives, *ati'us*, means "flatus," whereas the original form *a-ti'-ŭs*—more appropriately written *ati'as*—means "my father."

One solution to the problem of diacritics is to substitute different symbols for them. In Sioux, for example, some linguists use an h following a consonant to indicate aspiration instead of the raised inverted comma (') employed by others. This substitution, a good orthographic convention, yields words like *phaha*, to which many native Sioux people object, either because by analogy with English orthographic usage it looks like it should be pronounced as *faha*, or because it demonstrates a disregard for the missionary alphabet they already know. Such substitutions can also introduce ambiguity into a writing system. In Arikara, for example, one might be inclined to write the phoneme *š* as *sh* (as is done in English), but since there are words that have the sequences *s + h* (for example, *shaánu'*, "creek valley"), this substitution is untenable.

Clearly, writers must press publishers to recognize the necessity of printing linguistic material with diacritics and nonstandard symbols so that the integrity of Indian languages is maintained and the quality of historical scholarship is thereby improved—so that these fundamental principles are not sacrificed because of a failure to appreciate their significance.

Historical Relationships Among Languages

The comparative study of languages—the search for linguistic similarities and the formulation of explanations for them—provides significant information for the reconstruction of culture history. By this means it is possible to determine relationships among languages and their speakers and to determine whether these relationships reflect historical contact or genetic ties. Language comparison also reveals how a group of genetically related contemporary speech forms have developed over time from a putative ancestral language. For unwritten languages this technique yields vital historical information about interrelationships among the groups of language speakers and allows reconstruction of the chronology of their separations—information that in the New World predates earliest historical records by millenia and helps us to understand the geographical distribution of languages during the period of recorded history.

Levels of Linguistic Diversity

At the outset of his book *American Indians*, William Hagan describes how for the tribes of the United States, "physical variations, coupled with the hundred of different dialects spoken (although scholars have classified them in six major language groups), offer the best evidence that migrations from Asia began perhaps 30,000 years ago."[24] To take another example, W. David Baird writes that the Quapaws, Omahas, Osages, Kansas, and Poncas are "components of the Dhegiha Sioux family, all of whom . . . speak the same language."[3] Such indiscriminate uses of the terms *dialect*, *language*, and (language) *family* are common among writers on the American Indian, who often use *dialect* and *language* interchangeably, as if they were synonymous, and use *family* for any level of grouping of related dialects or languages. Hence it is important to distinguish between the levels of linguistic diversity that are found both within and among speech communities and to define precisely the terms for each level to forestall ambiguity.

The lowest level at which speech variation is found is that of the individual, whose total speech habits constitute an *idiolect*. Each individual in a speech community is characterized by a distinctive pattern of speaking that, no matter how slight, differs from those of the people about him. Generally there is no purpose in studying individual speech habits; it is the habits of a group of people—those of a village, tribe, or region—that are the usual object of description and study. But the notion of idiolect is important because higher levels of diversity—dialects and languages—in the last analysis comprise a totality of idiolects.

A *dialect* is a patterned set of speech habits that distinguishes a group of people within a larger speech community so that their speech differs from that of other members; usually this does not preclude mutual intelligibility. Two types of dialects are distinguished: first, the social dialect, characteristic of stratified or complex societies with social classes or occupational groups whose members develop distinctive speech patterns or vocabulary that contrast with other members of their community; and second, the regional dialect, which develops when one group removes itself from other members of the speech community and remains geographically or socially isolated over a sufficient length of time for speech differences to develop that distinguish it from the original community.

It is the latter, regional dialects, that are most commonly represented in native North America. In fact, on the Plains there is abundant historical evidence to indicate that many tribes which have had little dialectal differentiation during the past century—after their populations shrank drastically and formerly autonomous groups had coalesced—were much more linguistically diverse during the eighteenth century. For example, Tableau, the French fur trader who lived among the Arikaras in 1803–1804, remarked that each of the ten "tribes" formerly composing the Arikaras had its own dialect and that in the three recently consolidated villages he visited, this dialectal diversity was yet maintained. [1, p. 126] Similar diversity previously characterized the southern Caddoan groups now known as the Wichitas and Caddos as well as the Pawnees [51, 52]. And in 1899 when Kroeber engaged in field work among the Arapahos, he found evidence to suggest five former dialects of that language [39]. Only two survive today: Arapaho itself (with minor differences that have recently developed between southern and northern varieties) and Gros Ventre (sometimes called Atsina).

A *language* is generally defined in terms of mutual intelligibility—a speech community all of whose members are able to understand one another. Ordinarily this definitional criterion is sufficient to distinguish between two languages: if two groups understand the speech of the other, they share a single language; if not, they speak separate languages. But on the Plains as elsewhere in North America, there are many instances in which the speech of two groups has diverged so dramatically over time that they border on being considered as dialects of one language or as constituting separate languages. Arikara and Pawnee are one such example. Pawnee speech occurs in two dialectal forms—Skiri and Pawnee proper (frequently called South Band Pawnee)—that are unmistakably mutually intelligible for members of both speech communities, whereas Arikara has moved just beyond the point of mutual intelligibility. Changes in the Arikara sound system have phonetically masked words that are either identical to or only slightly variant from their Pawnee cognates, making it virtually impossible for speakers of Pawnee and Arikara to understand one another in normal speech. Yet members of both groups will maintain that they speak the same language [52].

The question is whether such a set of speech groups is better considered to represent one language or two. Is Arikara to be treated as a dialect, albeit aberrant, of the other two Pawnee dialects, or is it to be treated as a separate language? The answers are largely arbitrary, in which sociopolitical criteria seem as significant as linguistic ones. In Europe, where no unequivocal linguistic boundary can be drawn between, say, Dutch and German, because these speech varieties form a dialect continuum from the North Sea to the Swiss Alps and unintelligibility only appears at opposite ends of that geographical continuum, linguistic boundaries are made to coincide with political ones, so that the Dutch language extends to the national boundary separating the Netherlands and Germany, where the German language begins. In like manner in native North America it seems that language boundaries are best drawn between two divergent dialects if their speakers are geographically separated and politically autonomous as well as unable to understand one another. Utilizing these criteria, we must consider Arikara and Pawnee separate languages, even though their separation may only extend back in time several centuries.

After language boundaries are identified, two caveats must be specified to put to rest popular notions that language boundaries coincide with both cultural and social ones. In fact, there is no necessary congruence. For example, the Crows formerly were divided into two social groups, the River Crows, who lived along the lower Yellowstone River, and the Mountain Crows, who wintered in Wyoming but joined the River group in the spring. Both were distinct social units yet they shared the same culture and spoke the same language [42]. The Sioux groups provide a slightly contrastive example. The Tetons, or Western Sioux, formed a set of closely related social groups (bands) who were quite distinct from the Santees, or Eastern Sioux, who formed another set. These social groups spoke distinctive dialects of the same language. But in contrast to the Crows, the Tetons and Santees represented considerable differences in culture. The Santees practiced an Eastern Woodlands life-style that contrasted with the nomadic, High Plains culture type characteristic of the Tetons. It is an anthropological truism that there is no necessary correlation between language and either social or cultural boundaries. (For a classic discussion of the disjuncture of linguistic and social boundaries, see [9, pp. 6–14]).

Types of Relationships

When similarities between distinct languages are found—resemblances in vocabulary, sounds, grammar, and so on—they are to be explained as the result of one of two possible causes (assuming they are not merely fortuitous): either they have resulted from borrowing in the course of historical contact, or they are common inheritances from an ancestral speech form from which both have developed—or they represent a combination of these. Both explanations are historical, stemming from previous links between groups of people, but the former suggests nothing more than the social contact necessary for linguistic borrowing or diffusion to take place, whereas the latter establishes a relationship based on former unity among languages, the ancestral form of which over time differentiated into new and separate ones.

Diffusion and Areal Features. On the Plains there has been little study of areal features resulting from diffusion. Hollow and Parks [31] illustrate one areal trait, a form of consonantal symbolism, that appears as an old feature of Siouan languages and that also occurs in Arikara but no other Caddoan language, suggesting that diffusion from the Siouan groups to the Arikaras seems the most plausible explanation, especially since the Arikaras have a long history of contact with the Sioux, Mandans, and Hidatsas. This symbolism consists of consonantal changes among spirants to indicate semantic gradations in intensity. In Dakota, for example, there are sets of words like *zi*, "yellow," *ži*, "tawny," and *ǵi*, "brown." Mandan has a corresponding set: *síre*, "yellow," *šíre*, "light brown," and *xíre*, "brown." In Arikara there is a similar sort of spirantal symbolism, in which the phonemes *x* and *š* are replaced by *s* to indicate a diminutive or small object. For example, *kunahúx*, "old man," and *kunahús*, "little old man"; *súxtit*, "old woman," and *sústit*, "little old woman"; *xaatš*, "dog," and *saats*, "a newborn puppy."

Other areal features characteristic of the Plains are mentioned by Sherzer in an article that provides a history of typological studies in North America and describes each linguistic area in terms of its distinctive traits [70]. It is a general survey, restricted to a preselected list of traits and restricted by the availability of descriptive materials and therefore must be understood as an initial study, more suggestive than definitive. It omits mention, for example, of such promising traits for areal study as vowel devoicing (or whispering) that is characteristic of Arikara, Assiniboine, Cheyenne, and Comanche, among other Plains languages.

Genetic Relationships and Classification

During the past two centuries of American Indian language study, there has been a consistent and at times compelling interest in classification. Before the development of the comparative method in Indo-European studies in the mid-nineteenth century, most scholars confused or failed to distinguish between *genetic* groupings based on historical unity and *typological* classifications that categorize languages according to structural characteristic(s), the latter exemplified by Duponceau's categorization of American languages as poly-synthetic. Nineteenth-century interest in linguistic taxonomy was motivated by two complementary goals: to reduce the chaos of hundreds of individual languages to a manageable schema, and to establish their relationship with the languages of Asia in order to fit the New World into the Biblical conception of human history.

Although motivations for genetic classification have shifted over the past century as linguistic and anthropological scholarship have advanced, classification continues to be one of the primary goals in the study of New World peoples, in part because the more our understanding of the intricate details of language relationships increases, the deeper our knowledge of the history of tribal interrelationships becomes. And if scholars are to continue to extend our reconstruction of American Indian culture history further back in time, it will be based to no small extent upon the continued refinement of genetic classifications.

Albert Gallatin, American statesman and linguistic scholar, produced the first major classification of Indian languages. He published two versions of it, the first in 1836 and a new, expanded one in 1848 [16, 17]. Based on vocabulary comparison to establish *families* of languages—the same methodology used by Indo-European scholars—he was able to ascertain thirty-two genealogical groups. Following Gallatin's work no major classification appeared until 1891, when John W. Powell published his monumental "Linguistic Families of North America North of Mexico," in which he established fifty-eight families [59]. Like Gallatin's, Powell's classification was based on lexical comparision, but unlike Gallatin's, his was comprehensive. It was, as Sapir wrote in 1917, "the cornerstone of the linguistic edifice in North America . . . [which] has served . . . as the basis of all classificatory work in North American linguistics [66]."

Work in American Indian language classification after Powell has revolved around two approaches, one seeking to refine the relationships *within* language families and the other searching for proof of remoter relationships *among* families. The next influential classification to appear after Powell's illustrates the latter endeavor. It is the classification of Edward Sapir, first presented in 1921 and slightly modified in 1929 [67, 68]. Admittedly hypothetical, it was an attempt to interrelate as many families of Indian languages as possible into larger groupings. The result, based partially on morphological similarities and intuition, was a schema in which language families were grouped into *stocks*, which in turn were classified into only six *superstocks*. Sapir's taxonomic lumping has served as the basis for subsequent work designed to prove or disprove the details of his classification and to stimulate investigation of other possible relationships among families.

In 1964 a conference on American Indian language classification convened at Indiana University to assess the consensus of Americanist studies that had developed since Sapir. The classification to emerge from it, which recognizes eight linguistic stocks, each consisting of varying numbers of families, follows Sapir's in outline [78].

Currently, the most authoritative appraisal of the historical study of American Indian languages is embodied in a set of papers presented at a conference entitled "American Indian Linguistics: An Assessment," held in Oswego, New York, in 1976. The published proceedings survey all of North America and offer a comprehensive, detailed statement of current knowledge. The introduction to this volume, by Campbell and Mithun [11], and two papers by Mary R. Haas [23, pp. 110–29, 130–63], present insightful histories of Indian language classification and the intellectual milieu in which its major contributors worked.

In contrast to the conservative classificatory appraisal to emerge from the Oswego Conference is a recent, bold presentation by Joseph Greenberg of a genetic scheme encompassing all the indigenous languages of both Americas. His classification recognizes three "maximal" groups—Eskimo-Aleut, Na-Dene, and Amerind—the last composed of languages from northern Canada to Tierra del Fuego grouped into eleven subgroups. Although Greenberg offers extensive lexical and grammatical evidence, based on massive comparisons, to support his radical new proposal, he eschews the forms of evidence normally required by linguists to prove genetic relationships among languages; hence, his classification will undoubtedly remain controversial for some time [21].

The status of the comparative study of language families represented on the Plains is not significantly different from that of other areas of North America. For each of the families represented there— Siouan, Caddoan, Algonkian, Kiowa-Tanoan, Athapascan, and Uto-Aztecan—there are generally satisfactory provisional schemes of family subgroupings, but many have internal problems that will persist until adequate descriptive materials become available and detailed comparative work utilizing them has been accomplished.

A preliminary reconstruction of the phonology of the Caddoan family which was made by Allan R. Taylor [73], for example, confirmed the general subgrouping scheme presented by Alexander Lesser and Gene Weltfish [41] three decades earlier. But Taylor's study as well as subsequent work has not taken account of Kitsai, a language now extinct, although recorded by Lesser before its last speakers died. Moreover, thorough comparative study of Caddoan linguistic history has until recently been hampered by a lack of detailed descriptive studies which have only recently been completed or are still in progress and are yet unpublished. Therefore, one pressing desideratum for Caddoan, as indeed it is for most language families on the Plains, is the publication of basic reference works (dictionaries, grammars, and collections of texts) for every language (see [31]).

Even if the historical study of most Plains language families has not reached full development, work accomplished to date does answer many fundamental questions about the culture history of specific groups and in some instances clarifies previously misleading assumptions about the origin of contemporary social groups. The relationship of the Arikaras to the Skiris and other Pawnees to the south is one example. Based on oral tradition, many writers have asserted that the Arikaras are an "offshoot" of the Skiris, from whom they are reputed to have branched off (for example, [22, 29, 33]). Comparative study of these dialects—Arikara, Skiri, and Pawnee proper—reveals, however, that the Arikara dialect developed (or separated) from an earlier form of Pawnee before the differentiation of Skiri and Pawnee proper had occurred, a linguistic observation first made by Lesser and Weltfish [41] and corroborated by Taylor [73] and Parks [52]. Thus it is inaccurate to maintain that the Arikaras are genetically more closely related to the Skiris than they are to the other groups. In fact, these writers have confused actual genealogical relationship with the perceived affinity that resulted from social contact between the Arikaras and Skiri Pawnees during the late eighteenth and early nineteenth centuries, a social relationship which subsequently became reformed in oral traditions as a closer genetic tie.

A similar misconception based on oral tradition asserts that the Assiniboines branched off from the Yanktonai Sioux. William Keating, the chronicler of the Long expedition, recorded this tradition from a Sioux in Minnesota in 1823 when it was current, and it was repeated by other nineteenth-century writers (for example, [16, 62]), so that today many historians and anthropologists perpetuate it as accepted fact (for example, [25, 60]). A preliminary comparative study of Sioux and Assiniboine dialects, however, suggests that the split between Assiniboine and Sioux occurred at a period in the history of the language long preceding the one existing at the turn of the nineteenth century, before Sioux dialects were as highly differentiated as they were a century ago and are today [54]. Thus it would be incorrect to derive Assiniboine from any one contemporary Sioux dialect, since it developed before, or perhaps at the same time as, those dialects developed, but certainly not after they had become fully differentiated.

What these examples illustrate is a pattern by which myth is embedded in the historical literature and becomes uncritically accepted as fact. The comparative linguistic study of dialects, however, has shown that in at least two instances the traditional explanations of social origins are untenable and thus suggests that similarly based interpretations for other groups should be examined in the light of comparative linguistics.

Dating Historical Relationships

Dating the separations of languages postulated by linguists in comparative studies is a topic of no little interest in the study of culture history. There are two methods for deriving such dates, but neither yields fully satisfactory results.

One method is to make an *impressionistic* judgement of time depth: a linguist familiar with two or more closely related languages can estimate the number of years likely to account for the differences between them. This means of dating is purely subjective, an educated guess that is not independently replicable. However, it frequently provides more realistic dates than the other method, *glottochronology*, particularly when the linguist knows the languages well and can compare their differences and similarities with comparable pairs of European languages for which dates of separation are historically documented.

When it was first proposed in the 1950s as a method of assigning dates using an explicit operational procedure, glottochronology promised to be a scientifically accurate means of gauging time depth between pairs of languages. Its accuracy as a dating technique hinges on two critical assumptions: that all languages share a small common

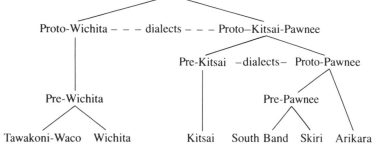

Fig. 7-1. Subgrouping of the Northern Caddoan Languages. Based on a chart originally printed in Douglas R. Parks, "The North Caddoan Languages: Their Subgroupings and Time Depths," *Nebraska History* 60(1979):206.

core vocabulary of words highly resistant to replacment, and that the rate of replacement of such vocabulary is measurably constant over time. Devising a list of the core vocabulary has in many cases presented sufficient problems to vitiate the statistical reliability of the results, but perhaps more importantly, the critical assumption that the rate of lexical replacement is constant over time has been seriously questioned (for example, [5].) Because of these shortcomings, the consensus is that there is little validity to the dates derived by glottochronology.

Several glottochronological studies have been reported for Plains languages. The most ambitious is that by Robert K. Headley, who applied the technique to the languages of the Siouan family [27]. Rood critically evaluated this study, questioning the reliability of the data, and concluded that although glottochronology seems to be able to measure relative time depth between subgroupings within a language family, Headley's results remain inconclusive [65]. In a study of the time depth of differentiation among northern Caddoan languages, Parks compared the results of glottochronology with a set of impressionistic dates previously proposed [52]. He concluded that although most of the dates that the statistical technique yielded did not appear realistic, they did in fact support his proposed subgrouping (Fig. 7-1).

Ethnonymy

The identification and explanation of names of social groups as reported in the historical literature is a linguistic topic of no little significance for the interpretation of culture history. When studying the early accounts of explorers, traders, missionaries, and other Europeans who wrote about Indians, one inevitably encounters problems in identifying the myriad names appearing in various forms. Not only are they written in varying shades of transparency, but some appear in one period but not another, while other names present conflicts in identification with contemporary or later groups. Resolving enigmatic forms can be exasperating—indeed, seemingly impossible at times—but solutions can frequently be achieved through the study of ethnonyms and their linguistic composition. A knowledge of the latter, moreover, can provide historical and ethnographic insights that might otherwise be overlooked. (See also [72].)

Most histories and ethnographies, generally at their outset, include a perfunctory statement of a people's name for themselves and for their major subdivisions, together with translations of these names and attempts to explain their origin or significance. Frequently the source for this information is the *Handbook of American Indians* [29], but often it may be taken from some earlier ethnographer, historian, or other writer. Sometimes the information is more or less correct, but all too commonly it suffers from one or more inadequacies: the transcription may be incorrect; the translation may be inaccurate; and most often the explanation of the origin or significance is either conjectural or demonstrably erroneous. Most citations and explanations, in fact, can ultimately be traced back to a single source, the basis of which was either oral tradition or an idiosyncratic interpretation that an early writer accepted and subsequent writers have uncritically repeated.

Because of these two interrelated problems—enigmatic forms in early sources and misleading or erroneous explanations of ethnonyms—the following discussion will focus on some of the fundamental issues in studying names and their etymologies.

Levels of Social Division

Determination of the level of social division denoted by a term is a crucial issue that pervades the enterprise of identifying and interpreting names in a historical source. Writers all too often construe such denotations for social units as *tribe* and *band* as givens that are to be uncritically accepted, either as a source designates a group or as the writer himself assumes the term to be understood in contemporary usage. Unfortunately there was little consistency in terminological usage among early writers. *Tribe* and *nation* are generally used synonymously, although frequently the term *tribe* is used to designate a subdivision of a nation, especially when the population is large and composed of relatively sizable, autonomous groups. A *band* is generally a subdivision of a tribe, but not infrequently the two terms are used interchangeably. For example, the Sioux are generally designated a nation divided into the Teton, Yankton, and Santee tribes, while the Tetons in turn are subdivided into bands, for example the Oglalas and Hunkpapas. A rapid perusal of the treaties between the Sioux and the United States government recorded in Kappler illustrates the lack of consistency in this historical genre [37]. In one treaty (1815) the Tetons are designated a "tribe" whereas in another one ten years later (1825) they, the Yanktons, and Yanktonais are called "bands." In individual treaties, moreover, two terms may be used synonymously, as in the "Treaty with the Sioune and Oglala Tribes, 1825" in which the groups are "tribes" in the title but "bands" in the text.

Although in the contemporary literature on American Indians the conspicuous terminological inconsistencies of the nineteenth century and earlier have given way to more conventionalized usages that are partly the result of past government treaty designations and partly the acceptance of anthropological taxonomy, two recent developments have occurred which reintroduce ambiguity, or at least uncertainty, into the use of familiar designations. One is the political movement among American Indians to assert tribal sovereignty, in which the term *nation* has been resurrected to designate what have heretofore been called tribes. The second trend results from academic self-examination: anthropologists assessing their own use of the terms *tribe* and *band*, acknowledging the lack of consensus concerning exactly what these social units denote, and introducing a conscious indeterminacy to the familiar taxonomy that has yet to be resolved (for example, see [28]). The effect of this appraisal has been to make many anthropological writers uncomfortable with the terms, since their use has been questioned but no satisfactory substitutions have been offered and accepted.

Instructive contrasts to the Western classification of social divisions are native taxonomies based on their own terminology. The Pawnees and Arikaras afford one example. They distinguish only two social levels: the village (*ituuru'*) and the band or tribe (*akitaaru'*), the latter a term that refers to any recognized social grouping larger than the village. Thus the Skiris, Chawis, and other so-called "bands" of the Pawnees are denoted as *akitaaru'*, just as are the Osages, Poncas, and other tribes. However, the etymology of many ethnonyms contrasts with this terminological usage. Many tribal names are composed of the term *ituuru'* followed by a modifier, for example, *tuhkaaka'*, "Crow" (lit., "Raven Village"), *tuhkiwaku'* (designation uncertain; lit., "Fox Village"), and Arikara *tuhkanihnaáwiš*, "Arapaho" (lit., "Gray Stone Village"). So, too, are Skiri and Arikara village names, for example, Skiri *tuurawi'u'*, "Part of a Village" and *tuhwaahukasa*, "Village Across a Hill," and Arikara *tuhkasthaánu'*, "Buffalo Sod Village."

The nomadic Sioux and Assiniboines, who differ from the semisedentary northern Caddoan peoples in social organization, provide another illustration. They, too, made only a bipartite distinction in named social levels. The smaller, or basic, structure is called *t'iyošpaye*, which denotes an extended family or kin-based band; the more inclusive unit is called *oyate*, a term meaning "people" that is used to designate any autonomous ethnic group larger than the extended family or kin-based band—what we would term a band, tribe, or nation. Many Sioux and at least two Assiniboine band names are composed of the term *t'u*^n*wa*^n, "village, settlement," together with a modifier, much like Pawnee and Arikara names, for example, *iha*^n*kt'u*^n*wa*^n, "Yankton" (lit., "End Village"), *waxpet'u*^n*wa*^n, "Wahpeton" (lit., "Leaf Village"), and the Assiniboine *watop'axnat'u*^n*wa*^n (meaning not certain). One tribal designation is also based on this noun: *xaxat'u*^n*wa*^n, "Chippewa" (Teton), "Gros Ventre" (Assiniboine) (lit., "Falls Village"). But in both Sioux and Assiniboine, band names and ethnonyms more frequently employ *wic'aša* (Assiniboine *wi*^n*cašta*), "man" as the base of the form. In Assiniboine there is, for example, *t'eha*^n *wi*^n*cašta*, "Stonies" (lit., "Far Away Men"), *we wi*^n*c'ašta*, "Bloods" (lit., "Blood Men"). However, when speaking of these groups, the term *oyate* is used, as in *sihasapa oyate*, "Blackfeet Tribe (people)."

These groups of Plains peoples, then, shared a classification of social divisions that recognized only two levels. The Sioux and Assiniboine *t'iyošpaye* is the analogue of the Pawnee and Arikara *ituuru'* ("village"), and the *oyate* designates the same type of group as the term *akitaaru'*. This bipartite native classification differs from the usual Western taxonomy, which distinguishes at least four levels: the family group or village, band, tribe, and nation. The latter set, however, is not actually more specific or precise than its native counterpart, nor is it used systematically, either in historical sources or contemporary anthropological practice. Hence it is incumbent upon the historian to interpret the level of social organization represented by an ethnonym within the context of the cultural organization of the people or group of peoples existent during the period in which the document was written.

When attempting to identify ethnonyms in historical sources, however, one should not begin by interpreting social units or simply seeking an identification with some modern tribe. The first problem is to determine the language of the name; for example, is it Arikara, Kiowa, or what? Once the language has been established, it is then possible to evaluate the reliability of the transcription for phonemic accuracy or recognition and, as part of the second step, try to ascertain its meaning. Finally, after both language and meaning of the name have been identified, it is appropriate to interpret the level of social organization that it represents.

The procedure, and the conclusions that it allows, may be illustrated by reference to a Spanish document recording a visit in 1795 to San Antonio, the seat of government for the Spanish province of Texas, of a group of Pawnees in company with some Wichitas and Taovayas. The Pawnees, who were members of a group that had fled before the American advance and had gone to live with the Wichitas, had been sent by their chief to report injuries received at the hands of the Americans and make peaceful overtures to the Spanish. During their visit they furnished the Spanish officials with a list of thirty-three "nations" (*naciones*) with whom they had friendly relations.

In 1964 Rudolph C. Troike published portions of the document, identified the Pawnees as Skiris, and listed the names of the thirty-three nations together with suggested identifications with known groups [76]. He was able to identify fourteen names with certainty. Table 7-1 presents in the first column a partial list of the names from the Spanish document preceded by the numbers they are given in Troike's article; in the second column are the Skiri names in phone-

Table 7-1. Partial List of Nations Known to the Skiri in 1795.

Spanish List		Pawnee Form	Identification
1	Guitaguirat	*piitahaawiraata*	Pitahawirata
2	Chagui	*cawii'i*	Chawi
3	Guitcajitquit	*kitkahahki*	Kitkahahki
6	Guacoti	*pahkuta*	Ioway
11	Astaray	*astarahi*	Astarahi
14	Alicara	*arikara*	Arikara
19	Sauto	*sáw't'uh*	Comanche [Caddo]
20	Tupascas	*tuhpakskac*	? lit., "White-Headed Village"
23	Tuchariabis	*tuhkarihaawis*	Arapaho
28	Turucatugu	*tuurukaataku*	Village on a Bank
30	Naucat	*rahuukaata*	By the Water
32	Aquisto	**akictu'*	unidentified

mic form, and in the third are identifications with modern or historically attested groups. (The forms in column two and identifications
in column three are my own.)

As suggested above, when confronted with a document such as
this, the first question is: What language are the names? In the document the visitors are identified as "Ahuahes," whose chief is called
"Yrisac." Since the Wichita name for the Pawnees is *awaahiih* and
the Tonkawa term is *awaahey*, the group would clearly seem to be
Pawnee, as indeed the words in the list are. But the next problem is
to determine *which* Pawnees they are. Troike does this by adducing
several lines of evidence: historical references to a group of "Pani-
mahas," the eighteenth-century designation for the Skiris, who were
living with the Taovayas at that time; the identification of their chief,
"Yrisac," as a Skiri personage; and the fact that the first three names
on the list represent the other Pawnee groups: Pitahawirata, Chawi,
and Kitkahahki.

There is, in addition, a piece of linguistic evidence to corroborate
the conclusion. The name given as "Tuchariabis" (no. 23) is phonemically reconstructable as *tuhkarihaawis*, a name for the Arapaho
that literally means "Colored Stone Village." If this name were a
Pawnee proper dialect form, it would be *tuhkarihraawis*, with an *hr*
consonant sequence resulting from the contraction of two elements,
the stem for "stone" and a qualifier, "colored." But instead the consonant that comes from the contraction is simply *h*, which is the
expected Skiri reflex or correspondence of *hr* in Pawnee proper.

Thus it is clear that this name is a Skiri form rather than one in Pawnee proper.

Once the names on the list have been determined to be Skiri, it is possible to establish their phonemic forms and meanings. Reconstructing phonemic forms is achieved in two complementary ways, both of which require knowledge of Pawnee linguistics. The first tactic is to search through the list for easily recognized Pawnee words. The other procedure is to undertake an internal reconstruction of the probable phonemic forms of words by comparing the recordings with one another and with the easily recognized Pawnee words in order to determine how the writer represented the sounds of Pawnee. Part of this analytic precedure, which requires familiarity with the sounds and orthographic conventions of eighteenth-century Spanish, has been mentioned previously. By a combination of these methods it is possible to correlate known Skiri ethnonyms with those on the Spanish list.

There is, however, a residue of problems, some of which are worth mentioning to exemplify how they might be handled. The form "Sauto" (no. 19) is not recognizable as a Skiri word, but is too close in shape to the Caddo word *saw't'uh*, "Comanche" to be merely fortuitous. Since the Pawnee name for the Comanche, *raarihta*, is not on the list, this one form is apparently the Caddo word. (Why a Caddo name should appear on the list is another matter.)

Another problem is illustrated by the form "Tupascas" (no. 20), which is clearly a Skiri word made up of three morphemes (*ituur-*, "village"; *paks-*, "head"; and *kaac*, "gray, white") meaning, literally, "White-Headed Village." Although this is not a modern Skiri designation for any known tribal group, the name does appear in late-eighteenth- and early-nineteenth-century sources as the name of a tribe with whom the Arikaras traded. (See, for example, Lewis and Clark's mention of the Arikara name "To-pah-cass," which they translated as "White Hair's" in [74].) Because the identification of this group remains a problem, it illustrates how there are some names that can be easily analyzed linguistically and can be identified with other historical references to unknown groups but cannot be linked to a recognized modern group.

A different problem is illustrated by the form "Aquisto" (no. 32), which is an unrecognized name. Troike suggests that it is a Wichita band, *akʷiits*, but this does not seem to be the form the writer was attempting to represent. Based on his orthographic usages elsewhere, the probable form of Aquisto should be more like *akictu'* or even *rakictu'*. Neither of these forms, however, are Skiri words, although both are certainly phonemically plausible. In a case such as this one, the name must remain unidentified and continue as a problem for future study.

The final question to be resolved is the nature of the social groups in the list. For the Spanish recorder, each of the names was a "nation," presumably a politically autonomous group that today would be called a tribe; for the Skiri visitors, each was undoubtedly an *akitaaru'*. Of interest, then, to the modern student is the inventory of what the Spaniards gave as nations and the Skiri as *akitaaru'*. Some, of course, are groups that we recognize today as tribes: the Missouris, Ioways, Comanches, Arapahos, and so on. But listed co-ordinately with these are other social groups that are now classed as smaller social units. The Pitahawiratas (no. 1), Chawis (no. 2), and Kitkahahkis (no. 3) are termed bands by modern writers. But clearly in 1795 they were perceived differently, at least by the Skiris, who gave them a rank equal to alien tribes. Similarly, in addition to the group called "Arikara" (no. 14) and one named "Astarahi" (no. 11), which Lewis and Clark identified as the "primitive" name of the Arikaras [74, vol. 6, p. 88], there also occur most of the names of what are today termed Arikara villages (for example, nos. 28 and 30). Consequently it must be inferred that these, too, were in 1795 at a "tribal" level and not merely villages under some tight form of organization. Precisely what their status was is a separate problem [51]. But their status here on this list is instructive: they were autonomous groups, ranked equivalent to alien tribes in the minds of the Skiris, a classification that historians must consider when interpreting "tribal" names in early sources.

Etymologies

An interest in the origin and significance of names—whether personal names, toponyms, or ethnonyms—has been as general among American Indian peoples as it has been among the non-Indians who have visited or studied them. Early writers nearly invariably included statements about the source or underlying meaning of the names they recorded, undoubtedly because they thought that these putative etymologies provided historical explanations of the people or topographic features they denoted. Early visitors to the Eastern Sioux in what is now Minnesota illustrate this interest. William Keating, chronicler of the Long expedition (1823); Joseph N. Nicollet, in the course of cartographic expeditions (1838–39); and Stephen R. Riggs, missionary to the tribe (1837–83), all recorded the names of social divisions of the Sioux together with literal meanings and explanations of them, the latter provided by individual Dakotas or their interpreters in interviews or, as with Riggs, in the course of a long association with the people.

The recordings of these three men illustrate the range of value of such etymologies. The composition of some of the names is quite apparent, posing neither a linguistic nor a referential problem. *Mdewak'a^{n}t'u^{n}wa^n*, the name of a Santee division, is clearly a compound of *mde*, "lake" + *wak'a^n*, "holy" + *t'u^{n}wa^n*, "village," just as each recorder noted, and is no doubt derived from the former residence of this group by the lake of that name (now Mille Lacs), as stated by Riggs [62, p. 156]. The linguistic composition of the name of another Santee division, *waxpek'ute* "Leaf Shooters," is equally recognizable, consisting of *waxpe*, "leaf," and *k'ute*, "to shoot." What is not clear, though, is the significance of the form. Keating [38, p. 402] says that it derives from an incident when some of these people shot at leaves, mistaking them for deer, while Riggs more prudently states that the circumstances occasioning the name are not known.

In contrast to these examples is the name of the Sissetons, its phonemic form *sisit'u^{n}wa^n*. The name is a compound composed of *sisi* + *t'u^{n}wa^n*, "village," but what *sisi* means or derives from is a matter of varying opinions. Nicollet [13, p. 258] recorded two versions: Sleepy Eyes told him these people lived where there were many fish and they were always dirty with the smell of them, while someone else said the name signified a village in a cleared or treeless area. Neither source agreed on the first element of the name *sisi*; Sleepy Eyes said it came from a form "asinsin" "to be dirty, impregnated," while the other source derived it from "sisin" "level, flat, slippery." Note that neither form, "asinsin" or "sisin," is the same as *sisi*, which lacks the nasal vowel or vowels of the others. Riggs gives similar explanations for its etymology. In his dictionary [61, p. 435] he lists a stem *sisi*, "swampy" provided by Joseph Renville, the mission's translator, while in his grammar [62, p. 158] he abandons the "swamp villagers" explanation in favor of a tradition Renville told about this people's affinity for fish and their village's characterization by an accumulation of piles of scales and entrails that in appearance were *si^nsi^n*, "dirty."

The three examples—explanations of the sources of the names Mdewakantonwan, Wahpeton, and Sisseton—provide illustrations of what is typically found in the literature. For Mdewakantonwan the sources give accurate explanations of linguistic composition and probable origin, whereas for Wahpeton the linguistic explanation is correct but the statement about its source is probably nothing more than a contrived story. And for Sisseton neither its proposed linguistic composition nor the conflicting traditions of its significance is plausible. The form *sisi* was apparently already obsolete in the early nineteenth century, and the traditions purporting to elucidate it and the origin of the name were just as apparently the result of native attempts to find an explanation for what was no longer known.

Seeking plausible explanations for opaque linguistic forms, whether they are partially or totally unanalyzable, is a natural part of language—something that occurs in all cultures—and results in *folk etymologies*. Ives Goddard, in a survey of the pitfalls encountered in the study of native North American ethnonymy, defines the folk etymology as "an (ad hoc or traditional) interpretation of a synchronically opaque name based on an incorrectly assumed derivational connection with other words or elements." He then illustrates it with an array of examples from the historical and ethnographic literature of the southwestern and northeastern United States [19]. The Plains Indian literature is replete with examples, too, a small selection of which will demonstrate the basis and scope of error or misapprehension occasioned by attempts to etymologize.

Perhaps the most pernicious type of folk etymology is one created by the culture historian who fails to correctly identify a form in an early source, especially when the data allowing proper recognition are available but not utilized. In *Oglala Religion*, a book that abounds in more folk etymologies than any other modern work on Plains Indians, William K. Powers remarks that during a stay with the Oglalas in 1846, Francis Parkman recorded the common Lakota word for white man as *meneaska*, which Powers identifies as *mniaška^n*, "moves on water," to support his assertion that the Oglalas likened the white man to a supernatural power [60]. Here Powers's contention about early Oglala perceptions may be valid, but his example is not. Parkman's recording [49, p. 256] is clearly a pho-

netically poor but recognizable rendition of *minaha^nska*, an early
Sioux and Assiniboine term for Americans that today occurs in the
Teton dialect in two forms, *minaha^nska* and *milaha^nska*. Its literal
meaning is "long knife."

Another example of the failure of modern writers to search
through source material adequately is provided by the speculation on
the identity of a group of Indians from the headwaters of the Mississippi who visited Fort Crevecoeur on Lake Peoria in 1680 and whose
name Robert Cavelier de la Salle records as "Chaa" [43, vol. 2, p.
54]. Since LaSalle was himself being hosted by Illinois Indians, one
obvious possibility for identifying the name "Chaa" is to look for it
in the Illinois language. And indeed this name is found there in two
early-eighteenth-century Illinois dictionaries [20, p. 109; 4, p. 288],
which cite it as the Illinois name for the Dakota Sioux (see [80, p.
116]. Several modern writers [35, p. 2; 84, p. 53], however, have
argued that the "Chaa" were Cheyennes only because the form superficially resembles a widespread set of names for the Cheyennes
found in several other Plains languages (for example, Arikara *šaahé*;
Sioux *šahiyena*) and in spite of the fact that the Cheyenne name for
themselves, *tsétsehéstahese*, is entirely different [48, p. 201]. Ironically, George Hyde [33, p. 179] correctly identifies La Salle's
"Chaa" as Sioux, but he does this by using the same fallacious
method of Jablow and Wood: he associates "Chaa" with the first
syllable of the Pawnee name for Sioux, *cararat*, the last two syllables of which he glosses as "enemies." This etymology has no
linguistic basis whatsoever. (What Hyde apparently did not also realize was that the French rendition would have been pronounced *ša*,
not *ča* as in the Pawnee word, so that what he thought were identical
syllables were in reality phonetically different.)

The proclivity of writers to explain etymologies on the basis of
partial resemblances among random words is no more than the
speculation of amateurs and is a procedure fraught with almost inevitable error. Powers [60, pp. 26–27], for example, suggests that
the name "Saoni" or "Saone" (Nicollet in [13, p. 259]; Tabeau in
[1, p. 103]; Lewis and Clark in [74, vol. 6, p. 97]), an early-nineteenth-century Teton group, "is probably an orthographic corruption
of *canoti* . . . 'forest dweller.' " Powers does not define what an
"orthographic corruption" is, nor does he mention that most recorders write this name with an initial *s* so that the first syllable *sa* (or
perhaps *sa^n*) is clearly not the morpheme *c'a^n* "wood" of "wood (or

forest) dweller." (Powers does not write aspiration when citing Sioux forms; hence his orthography is not phonemic. His *canoti* is actually *c'a^not'i*.) Likewise, *ni* or *ne*, the final syllable of Saoni, is clearly not the morpheme *t'i*, "dwell," the final syllable of "wood dweller." Powers's suggestion that Saoni is actually *c'a^not'i* is the result of his ignoring phonemic distinctions. He, like others who look only for superficial resemblances among unrelated words, assumes that phonemic differences are inconsequential when trying to relate words he seeks to identify.

Some of the problems of establishing with certainty the historical meaning of the elements in an ethnonym and separating folk from true etymology are illustrated by the Arikara and Pawnee words meaning "Hidatsa." The Arikara form is *wiitatshaánu'* and is composed of two elements: *wiíta*, "man" and *tshaánu'*, a descriptive stem that means "proud, as someone who wears fancy attire" and only occurs in one other compound ("war shirt," which is literally "proud shirt") and a verb ("to act proudly"). Contemporary Arikara speakers usually explain the underlying meaning of the name as deriving from a penchant for fancy attire among Hidatsa males. This interpretation, coupled with the highly restricted occurrence of the stem meaning "proud," suggests that it might be a folk etymology. And indeed when the Arikara name is compared with its Pawnee cognate, that possibility seems more likely. In Pawnee the word is *piitakicahaaru'*, composed of the same two elements that comprise the Arikara word. The difference is that in Pawnee *kicahaaru'* (which is cognate with *tshaánu'*, the latter derived from the former by a set of regular historical sound changes) means "marsh, swamp, well-watered place,' so the literal meaning of the Pawnee name is "marsh man." The problem, then, is to decide if the meaning of *tshaánu'* was something like "marsh" and changed because of a tradition about the attire of Hidatsa males, thereby taking on a new meaning, or if the stem had two meanings earlier in the history of the language, one of which was preserved in Arikara and the other in Pawnee.

Historical references do not clarify the matter. In the mid nineteenth century Hayden [26, p. 357] recorded the meaning of the Arikara word as "well-dressed men," whereas Washington Matthews [44, p. 36] said it meant "well-dressed people" and "people at the water," the latter meaning said to be a reference to the Hidatsas' former residence at the ford of the Knife River. Arguments could be made for either interpretation—primacy of the meaning in Pawnee and a shift in its meaning in Arikara because of a folk tradition, or two former meanings that parted, one remaining in Arikara and the other in Pawnee—but the true explanation of the name's origin is going to be uncertain unless further study of the linguistic history of the northern Caddoan languages should provide a decisive solution.

Still another perspective on folk etymologies is provided by two examples of the reaction of some contemporary Indian people to the English translation or presumed meaning of an ethnonym designating themselves. The first one also illustrates a folk etymology in the making. Among the Assiniboines there is a band whose name is *šu^{n}kc'epina* (also *su^{n}kc'epi*), meaning "Dog Penises." This band name, like many others, derives from the name of a chief, *šu^{n}kc'e*, "Dog's Penis," who settled with his people on the White Bear Reserve in Saskatchewan in the nineteenth century. The band name is formed by adding the plural suffix of *pi* to the chief's name, and frequently *na*, a common diminutive suffix used in forming names. Some contemporary Assiniboines argue that the form *šu^{n}kc'epina* or *šu^{n}kc'epi* is incorrect and is really a misreading for *šu^{n}kc'epa*, "Fat Dog," which resembles the former name. Historical evidence and contemporary testimony from a wide sample of older Assiniboine speakers, however, attests to the correctness of the name *šu^{n}kc'epina* and illustrates how the historical form of the name is being reinterpreted because its English meaning offends contemporary sensibilities.

The name "Sioux" is a similar but contrasting example: it has become anathema to some contemporary Sioux and even some scholars (for example, [60]) because of the erroneous notion that the name means "snake" and thus—according to modern American standards—is a pejorative designation. Goddard [19, p. 105] has carefully examined the history of the name and concludes that Sioux is actually meaningless in any Indian language. It is a French shortening of Nadouessioux, which ultimately was a borrowing from Ojibwa *na·towe·ssiwak*, a form in the Ottawa dialect that was used only as a tribal name, never as a designation for snakes. The Ottawa form was in turn derived from another ethnonym, *na·towe·*, "Iroquoian," which happened also to be used as the name for the massasauga rattlesnake. Goddard convincingly argues that "it is the snake that is being called an Iroquoian rather than the other way around, since this word matches . . . the Proto-Algonquian verbal element *-a·towe· 'speak a (foreign) language.' By the most likely analysis, then, Proto-Algonquian *na·towe·wa 'Iroquoian' would mean etymologically 'speaker of a foreign language.' "

The preceding examples are sufficient to demonstrate how in practice many culture historians fail to distinguish between a linguistically valid etymology and a folk etymology of an ethnonym. The distinction, in fact, is rarely even acknowledged by writers, so folk etymologies are commonly cited as though they were linguistically accurate and function as the basis for historical interpretation, when in fact they serve only to distort and obfuscate the past.

A valid etymology reveals the history of a word by discovering its antecedent forms in the same language or group of dialects and by finding cognate forms in related languages. The search for these related forms is carried out through careful lexicographical study and comparative analysis based on laws of sound change, not by the detection of superficially similar forms hastily concluded to be cognate. A folk etymology, in contrast, is a fictive account of the history of a word that is based on a cultural tradition or individual reinterpretation and generally develops when the actual history of a word has become obscure. Because the study of ethnonyms can be historically and ethnographically revealing and can significantly aid in the reconstruction of the past, it is essential that historians and anthropologists be cognizant of the distinction and develop a more critical eye for distinguishing between them. If the study of the history of the American Indian is to continue to progress, there must be a conscious demand for sound histories of linguistic forms to replace the facilely deceptive ones already established in the literature and occasionally yet appearing in new works.

Conclusion

During the century since Powell and Boas wrote their programmatic statements about the fundamental importance of language for understanding the cultures and history of native North America, the study of American Indian languages has taken a progressively more specialized course of development. Boas sought to make linguistic study an integral part of the training of every anthropologist. But he also trained Edward Sapir, who, together with linguists trained in the Indo-European tradition, helped to chart a more independent development for linguistics as an academic field and American Indian language study as a part of it. Although two primary goals of linguistics throughout this century have been grammatical description and the study of historical relationships among languages, there has also been a strong interest in methodology, which thirty years ago shifted to an aggressive interest in theory—to what is universal in human languages and what a theory of language structure is. The latter concern diverted linguistic goals away from the creation of descriptive reference works to studies of specific aspects of language structure and linguistic processes.

While linguistics was evolving towards academic autonomy, anthropology was moving away from descriptive language studies and the role that Boas had established for linguistics within the field. By 1940, in a tribute to John R. Swanton, Kroeber [40, p. 6] remarked that the compilation of dictionaries was no longer a goal of anthropological linguistics. For anthropology there has been a progressively greater concern with the sociological aspects of language and what has been termed the "ethnography of speaking" [34].

Because of these developments in anthropology and linguistics, few scholars in recent decades have focused on the goal of producing descriptive reference works for American Indian languages— dictionaries, grammars, and collections of texts. The outcome for an area like the Plains is a paucity of adequate linguistic sources for the study of the region's culture history.

In the field of Indian history the attitude towards linguistics and the study of American Indian languages has been ambivalent: ethnohistorians from the anthropological tradition have acknowledged the importance of these subjects but rarely incorporated them into their own work, and historians have ignored Indian languages almost altogether. Consequently, there has been little progress during the past century in the quality of citation of linguistic data, the description of speech communities and their relationships through time, and the historical understanding of the etymologies of Indian tribal and place names.

To achieve a state in which the study of Indian languages and linguistics is making these contributions, historians, anthropologists, and linguists must work jointly on common problems. Historians and anthropologists must demonstrate active concern for the importance of language study—to make new efforts to study specific languages and learn the fundamentals of linguistic analysis—while linguists must participate more actively in the process of historical research, familiarizing themselves with the specific problems of history and producing the language reference works that are essential tools in this endeavor. Such efforts will surely bring significant progress to the historical study of the American Indian.

References

1. Abel, Annie Heloise, ed. 1939. *Tabeau's Narrative of Loisel's Expedition to the Upper Missouri*. Norman: University of Oklahoma Press.
2. Anderson, Irving W. 1978. "Sacajawea, Sacagawea, Sakakawea?" *South Dakota History* 8: 303–11.
3. Baird, W. David. 1980. *The Quapaw Indians: A History of the Downstream People*. Norman: University of Oklahoma Press.
4. Belting, Natalia M. 1958. "Illinois Names for Themselves and Other Groups." *Ethnohistory* 5:285–91.
5. Bergsland, Knut, and H. Vogt. 1962. "On the Validity of Glottochronology." *Current Anthropology* 3:115–58.
6. Berkhofer, Robert F., Jr. 1965. *Salvation and the Savage: An Analysis of Protestant Missions and American Indian Responses, 1787–1862*. Lexington: University of Kentucky Press.
7. Berthrong, Donald J. 1963. *The Southern Cheyennes*. Norman: University of Oklahoma Press.
8. Boas, Franz. 1889. "On Alternating Sounds." *American Anthropologist*, o.s. 2:47–53.
9. ———. 1911. *Handbook of American Indian Languages*. Part 1. Smithsonian Institution, Bureau of American Ethnology Bulletin 40, vol. 1. Washington, D.C.: Government Printing Office.
10. Buechel, Eugene, S.J. 1970. *A Dictionary of the Teton Dakota Sioux Language*. Ed. Paul Manhart, S.J. Pine Ridge, S.Dak.: Red Cloud Indian School.
11. Campbell, Lyle, and Marianne Mithun. 1979. *The Languages of Native America: Historical and Comparative Assessment*. Austin: University of Texas Press.
12. Clark, Ann. 1944. *Brave Against the Enemy: T'oka Wan Itkok'ip Ohitike Kin He*. Lawrence, Kans.: Haskell Institute.
13. DeMallie, Raymond J., trans. and ed. 1976. "Nicollet's Notes on the Dakota." In *Joseph N. Nicollet on the Plains and Prairies*, ed. Edmund C. Bray and Martha Coleman Bray, pp. 250–81. St. Paul: Minnesota Historical Society Press.
14. [Dunbar, John.] 1836. *Lawyrawkvlarits Pany Kwta* [Pawnee First Book]. Boston.
15. Duponceau, Peter S. 1838. *Mémoire sur le Systeme Grammatical des Langues de Quelques Nations Indiennes de l'Amérique du Nord*. Paris: A. Pihan de la Forest.
16. Gallatin, Albert. 1836. *A Synopsis of the Indian Tribes Within the United States East of the Rocky Mountains, and in the British and Russian Possessions in North America*. Transactions of the American Antiquarian Society, vol. 2. Cambridge.

17. ———. 1848. *Hale's Indians of North-West America, and Vocabularies of North America; with an Introduction.* American Ethnological Society, Transactions, vol. 2.
18. Gibson, Arrell M. 1963. *The Kickapoos: Lords of the Middle Border.* Norman: University of Oklahoma Press.
19. Goddard, Ives. 1984. "The Study of Native North American Ethnonymy." In *Naming Systems*, ed. Elisabeth Tooker, pp. 95–107. 1980 Proceedings of the American Ethnological Society. Washington, D.C.
20. Gravier, Jacques. [Ca. 1700–1701.] "Dictionary of the Illinois Language." Manuscript in Watkinson Library, Trinity College, Hartford, Conn. Copy in the National Anthropological Archives, Smithsonian Institution.
21. Greenberg, Joseph. 1987. *Language in the Americas.* Stanford: Stanford University Press.
22. Grinnell, George Bird. 1890. *Pawnee Hero Stories and Folk-Tales.* New York: Charles Scribner's Sons.
23. Haas, Mary R. 1978. *Language, Culture, and History: Essays by Mary R. Haas.* Selected and Introduced by Anwar S. Dil. Stanford: Stanford University Press.
24. Hagan, William T. 1961. *American Indians.* Chicago: University of Chicago Press.
25. Hassrick, Royal B. 1964. *The Sioux: Life and Customs of a Warrior Society.* Norman: University of Oklahoma Press.
26. Hayden, F. V. 1862. *On the Ethnography and Philology of the Indian Tribes of the Missouri Valley.* Transactions of the American Philosophical Society, n.s., vol. 3, part 2. Philadelphia.
27. Headley, Robert K., Jr. 1971. "The Origin and Distribution of the Siouan Speaking Tribes." M.A. thesis, Catholic University of America.
28. Helm, June, ed. 1968. *Essays On the Problem of Tribe.* Proceedings of the 1967 Annual Spring Meeting of the American Ethnological Society. Seattle: University of Washington Press.
29. Hodge, Frederick Webb. 1907–10. *Handbook of American Indians North of Mexico.* 2 vols. Smithsonian Institution, Bureau of American Ethnology Bulletin 30. Washington, D.C.: Government Printing Office.
30. Hollow, Robert C., Jr. 1970. "A Mandan Dictionary." Ph.D. diss., University of California, Berkeley.
31. ———, and Douglas R. Parks. 1980. "Studies in Plains Linguistics: A Review." In *Anthropology on the Great Plains*, ed. W. Raymond Wood and Margot Liberty, pp. 68–97. Lincoln: University of Nebraska Press.
32. Hyde, George E. 1937. *Red Cloud's Folk: A History of the Oglala Sioux Indians.* Norman: University of Oklahoma Press.
33. ———. 1951. *Pawnee Indians.* Denver: University of Denver Press.
34. Hymes, Dell H. 1962. "The Ethnography of Speaking." In *Anthropology and Human Behavior*, ed. Thomas Gladwin and William C. Sturtevant, pp. 13–53. Washington, D.C.: Anthropological Society of Washington.
35. Jablow, Joseph. 1950. *The Cheyenne in Plains Indian Trade Relations,*

1795–1840. American Ethnological Society Monograph 19. New York: J. J. Augustin.
36. Jones, A. Wesley, 1979. *Hidatsa-English, English-Hidatsa Wordlist.* Bismarck, N.Dak.: Mary College.
37. Kappler, Charles J. 1904. *Indian Affairs: Laws and Treaties, Vol. 2 (Treaties).* Washington, D.C.: Government Printing Office.
38. Keating, William H. 1824. *Narrative of An Expedition to the Sources of St. Peter's River.* 2 vols. Reprint ed., Minneapolis: Ross & Haines, 1959.
39. Kroeber, A. L. 1916. "Arapaho Dialects." *University of California Publications in American Archaeology and Ethnology*, vol 12, no. 3, pp. 71–138.
40. ―――. 1940. "The Work of John R. Swanton." In *Essays in the History of Anthropology of North America Published in Honor of John R. Swanton*, pp. 1–9. Smithsonian Miscellaneous Collections 100. Washington, D.C.: Anthropological Society of Washington.
41. Lesser, Alexander, and Gene Weltfish. 1932. "Composition of the Caddoan Linguistic Stock." *Smithsonian Miscellaneous Collections*, vol. 87, no. 6.
42. Lowie, Robert H. 1935. *The Crow Indians.* New York: Farrar & Rinehart.
43. Margry, Pierre, ed. 1876–86. *Découvertes et Établissements des Français dans l'Ouest et dans le Sud de l'Amérique Septentrionale (1614–1754); Mémoires et Documents originaux.* 6 vols. Paris: D. Jouast.
44. Matthews, Washington. 1877. *Ethnography and Philology of the Hidatsa Indians.* United States Geological and Geographical Survey, Miscellaneous Publications, vol. 7. Washington, D.C.: Government Printing Office.
45. Merrill, Moses. 1834. *Otoe Hymn Book.* Shawannoe Mission: J. Meeker.
46. Milner, Clyde A., II. 1982. *With Good Intentions: Quaker Work Among the Pawnees, Otos, and Omahas in the 1870s.* Lincoln: University of Nebraska Press.
47. [Montgomery, William B., and W. C. Requa.] 1834. *The Osage First Book.* Boston: Crocker & Brewster.
48. Northern Cheyenne Language and Culture Center. 1976. *English-Cheyenne Dictionary.* Lame Deer, Montana.
49. Parkman, Francis. 1969. *The Oregon Trail.* Ed. E. N. Feltskog. Madison: University of Wisconsin Press.
50. Parks, Douglas R. 1976. *A Grammar of Pawnee.* New York: Garland Publishing, Inc.
51. ―――. 1979a. "Bands and Villages of the Arikara and Pawnee." *Nebraska History* 60:214–39.
52. ―――. 1979b. "The Northern Caddoan Languages: Their Subgrouping and Time Depth." *Nebraska History* 60:197–213.
53. ―――. 1986. "Pawnee and Arikara Dialects." Unpublished manuscript.

54. ——, and A. Wesley Jones. 1980. "The Sioux Dialect Survey: A Progress Report." *Siouan and Caddoan Linguistics.* (Newsletter, Department of Linguistics, University of Colorado.) March:10–15.

55. ——, and Waldo R. Wedel. 1985. "Pawnee Geography: Historical and Sacred." *Great Plains Quarterly* 5:143–76.

56. Petter, Rodolphe. 1913–15. *English-Cheyenne Dictionary.* Kettle Falls, Wash.

57. Pickering, John. 1820. *An Essay on a Uniform Orthography for the Indian Languages of North America, as Published in the Memoirs of the American Academy of Sciences.* Cambridge: University Press.

58. Powell, J. W. 1881. *First Annual Report of the Bureau of Ethnology to the Secretary of the Smithsonian Institution, 1879-'80.* Washington, D.C.: Government Printing Office.

59. ——. 1891. "Indian Linguistic Families of America North of Mexico." Smithsonian Institution, Bureau of Ethnology, *Annual Report* 7:1–142. Washington, D.C.: Government Printing Office.

60. Powers, William K. 1977. *Oglala Religion.* Lincoln: University of Nebraska Press.

61. Riggs, Stephen Return. 1890. *A Dakota-English Dictionary.* Ed. J. Owen Dorsey. Contributions to North American Ethnology, vol. 7. Washington, D.C.: Government Printing Office.

62. ——. 1893. *Dakota Grammar, Texts, and Ethnography.* Ed. J. Owen Dorsey. Contributions to North American Ethnology, vol. 9. Washington, D.C.: Government Printing Office.

63. Robinson, Doane. 1904. *A History of the Dakota or Sioux Indians.* South Dakota Historical Collections, vol. 2. Pierre, S.Dak.

64. Ronda, James P. 1984. *Lewis and Clark Among the Indians.* Lincoln: University of Nebraska Press.

65. Rood, David S. 1979. "Siouan." In *The Languages of Native North America: Historical and Comparative Assessment,* ed. Lyle Campbell and Marianne Mithun, pp. 236–98. Austin: University of Texas Press.

66. Sapir, Edward. 1917. "Linguistic Publications of the Bureau of American Ethnology, A General Review." *International Journal of American Linguistics* 1:76–81.

67. ——. 1921. "A Bird's-eye View of American Languages North of Mexico." *Science* 54:408.

68. ——. 1929. "Central and North American Languages." *Encyclopaedia Britannica,* 14th ed., vol. 5, pp. 138–41.

69. Schoolcraft, Henry Rowe. 1845. *Oneota, or Characteristics of the Red Race of America. From Original Notes and Manuscripts.* New York & London: Wiley & Putnam.

70. Sherzer, Joel. 1973. "Areal Linguistics in North America." In *Current Trends in Linguistics,* ed. Thomas A. Sebeok, vol. 10, pp. 1164–1209. The Hague: Mouton.

71. [Stevens, Jedediah D.] 1836. *Sioux Spelling-Book. Designed for the Use of Native Learners.* Boston: Crocker & Brewster.

72. Swanton, John R. 1909–10. "Indian Names in Historical Documents."

Proceedings of the Mississippi Valley Historical Association 3: 341–46.
73. Taylor, Allan R. 1963. "Comparative Caddoan." *International Journal of American Linguistics* 29:113–31.
74. Thwaites, Reuben Gold, ed. 1904–1905. *Original Journals of the Lewis and Clark Expedition, 1804–1806.* 8 vols. New York: Dodd, Mead.
75. ———, ed. 1906. *Early Western Travels, 1748–1846,* vols. 22–24, *Maximilian, Prince of Weid's Travels in the Interior of North America, 1832–34.* 3 vols. Cleveland: Arthur H. Clark.
76. Troike, Rudolph C. 1964. "A Pawnee Visit to San Antonio in 1795." *Ethnohistory* 11:380–93.
77. Vestal, Stanley. 1932. *Sitting Bull: Champion of the Sioux.* Boston: Houghton Mifflin.
78. Voegelin, C. F., and F. M. Voegelin. 1965. "Classification of American Indian Languages." Languages of the World, Native American fascicle 2, section 1.6. *Anthropological Linguistics* 7:121–50.
79. Washburn, Wilcomb E. 1971. "The Writing of American Indian History: A Status Report." *Pacific Historical Review* 40: 261–81.
80. Wedel, Mildred Mott, and Raymond J. DeMallie. 1980. "The Ethnohistorical Approach in Plains Area Studies." In *Anthropology on the Great Plains,* ed. W. Raymond Wood and Margot Liberty, pp. 110–28. Lincoln: University of Nebraska Press.
81. Weltfish, Gene. 1965. *The Lost Universe: With a Closing Chapter on "The Universe Regained."* New York: Basic Books.
82. White, Richard. 1982. "The Cultural Landscape of the Pawnees." *Great Plains Quarterly* 2:31–40.
83. ———. 1983. *The Roots of Dependency: Subsistence, Environment, and Social Change Among the Choctaws, Pawnees, and Navajos.* Lincoln: University of Nebraska Press.
84. Wood, W. Raymond. 1971. *Biesterfeldt: A Post-Contact Coalescent Site on the Northeastern Plains.* Smithsonian Contributions to Anthropology 15. Washington, D.C.: Government Printing Office.
85. Zeisberger, David. 1827. *Grammar of the Language of the Lenni Lenape or Delaware Indians.* Trans. Peter S. Duponceau. Transactions of the American Philosophical Society, n.s., vol. 3. Philadelphia.

CHAPTER 8

That Other Discipline: Economics and American Indian History

RONALD L. TROSPER

Behind the political and military studies that have long dominated Indian history lies a story of centuries of Indian participation in the fur trade, disruption of traditional subsistence cycles, erosion of tribal land bases, growing dependency, internal colonialism, and repeated adjustment to new economic conditions. Yet Indian economic history remains a relatively underdeveloped field of inquiry.

In this chapter, a Harvard-trained economist, who has returned home to his reservation to assist the tribe in achieving self-determination and economic advancement, considers some of the reasons why historians have not adequately incorporated economic analysis into the study of Indian history. Confronted with complicated theories, sloppy analysis, and occasional oversimplification, historians have often thrown out the baby with the bath water in their rejection of economics instead of selecting the most useful models and drawing upon a vast amount of underused data. Whereas other chapters in this volume review the recent literature, Ron Trosper also draws upon his own experiences on the Flathead reservation to provide a commentary on how historians can apply economic theory as a key to understanding Indian as well as non-Indian behavior over time.

The economic history of American Indian communities remains largely untouched by scholars, in spite of the fact that so much of the motivation behind European expansion was economic. I see several reasons for this. First, the negative effects of transfering land from Indians to non-Indians is obvious and might be considered the whole story. Second, the political aspects of Indian-European relations grab much more attention. I want to explore a third reason: the difficulties economic analysis presents for noneconomists. Introductory economic courses usually emphasize simple models and unrealistic assumptions. Among these are the assumptions that people act as isolated individuals with private gain as their primary goal, that spillover effects are not an important aspect of economic decisions, and that everyone involved in an economic transaction has the same information. A historian may never get to subsequent courses in which these assumptions are dropped.

Much of a historian's work is interdisciplinary, requiring sophisticated use of insights developed by sociology, psychology, political science, anthropology, and economics. Of these, the insights of economics are the least accessible. Further, when studying non-Western cultures, some of the cultural biases of economics make the profession seem unappealing as well as obscure. The first part of this essay examines three applications of economic theory to American Indian history: labor supply, barter, and open-access resources. These examples suggest that economic analysis can assist the historian in clarifying and analyzing past events. After considering these examples, I recommend some economists whose work may prove helpful to historians.

The final part of this chapter raises a number of economic questions we are now studying on my reservation. These questions are important today not only on the Flathead reservation, but they raise problems economic historians can address in other contexts. As a result, unlike the other bibliographic chapters in this volume, my chapter is devoted more to what I would like to read than to what I have read.

Historians and anthropologists have complained about the application of "western bourgeois" economic theory to non-European cultures. As I understand them, these critics object to separating exchange of commodities from the institutions and values of society. They object to the conception of "economic man" as interested only in personal gain; generosity, a need for security, and concern for the environment are omitted in conventional analysis. They identify markets exclusively with capitalism. Finally, they object to assuming labor and land can be treated as commodities. That some economists are guilty of these errors does not mean that all are. Those critical of economics often choose poor examples, usually ones which are not representative of good economic analysis. Some of the critics' targets contain errors that are so elementary that noneconomists can spot them. When bad economics come to represent all economic theory, rejection is understandable.

While sloppy economic analysis reduces the standing of the "dismal science" among historians, arguments among economists only make matters worse. Even the qualities of "good work" are subject to debate. Nevertheless, economic theory has progressed far from the model of perfect competition featured in introductory texts and the simple-minded justifications used by American politicians during President Reagan's reign. Mathematical complexity has gone along with advances in understanding, and there are many sensible models of economic behavior. Unfortunately this new complexity often leaves historians cold. As a result, communication across disciplinary lines has become more difficult.

I certainly do not want to defend that part of economics known as the "neoclassical faith," which can be faulted for failure to address important questions (such as the significance of highly concentrated wealth) and for omitting important factors. Neoclassical analysts assume that exchange of the services from labor, land, and capital can be understood with the same analysis used for bread, movies, and other commodities. Economics was first called dismal because Malthus and other classical economists predicted ruin from overpopulation; modern usage applies the same term to the neoclassical economist's narrow outlook.

I have three examples that illustrate useful applications of economics theory to American Indian history. The first is the shape of labor supply curves. The second is the application of economic theory to a barter economy. The third is analysis of open-access resources. In each case I offer an explanation from economics which I believe provides answers to particular puzzles. Once these topics are covered, we may proceed to an examination of how modern economic theory can contribute to the future of American Indian history.

Labor Supply Curve

In his prologue to *Keepers of the Game* [21], Calvin Martin criticizes some applications of economics to Indian history. "The problem with the conventional economic explanation for the Indian's motivation and participation in the Eastern Canadian fur trade is that it creates an artifical and misleading behavior model (p. 11)." Martin agrees with members of the "substantivist" school of economic anthropology when they "argue that pre-industrial peoples are devoid of a systematic, empirical sense of 'economics.' " He states that "the substantivist approach is the more fruitful way of scrutinizing the Indian's position in the Eastern Canadian fur trade" (p. 12). His example to prove this point is the choice between work and leisure; the economic or "Western bourgeois" approach is not fruitful because it predicts that any increase in the price of beaver should cause more beaver to be supplied, which is not what was observed. In addition, "It is my contention that the formalist way of thinking, predicated on the insatiability of human needs and the chronic insufficiency of goods, breeds the sort of 'economic seduction' rationale . . ." which explains the extermination of furbearers. Martin's refutation of formalism rests in part on the fact that hunters and gatherers have now and have always had leisure time. Formal economics would assert otherwise. Martin, therefore, rejects all economic thinking rather than the formalists alone. Later in his book, particularly in the last chapter, Martin shows himself well able to make solid economic analysis and to report significant data from his historical research.

The following quotation summarizes a problem in labor supply as reported by fur traders:

As seasoned traders had pointed out many times, to raise the price of Indian furs would result in the surrender of fewer rather than more beaver skins. The reason for this inelastic supply seems to be that Indians, at least until the early nineteenth century, insisted on viewing the trade as a form of gift exchange. ... . Fret as they may, HBC merchants could never persuade the tribesmen that human wants can and should be insatiable. [21, p. 10, note b]

In an essay generally critical of Martin's book, Dean Snow agrees with this point, as follows:

Indeed, increased prices seemed to lead to decreased pelt supplies. Martin cites E. E. Rich's explanation that Indians in this time and in this region still treated trade as a form of gift exchange, and the emphasis was still upon maintaining a constant flow of European goods. The observation makes very good sense to anyone familiar with Native American cultures." [27, p. 69].

Thus, gift exchange is seen as different from market exchange, because increased prices for the product of labor, pelts, led to a decrease in the amount supplied. It may be true that the economic analysis, particularly neoclassical economics, fails to include insti-

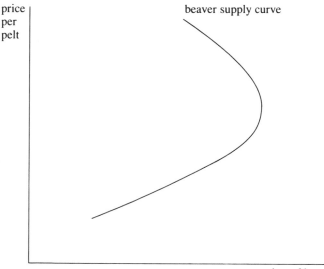

Fig. 8-1. Beaver Supply Curve

tutional and cultural factors. But this example is poorly chosen, for it truly is an attack on a straw man; economists have examined the work-leisure choice, and widespread agreement exists that what was observed by the traders is just what would be expected at higher beaver prices.

Fig. 8-1 presents the supply curve for beaver, shown as a graph of the relationship between the price of beaver and the quantity supplied. The vertical axis is the price of beaver; the horizontal axis is the quantity of beaver. The supply curve rises to the right for low beaver prices, showing the expected result. As the price rises, the supply curve goes vertical and then bends backward. At the highest prices, increases in the beaver price reduce the quantity supplied. This is the "unexpected" result. No modern economist would be surprised by that graph. It looks like the supply curve for labor. Since labor was the main input in harvesting beaver, the supply curve for beaver should look like the supply curve of labor.

Economists would explain the "unexpected" shape of the beaver-supply curve by distinguishing the "substitution effect" and the "income effect." The substitution effect is the increase in work which should result when a wage increases and income does not; this is the response the traders expected. In other words, at the outset, people will work harder to raise their income. The income effect is the reduction of work which occurs because of an increase in income. Later in the trade, prices are high enough that people can reduce their hours of work. As the price of beaver rises, the income effect becomes equal to the substitution effect, and the supply curve is vertical. As the price rises further, the income effect dominates, and the supply curve bends backward.

Whether or not the income effect will dominate is an empirical matter. In studies of the modern economy, we have found that the income effect is negative. In the American economy in the twentieth century, real wages have risen with time, and average weekly hours of work have fallen [3, p. 617]. I have studied Indian and white hours of participation in the labor force using data from 1975 [30]. Although there were some differences between the groups in the magnitudes of response to wage and income changes, the signs were always the same. Increases in income reduced the hours of work for both groups, as has been found in many other statistical studies as well. Cain and Watts summarized the evidence [4].

The assumed reason the income effect is negative is that the consumption of leisure is a normal good. Normal goods are those for which consumption increases when income increases. If leisure is a normal good, then an increase in income should reduce hours of work, other things held constant.

For some readers, this example may raise further problems because it takes a fact from the twentieth century and applies it to the sixteenth and seventeenth centuries and because it appears to treat labor as a commodity. As a matter of theory, the two effects can be of any size. Economic theory does not state with certainty that labor supply curves are shaped as shown in Fig. 8-1. Available evidence says they do. Martin discusses the presence of leisure in hunter-gatherer societies; his discussion shows that he, too, believes that leisure is a desired good [21, pp. 14–15]. Given that belief, Martin should not have rejected economic theory with the beaver supply curve. In fact, by emphasizing leisure, Martin is treating labor—not furs—as a commodity.

I do not want to review the literature which seeks to explain the extermination of furbearers, because my main focus is upon difficulties in the use of economics. As will be clear below, I would stress the open-access problems created on the frontier by competing hunters from different political systems.

Prices as Quantity Ratios

In spite of his apparent rejection of economic analysis, Martin shows good economic insights, particularly in his selection of data. My favorite is the following, which will introduce my second example of the application of economic analysis:

> Le Jeune was thus accosted one day by an incredulous Montagnais who facetiously announced: "The Beaver does everything perfectly well, it makes kettles, hatchets, swords, knives, bread; and, in short, it makes everything.' He was making sport of us Europeans, who have such a fondness for the skin of this animal and who fight to see who will give the most to these Barbarians, to get it; they carry this to such an extent that my host said to me one day, showing me a very beautiful knife, 'The English have no sense; they give us twenty knives like this for one Beaver skin." [21, p. 153]

The Indian described the virtues of trade and expressed his point precisely using an economist's main variable: price. In this case, one beaver skin can be traded for twenty knives.

A great many historians (and anthropologists) believe that the introduction of money into a barter economy is a significant event. From the point of view of economic theory, however, the introduction of money, while important, has a different importance than that attributed to it by historians. Economic theory is divided into microeconomics and macroeconomics. Microeconomic theory applies best to a barter economy and can also apply to a monetary economy. Macroeconomics requires money. Most of the questions asked by historians about economic variables are best dealt with by microeconomic analysis, in which the presence of money plays a small role.

When an economist says "price" in the context of microeconomic theory, he means a trading ratio between any two goods. Most people believe that a "price" requires money, since all prices now are stated in terms of money. But the price of a Hudson's Bay blanket in terms of beaver skins is what an economist would mean by price. In analysis of modern-day consumption, an economist's first step is to convert money prices into quantity ratios. This is done by forming a ratio and cancelling the money values. If butter costs $1.00 a pound and a gun costs $100, then the price of a gun is 100 pounds of butter, or the price of butter is 1/100 of a gun. Pick up any introductory text in microeconomics and look for the budget line and consumer indifference curves. Because money has no intrinsic value, economists assume that behavior is determined by the utility of goods and price ratios that describe how one good can be traded for another. Books on microeconomic theory typically assume one commodity becomes the *numéraire*. All other commodity prices are expressed in terms of the *numéraire*. Arrow and Hahn's *General Competitive Analysis* [2], for instance, seriously discusses money in only the last (fourteenth) chapter but uses a *numéraire* throughout. Unable to use British sterling as a unit of account, the Hudson's Bay Company chose "made beaver" as the *numéraire*. In their analysis of the fur trade, Ray and Freeman adopt the company's practice and report their wealth of data using made beaver throughout [24]. They examine the pattern of prices over time and location. (But in discussing the supply curve of beaver, they repeat Martin's mistake described in the previous section. [24, p. 245]).

Consider the case of a European establishing initial contact with the Indians. The Indian economy is portrayed as a barter economy and the European as a monetary economy. But this is not a particularly important distinction. Much more important is the fact that the prices and the list of goods available are different in the two economies. Trade following contact causes the prices in both economies to change. The consequences of these price changes are the significant events for an economist. Economic theory predicts that each economy will shift its production toward goods in which it has comparative advantage and that average real consumption in both economies will rise [2, chap. 6]. These results occur because of trade and changes in the prices of goods.

An example of this effect is Choctaw revitalization in the early eighteenth century, as described by Richard White [31]. White labors under the assumption that there is a unique entity called "the market." When Indians engage in this market, dependency results. The dynamic *capitalist* or *modern* market system can and does create dependency. White's view that "the market" is at fault overlooks the fact that capitalism arrives as a total onslaught: markets, armies, settlers, railroads, and so on. Prior to the start of modern economic growth in England in the middle of the eighteenth century, however, Indians faced the different and less effective system called "mercantilism."

When Europeans and Choctaws traded commodities, as predicted by the theory of comparative advantage, Choctaw living standards rose; the chiefs, as distributors of the new trade goods, increased in power. White sees this in his data and appears puzzled (pp. 41–52). In order to explain this positive effect of trade, White distinguishes "mere exchange" from "the market" as follows:

Dependence . . . was a political condition, not purely a material condition. The mere exchange of goods hardly represents dependence. What brought dependence to the Choctaws, for example, was not woolen goods or hoes or guns in and of themselves but the penetration of the market economy . . . which resulted in the destruction of native subsistence. [p. 204]

I would edit this statement, substituting "the colonial commodity market" for "mere exchange," and "the capitalist system" for "the market." There certainly were profound differences for Choctaw leaders when they had to deal with only the English and the new United States. Mercantilists were replaced by capitalists; expanding English capitalism created dependency, whereas the French and Spanish had not.

One must recognize that more than new market transactions accompanied capitalism. Colonial political institutions and settlers also arrived. Trade in industrial goods was not sufficient to acquire Indian land without dismantling Choctaw political institutions. When the Five Civilized Tribes moved to Indian Territory, they reconstituted their governments, which in turn required the United States to repeat the attack on Indian governments during the allotment era.

The Choctaws, Cherokees, and other southern Indians, having grown strong, resisted well both in the 1830s and the 1880s and 1890s. In both periods, strong Indian governments and prosperous Indian economies forced the United States to use political power to open Indian resources to non-Indians. White's case studies provide evidence of this. Despite his focus on "the market" he demonstrates that political factors were also important.

This analysis suggests the following questions: 1. What were the prices prior to contact? How much did the price of some significant goods change after contact? 2. What was the change in consumption? The answers to these questions are useful because they can explain changes in the patterns of production. When combined with data on the quantity of trade and with observations on living standards, one could estimate the change in real consumption. Economic historians

have found ways to estimate changes in living standards in periods
with no economy-wide surveys. Anderson [1], for instance, provides
data on colonial New England. The March, 1983, volume of the
Journal of Economic History contains a symposium in historical
measurement of living standards [12].

Evidence about prices can be used to discover possible inconsistencies in an analysis. For instance, in colonial times, trade with
Europeans may have changed the value of corn, produced by
women, relative to products of game. This in turn may have caused
changes in the roles of men and women in Indian society. The argument sounds plausible; one way to check it is to compare prices to
see if they did move as suggested. If the relative corn price rose,
this suggests that changes in gender roles we know did occur were
economically motivated rather than forced on the group in some
other manner.

Ray notwithstanding, comparing prices is difficult. Outside of the
records of the Hudson's Bay Company, probably few observations
exist. Prices vary seasonally and with geography. One cannot use a
single price given in a primary source as "the price" of a good. The
location, season, and year of the price also need to be recorded.
Primary sources should have more price data than historians report
in their works. Prices matter in daily life; I cannot believe the data
are as scant as they appear from reading historians debating issues
whose importance can be better understood by using information on
relative prices.

Open Access Resources

The ubiquity of prices compared to degree of monetarization is another simple example of an area where economic theory can increase
the precision and clarity of historical analysis. A more complicated
example of the value of "economic thinking" is the subject of open-
access resources. Here the economic theory is difficult and consensus
among economists is much less than in regard to analysis of trade or
the choice between work and leisure.

An open-access resource is one for which harvest is freely open to
anyone with the needed equipment. Fisheries and open range are two
common examples of open-access resources. Whales, beaver, buffalo, and timber are others. When equipment is sufficiently devel-

oped, failure to limit access to the resource dooms it either to extinction or depletion to the point that further harvest does not pay. Problems arise when the technical conditions of harvest or social institutions make control of access difficult.

Societies develop methods to control these problems. A great many economists believe that the resource can be preserved only by privatizing it. But in fact there are a variety of possible techniques to deal with open-access resource management. One is to limit harvests to a certain number over a defined period. Another is to limit the equipment available to extract the resource. If we assume that Indian societies had found ways to avoid the depletion of their resources, then they must have adopted one of these methods.

The spread of Europeans across the North American continent produced a succession of open-access problems for Indians and for Europeans, for several reasons. First, the frontier was an area where no government had effective control. Management of an open-access resource is much easier when governmental authority can be used. Second, the mercantile and industrial revolution in Europe provided increasingly effective weapons for hunting. Third, international trade provided the large market needed to amplify hunting intensity to levels which threatened resources.

Open-access resources become more interesting—and more difficult to describe—when one considers the (apparently) different attitudes towards private property that existed in Indian and non-Indian societies. In the frontier setting, Indian leaders claimed that all property was owned by the nation rather than by individuals. This claim made it possible to limit the cession of land by individual Indians to Europeans. It also, however, distorted the perception of Indian property rights systems. Indians, holding their land "in common," were seen to regulate it with a system less desirable than the European private property system. As the European ideology took hold, it allowed the allotment policy to be justified as benefiting Indians, when in fact it did not.

Leonard Carlson reviews both the ideology and the results of the allotment policy in *Indians, Bureaucrats, and Land: The Dawes Act and the Decline of Indian Farming* [5]. He finds that Indian agriculture before allotment was more vigorous than afterwards, primarily because of the loss of land. His chapter on preallotment agriculture, while good, assumes rather than proves that Indians had a private property system during the closed reservation period. In this, Carlson seems unaware that anything other than a private property system can be used to overcome the open-access problem.

One cannot deny the reality of the open-access problems when different nations are trying to use the same resource. The rational response to excessive harvest is to limit the harvest in some way. The assignment of hunting territories among the Montagnais Indians of Canada is an example of Indians responding with a control method, privatization of the resource [14, 16, 21]. There are also examples of non-Indians failing to adopt a successful policy; hunters virtually extinguished the nation's supply of buffalo and eliminated passenger pigeons. Many societies have devised successful methods for protecting their resources. The entire subject raises a variety of interesting historical questions: Was the problem perceived? What solutions were attempted? Was it possible to implement the solutions successfully? If not, why not; if successful, why?

Ford Carlisle Runge provides an excellent critique of mainstream assumptions that only privatization can deal with open-access problems [25]. Voluntary restraint in grazing the range can occur when herders share a common set of values and expectations. Neoclassical economists, with their predilection to assume that individual behavior will be governed only by simple views of the actions of others, fail to examine broader institutional possibilities. Some of these possibilities may be less expensive than the enforcement mechanisms needed for privatization, such as fences and title record-keeping.

Runge illustrates these differences by contrasting two different analogies from game theory: the prisoner's dilemma and the battle of the sexes. Games are depicted by payoff matrices. I have made a slight change from Runge by using the examples as explained by Luce and Raiffa [17, pp. 90–102].

In the prisoner's dilemma, the prosecuting attorney separates two prisoners accused of jointly committing the same crime and offers them both the same deal. For confession, the confessor will receive no jail sentence if the other prisoner does not confess and will receive a sentence of five years if the other confesses. Both know that if neither confesses, only a short sentence, one year, is possible. If no coordination of policy is possible, this set of payoffs practically forces each prisoner to confess, to their joint sorrow. Further, if they meet between interrogation and agree not to confess, there is great incentive to cheat. If prisoner one knows the other will not confess, by confessing prisoner one receives no jail at all. Only if both can enforce their joint agreement is it a stable outcome.

In the battle of the sexes, the game assumes that the husband prefers to go to the fights, the woman prefers to go to the ballet, and each prefers the company of the other. As in the prisoner's dilemma, cooperation is better than noncooperation. But unlike the prisoner's dilemma, once agreement is reached, there is not incentive to double-cross. Once the man knows the woman has agreed to go to the ballet, he will choose the ballet even though his payoff would be higher if both were to go to the fights. He does not want to go to the fights alone.

In moving to an open-access resource, one assumes that numerous people are playing the game and that the individual payoffs are similar. Is grazing the range more like the prisoner's dilemma or the battle of the sexes? If it is the former, then both communication and enforcement are required to prevent an undesirable outcome. If it is the latter, then only communication is required.

Runge defines "common property" as an institution involving tacit cooperation which can come into existence if the natural conditions of a resource are like the battle of the sexes. He asserts that the payoffs for the open range are like those of the battle of the sexes, where one option is to voluntarily restrain from overgrazing and the other is to graze to the limit. Neoclassical economists naturally discount the possibilities of cooperation without enforcement and see the problem as a prisonner's dilemma. They assume a tacit form of cooperation will not work.

The two analogies can be distinguished by examining the technical conditions of production and by examining social institutions. If communication of intent is sufficient to manage the resource, then existence of a common language is significant, since language is basic to understanding. If the battle of the sexes is the right analogy, then measures to reveal cheaters may be all that is necessary. But if communication is difficult, cheating is possible, and the prisoner's dilemma applies, then enforcement mechanisms are required.

Private property systems, as symbolized by the barbed-wire fence, have both communication and enforcement mechanisms. An open-access system, as symbolized by the nineteenth-century herds of buffalo on the Great Plains, has neither. In particular historical examples, one fruitful approach would be to characterize the communication and enforcement conditions of the resource under examination.

McManus [19] perceived a problem with the case of the Montagnais and Naskapi hunting territories as reported by Leacock [14] and Lips [16]: it appears that hunting territories were well defined and that owners had exclusive use. Yet the resource was overexploited. This is not what should happen under a system of private property. Upon investigation, however, McManus found that access was not restricted for purposes of gathering food. This gave intruders access to the private trapping reserves, which for McManus provides enough evidence to resolve the paradox; enforcement of private rights was not fully possible.

The open range of the Navajo reservation has received attention because of overgrazing. Federal policies to correct the problem did not do so and created other problems. The main references are Spicer [28], Parman [23], Libecap and Johnson [15], and White [31]. None analyze the story from the point of view that Runge's contrasting game theory models would suggest. Libecap and Johnson, neoclassical economists, predictably assume the prisoner's dilemma model and conclude that a private property approach enforced by an "outside agency" would be better. White examines the traditional range management institutions in use by the Navajos from the nineteenth century on [31, chaps. 10 and 11]. Changes were occurring rapidly, and Navajo political leaders had little actual power compared to federal officials. Livestock numbers were increasing at the same time that Navajo range was reduced by white immigration. Is the problem "too many sheep," unregulated and overgrazing the land, or is it "too little land," caused by non-Indian occupation of land traditionally used by the Navajo? When the BIA tried to cure range problems in the 1930s, they based policy on faulty scientific assumptions and followed these errors with hastily planned and poorly administered remedies. Furthermore, the whole sheep issue may well be a diversion of attention away from the non-Indian desire for Navajo mineral wealth and an uninterrupted flow of power from the area's hydroelectric projects.

Six Explanations

The open-access resource problem is one of the possible answers to a major question of Indian economic history: the causes of dependence. In his chapter "Unstable Symbiosis," Francis Jennings poses the following question: "Apart from the incessant demographic erosion of disease and war, what traits in Indian culture made the trade itself so deleterious?" [11, p. 102]. This question prejudges the answer by looking at cultural differences for the result. The question should be restated along these lines: "Why did the trade between Indians and Europeans lead to economic growth for Europeans and dependency for Indians?" Although answering the question lay outside of the major focus of his research, Jennings made a bold attempt to do so. His hypothesis is that Indian society did not value capital accumulation. Is this one of the answers offered by economics? Yes. But some other possibilities exist. Consider the following list:

1. Indian societies failed to accumulate capital.
2. Comparative advantage for Indians lay in the hunt, which uses a resource, game, that became vulnerable to open-access exploitation and resulting destruction.
3. Europeans had immigrants; Indians did not. This led to an overwhelming military advantage that allowed Europeans to take Indian property without payment to the owners.
4. The industrial revolution took place in Europe, thus introducing a new process, modern economic growth, beginning in the middle of the eighteenth century. Because technological progress there suddenly increased to a rate far greater than ever before, all other regions fell behind through no fault of their own. This economic growth augmented the military advantage obtained from population growth.
5. Europeans gained a monopoly position in trade with Indians. Those with monopoly can gain a larger share of the joint gain from trade than under competitive conditions.
6. Indians were unable to unify politically; because of the U.S. Constitution, Europeans successfully obtained unity.

These possibilities are not mutually exclusive; doubtless there is no answer which is correct in every place at all times. Some of the answers are analytically complex; others are quite simple. Jennings was referring to the colonial period. Quite possibly the vulnerability of the hunt to open-access destruction was much more important than the nature of Indian culture. The value of economic analysis, of course, is that it can help us understand behavior across vast ranges of time and space. This quality enables us to explore the connections between economic issues in the past and the present.

Useful Economists

Having read through the three examples—the labor supply curve, barter as exchange, and the problem of open access—many readers must wonder how to select and choose among the variety of economists they might consult. There are weaknesses in the mainstream approaches, but scholars should not reject the whole discipline; rather, they should learn to pick and choose among what is available.

Albert Hirschman's work is particularly useful. His collection, *Essays in Trespassing* [9], is a good place to start because he provides a guided tour through his own thinking and, consequently, through much of development economics. For example, the second essay in this collection is an enlightening critique of dependency theory as developed in Latin America. As is typical of Hirschman, who sees many sides of everything, he points out an advantage of being on the periphery of the capitalist system: policy makers at the center pay little attention to the periphery if it is perceived as small and unimportant. Consequently, gains can be made:

Because of the disparity of attention, dependent countries are in a favorable position to utilize what room for maneuver they have and may be able to widen this room: within limits that are often uncertain and constantly changing, the dominant country is unlikely to pay the attention and make the effort needed to counter or effectively rein in dependent countries straining to achieve a greater degree of autonomy. [9, p. 31]

He challenges dependency theorists to think about ways to solve the problems rather than to elaborate the complaints.

There is much other good advice from Hirschman in that book. I also recommend *Exit, Voice and Loyalty* [10]. "Exit" is a metaphor for economic incentives; "voice" represents political action. Choice among these, and management of that choice by Europeans, has occurred often for Indians and Indian tribes in their struggles for survival.

For analysis of the contemporary American economy, I recommend both John Kenneth Galbraith and Stephen Marglin. Many readers are doubtless aware of Galbraith. *Economics and the Public Purpose* [8] summarizes and extends the analysis in his earlier, more famous books. "The combination of a powerful thrust to the expansion of the firm in some parts of the economy with effective restraints on growth in other parts," he writes, "produces a remarkably skewed pattern of economic development" [p. 42]. The economy is made up of one thousand large corporations producing half of the private output of the economy and twelve million smaller firms comprising the other half. The thousand comprise the "planning system"; the rest are the "market system." The neoclassical model is helpful in analyzing the market system and of little help for the planning system. The application of this to Indian affairs is that we should clarify which half is affecting a particular Indian community in order to understand the consequences.

Marglin's *Growth, Distribution, and Prices* [20] complements Galbraith by investigating the determinants of economic growth in a capitalistic economy. He presents three alternative theories: neoclassical, neo-Marxist, and neo-Keynesian. He concludes with a model which combines the second two. He wants to know how well these models can explain differences in economic growth and distribution of income among capitalist countries. Why did Japan grow at a rate of 7 percent per year between 1953 and 1977, while Great Britain grew at only 2 percent? As he tries to answer this question, he sees a "prior problem": "How do we properly formulate and understand the three theories?" [p. 312]. His answer to this question is to construct a series of mathematical analogies which capture the character of real economies while also enabling him to compare different models of long-run economic growth. I like this book because a good model of capitalist growth should be helpful when one needs to understand the effect of such growth on other economies.

Although the book is mathematical, not all of the mathematics is essential to Marglin's points. The simple models use no more than high school algebra, with the exception of "stability analysis," which can be taken on trust. Most of the essential points are conveyed in the simple models. As with most analogies, the usefulness of the models lies in illuminating new or unexpected features of the object under study. I have found the book also shows which of the neoclassical tools serve a purely ideological function and which have more general usefulness.

One of the least satisfactory parts of economics is its conception of the individual, be he consumer, worker, or factory owner. Amartya Sen leads the field in criticizing and improving that theory. His works are collected in *Choice, Welfare and Measurement* [26]. The title of the fourth essay conveys the flavor of his work: "Rational Fools: A Critique of the Behavioural Foundations of Economic Theory." Fortunately Sen can construct as well as demolish models of human behavior.

Anthony Fisher's *Resource and Environmental Economics* [7] surveys economic models of the use of natural resources in a market economy. Since Indians had and have ownership of such resources, such models are relevant, as I have argued above in regard to open access. Fisher shares with me the odd role of simultaneously criticizing and defending economic analyses.

I do not wish to associate myself with the view of some others, usually economists, to the effect that there is nothing new or special about, for example, exhaustible resources, that everything worth knowing about [the economics of] these resources is already contained in the standard concepts and models, and/or that everything is best left to the market to decide. [p. 234]

Although his book also presents mathematical models, he interprets them clearly as well as illustrating the models graphically.

In addition to these, the books by McCloskey [18] and by Caves and Jones [6] can be helpful. McCloskey explains in detail why economists write, and therefore think, dismally. Caves and Jones deal with international trade and comparative advantage.

One odd aspect of the critique of neoclassical economic theory from the cited authors is that microeconomic theory may be more applicable to noncapitalist markets than to capitalist markets. Neoclassical theory deals with markets full of consumers and producers, with no advantages given to any group either by government action or by strategic position. I spent two summers in 1966 and 1967 working with anthropologists in the highlands of Chiapas, Mexico. The markets in the city of San Cristóbal were more like the neoclassical model than any around me on the Flathead reservation today. As a result of the land reform which followed the Mexican Revolution, each of the separate Mayan Indian and Spanish-speaking communities specialized in particular products. There were many market participants, with no obvious big players. In my community of Zinancantan, individuals stored corn in the fall to pay labor costs in the subsequent summer. A neighboring community provided labor, and another land.

Current Policy

As an economist who has returned to his home reservation and is trying to assist his own tribe in achieving self-determination and improved standards of living, I find policy applications of economic analysis particularly appealing. My current position prompts a number of questions that might interest academic scholars. Despite the danger of "presentism," these questions deserve serious attention. First, how do we go about dismantling the system of dependency? History helps answer this question because it shows what was put in place or destroyed as dependency was created. History also suggests that strengthening tribal governments might combat dependency. Dismantling these governments in the general allotment period left individual Indians on their own. Too often, the result of this abandonment was dependency. Although far from perfect, both the Indian Reorganization Act and the Indian Self-Determination and Education Act have been used to strengthen tribal government. Once the tribal government is in place, however, what should its policies be?

What were the development strategies or policies of Indian governments when they had the power to implement them? It would be interesting to know what was planned by tribal leaders during the periods when reservations were primarily Indian in population and when the Indian agent was relatively weak. Other similar questions arise: What kinds of investments were made by Indian leaders? What was immigration policy? What value did Indians put on the land when asked to sell?

On my reservation, for example, the federal government offered $15,000 for a railroad right-of-way in 1882; this sum was $10 an acre. The chiefs asked for $1,000,000 (nearly $700 an acre), complained that unauthorized whites were living in and grazing cattle on the reservation, and asked for the equipment and training that had been promised by treaty in 1855. In the end the government paid $16,000 for the land and $5,458 for improvements.

If the government had to have a right-of-way, it should have taken a route around the reservation; one chief indicated he had his own plans for the reservation:

ENEAS. Who established the lines of this reservation? It was the Great Father that got these lines established. Why does he want to break the lines? If we had no lines I would say no word. Lines are just like a fence. He told us so. No white man is allowed to live and work on the reservation. You know it is so in the treaty. That is the reason I say you had better go the other way. Why do you wish us to go away? It is a small country; it is valuable to us; we support ourselves by it; there is no end to these lands supporting us; they will do it for generations. If you say you will give us money for our lands, I doubt if we get it, because we didn't before. [U.S. Congress, Senate, *Report in Relation to Agreement with Flathead and Other Indians*, S. Exec. Doc. No. 44, 47th Cong., 2d sess., 1883]

Is it true that traditional values are inconsistent with economic development? There should be a variety of experiences. In some tribes, increases in income may strengthen traditional systems, while in others they may weaken. In Zinacantan, for instance, increased income led to an increase in the amount of traditional ceremonies. Which tribes are good case studies, and what forms of economic growth occurred in them?

On the Flathead reservation, one of our businesses provides jobs which closely mimic traditional hunting and gathering organization. Other enterprises employ nontraditional, bureaucratic structures. Both types have "worked," in the sense that tribal members can earn a living from them and the businesses can survive. Flathead Post and Pole supports traditional activities by purchasing lodgepole pine from tribal members who harvest with chainsaws and deliver with small trucks. The cutters neither sell labor services nor accept supervision; they sell a commodity, small-diameter lodgepole pine cut to seven- or eight-foot lengths. Small work groups (two to five) are efficient. The manufacture of the products occurs in an industrial framework.

The Salish and Kootenai tribes operate three educational institutions: Salish-Kootenai College, a two-year college; Kicking Horse Job Corps, a contractor to the Labor Department; and Two Eagle River School, an alternative high school. All three are fairly typical schools, although the course content and students may vary from those of other institutions. As one might expect, "full-bloods" tend to work for the post yard and "mixed-bloods" for the bureaucracies. (I use quotation marks because I refer to a cultural rather than racial classification.) Another major industry, cattle ranching, appears to lie on the "traditional" side. A third line of development has been to create enterprises in electronics, printing, and construction. In allocation of investment dollars, the tribal council favors the timber-based and grazing-land based sectors rather than the industrial or construction sectors. This may be because of values, but an alternative explanation is that benefits are greater when we build economic activity based on our natural resources. We also successfully operate a small-scale high-head hydroelectric facility, and we have just contracted (October, 1986) to manage the BIA's electric distribution system. As a new, college-educated core of tribal members move into managerial and technical positions, we are steadily eroding the export of materials in raw form and are dismantling the dependency apparatus.

Because the American economy has been technically ahead of Indians since the industrial revolution, there are a number of questions regarding the transfer of technology among the societies. How did Indians acquire capability in the use of the new techniques? What was the cost of acquiring them? What barriers were placed in the way? How fast did technology transfer occur? H. Craig Miner addresses some of these questions in *The Corporation and the Indian* [22]. His goal is to show how corporations reduced the sovereignty of tribal governments in Indian Territory between 1865 and 1907. This is one major part of the cost of new technology.

But there are other costs and there are other ways to acquire knowledge. And what were the *benefits* of the new relationships? It is important to look beyond a single force or economic event and build a broad picture of the tribal economy through time. For example, Indians learned from missionaries, spouses, lawyers, and Indian agents—not just from traders and businessmen. Leonard Carlson showed that Indians on reservations were rapidly learning to farm before the allotment policy [5]. I showed that Indian ranchers on the Northern Cheyenne reservation in 1967 were not behind their non-Indian neighbors [29]. Miner mentions that the Cherokees wanted to establish their own railroad and were prevented from doing so by the Office of Indian Affairs [22, pp. 23–27]

Economic questions asked about historic events are vitally important because Indian communities are still grappling with economic growth and the associated difficulties of surviving in a non-Indian economy. On the surface, the current circumstances differ from those of the eighteenth and nineteenth centuries because some of the worst aspects of capitalism have been contained by government regulation. But similarities remain. Neighboring non-Indians use Indian resources and pay below-market rates, as in coal leases on the Navajo reservation. A tribe has trouble borrowing funds while a lessee uses his leasehold interest on tribal land as security for a bank loan. Forest management focuses on stumpage sales rather than tribal use.

Indian economies continue to function in a hostile environment. Indian control of land can be limited by the BIA. States challenge tribal taxation powers. Tribal governments are sometimes compared to corporations, and in Alaska that identity is fixed in law. Some tribes incorporate their enterprises under tribal law and expect different styles of management. In tribal businesses non-Indian managers who are accustomed to cash bonuses tied to profit performance often find themselves at odds with owners who have other priorities. Alternatively, non-Indians incorporate Indians in management positions in order to qualify for Indian preference in government purchasing policy; this creates a reverse problem: Indians forced to inhabit a non-Indian hierarchy. The practice also brings to mind the use of "front men" in nineteenth-century leasing and land sales negotiations. Each of these analogies suggests a set of historical questions which can be explored through economic analysis.

Conclusion

Parts of this essay have argued that economic theory can contribute and has contributed to our understanding of historical events. Historians should consider a variety of economic models for interpreting Indian and non-Indian behavior. By way of conclusion, however, we should remember that differences between Indian and non-Indian economies continue to exist. For example, market behavior differs when governmental authority is absent compared to when it is present. A group of hunters wishing to preserve or to maximize the harvest can enforce mutual sanctions if there is structural political system available. Otherwise, the situation more closely resembles one of open access. A second distinction is between situations with slowly changing technology and those undergoing rapid change. The nineteenth and twentieth centuries have much greater rates of technological change than did the sixteenth and seventeenth.

Clearly, economic theory is sufficiently flexible to contribute to our understanding of Indian economic history. In fact, Jennings, White, and Martin might be surprised to discover that they are already using economic theory. Their objections to "formalist" economists may have misled them. I suspect that if one were to replace "formalist" with "neoclassical" or "hard-line neoclassical," at least the first barriers would come tumbling down. With the realization that there are economists on their side, scholars can reject economic arguments without rejecting economics altogether.

Some obstacles remain. Like all theories, economic theory involves oversimplification, abstraction, and a technical language. The mathematical "models" are really oversimplifications expressed in an intimidating manner. Good writers such as Hirschman, Galbraith, Fisher, and Marglin can convey the essence of the models to the nonmathematical reader. Readers with some experience in math need only algebra and the portions of calculus which explain how to compute slopes and areas. With their good grounding in data, and with the puzzles presented by that data to entice them, historians should find fresh insights in return for the time they spend with the work of economists.

References

1. Anderson, Terry L. 1979. "Economic Growth in Colonial New England: 'Statistical Renaissance.' " *Journal of Economic History* 39: 243–57.
2. Arrow, Kenneth J., and Frank Hahn. 1971. *General Competitive Analysis*. San Francisco: Holden Day.
3. Baumol, William J., and Alan S. Blinder. 1982. *Economics: Principles and Policy*. 2d ed. New York: Harcourt Brace Jovanovich.
4. Cain, Glen G., and Harold W. Watts, eds. 1973. *Income Maintenance and Labor Supply*. Chicago: Rand, McNally.
5. Carlson, Leonard A. 1981. *Indians, Bureaucrats, and Land: The Dawes Act and the Decline of Indian Farming*. Westport: The Greenwood Press.
6. Caves, Richard E., and Ronald W. Jones. 1973. *World Trade and Payments: An Introduction*. Boston: Little, Brown.
7. Fisher, Anthony. 1981. *Resource and Environmental Economics*. Cambridge: Cambridge University Press.
8. Galbraith, John Kenneth. 1973. *Economics and the Public Purpose*. Boston: Houghton Mifflin.
9. Hirschman, Albert O. 1981. *Essays in Trespassing: Economics to Politics and Beyond*. Cambridge: Cambridge University Press.
10. Hirschman, Albert O. 1970. *Exit, Voice, and Loyalty: Responses to Decline in Firms, Organizations, and States*. Cambridge: Harvard University Press.
11. Jennings, Francis. 1976. *The Invasion of America: Indians, Colonialism, and the Cant of Conquest*. New York: The Norton Library.
12. *Journal of Economic History* 43 (March 1983). Papers presented at the Forty-Second Annual Meeting of the Economic History Association.
13. Krech, Shepard, III. 1981. *Indians, Animals, and the Fur Trade: A Critique of Keepers of the Game*. Athens: University of Georgia Press.

14. Leacock, Eleanor. 1954. "The Montagnais' Hunting Territory and the Fur Trade." Memoir No. 73. *American Anthropologist* 56, no. 5, part 2.

15. Libecap, Gary D., and Ronald N. Johnson. 1980. "Legislating Commons: The Navajo Tribal Council and the Navajo Range." *Economic Inquiry* 18:69–85.

16. Lips, Julius E. 1947. *Naskapi Law*. Transactions of the American Philosophical Society, n.s. 37, part 4, pp. 379–492.

17. Luce, R. Duncan, and Howard Raiffa. 1957. *Games and Decisions*. New York: John Wiley and Sons.

18. McCloskey, Donald N. 1985. *The Rhetoric of Economics*. Madison: University of Wisconsin Press.

19. McManus, John C. 1972. "An Economic Analysis of Indian Behavior in the North American Fur Trade." *Journal of Economic History* 32: 36–53.

20. Marglin, Stephen A. 1984. *Growth, Distribution, and Prices*. Cambridge: Harvard University Press.

21. Martin, Calvin. 1978. *Keepers of the Game: Indian-Animal Relationships and the Fur Trade*. Berkeley: University of California Press.

22. Miner, H. Craig. 1976. *The Corporation and the Indian: Tribal Sovereignty and Industrial Civilization in Indian Territority, 1865–1907*. Columbia: University of Missouri Press.

23. Parman, Donald L. 1976. *The Navajos and the New Deal*. New Haven: Yale University Press.

24. Ray, Arthur J., and Donald Freeman. 1978. *Give Us Good Measure: An Economic Analysis of Relations Between the Indians and the Hudson's Bay Company Before 1763*. Toronto: University of Toronto Press.

25. Runge, Carlisle Ford. 1981. "Common Property Externalities: Isolation, Assurance, and Resource Depletion in a Traditional Grazing Context." *American Journal of Agricultural Economics* 63:595–606.

26. Sen, Amartya. 1982. *Choice, Welfare and Measurement*. Cambridge, Mass.: MIT Press.

27. Snow, Dean R. 1981. "*Keepers of the Game* and the Nature of Explanation." In Krech, *Indians, Animals, and the Fur Trade*, pp. 59–72.

28. Spicer, E. H. 1952. "Sheepmen and Technicians: A Program of Soil Conservation on the Navajo Indian Reservation." In *Human Problems in Technological Change*, pp. 185–207. Ed. E. H. Spicer. New York: Russel Sage Foundation.

29. Trosper, Ronald L. 1978. "American Indian Relative Ranching Efficiency." *American Economic Review* 68, no. 4:503–16.

30. ———. 1980. *Earnings and Labor Supply: A Microeconomic Comparison of American Indians and Alaskan Natives to American Whites and Blacks*. Publication No. 55. Boston: Social Welfare Research Institute, Boston College.

31. White, Richard. 1983. *The Roots of Dependency: Subsistence, Environment, and Social Change Among the Choctaws, Pawnees, and Navajos*. Lincoln: University of Nebraska Press.

CHAPTER 9

Toward a History of Indian Religion: Religious Changes in Native Societies

ROBERT A. BRIGHTMAN

Despite the fact that James Mooney's The Ghost Dance Religion and the Sioux Outbreak of 1890 *(Washington, D.C.: U.S. Government Printing Office, 1896) was written nearly a century ago, scholars have been reluctant to explore processes of religious change within American Indian communities. The bulk of modern scholarship on religious subjects has been concerned with religious systems and ceremonies rather than with the* history *of Indian spiritual life. The principal exceptions to this pattern have been studies of missions (a subject surveyed in an earlier Newberry bibliography, James P. Ronda and James Axtell,* Indian Missions: A Critical Bibliography *[Bloomington: Indiana University Press, 1978]).*

Åke Hultkrantz has provided an annotated bibliography for The Study of American Indian Religions, *edited by Christopher Vecsey (Washington, D.C.: American Academy of Religion, 1983), that will guide beginning students and scholars alike through the field. Robert Brightman's essay, however, focuses on a relatively new approach to the study of Native American spirituality: Indian religious history. He identifies recent publications which attempt to trace the process of change within native belief systems. This approach is less concerned with aboriginal spirituality or missionization than it is with the internal intellectual "unfolding" of Indian communities. Brightman's review both attempts to pursue this new approach and offers some suggestions for future research. He argues that focusing on religious change can free us from earlier categories of analysis ("Christian" versus "non-Christian," "traditional" versus "modern"), thereby fostering a more complete—and more accurate—picture of the Indian experience.*

This chapter tries to combine a review of recent writing on American Indian religious history and religious change with certain summary observations and suggestions regarding future scholarship in the field. As a reading of the recent literature makes clear, the topic is most profitably explored from an ethnohistorical perspective, that is to say, one which conjoins historical and ethnological expertise.

I have organized the chapter by informal "culture areas," a heuristic device whose artificiality will readily be evident to scholars who have traced the complex skein of reciprocal religious influence throughout North America. This particular grid was chosen only after reflecting that an arrangement by linguistic families would be more artificial still and that a topical organization ("missions," "revitalization," "syncretism," and so on) was impracticable given the multiple interests of many authors. The equivocal word *religion* is also somewhat arbitrary. It is used to signify complexes of belief and practice oriented towards reciprocally reactive superhuman or nonhuman entities and processes (cf. Horton [23]; Spiro [61]) and thus coincides in large part with our intuitive senses of what the subject entails. There is no necessary commitment to this definition as adequate in transcultural analysis. As Evans-Pritchard once remarked [14, pp. 84–85], long before the current preoccupation with reflexivity emerged, Western ethnological categories seemed too often to objectify Western ethnography. These categories themselves may stand in need of relativization (cf. Frake [17, p. 114–15]).

Eastern Canada and the Northeast

Studies of this area reflect the broad scope of recent writings on Indian religion. James Axtell's compendious *The Invasion Within* [2] addresses many aspects of the colonial encounter with the French and English, focusing in large part on the circumstances and consequences of the missionary enterprise. As Axtell astutely observes, the encounter had both political and economic dimensions, but it "remained primarily a contest between two concepts of spiritual power and the quality of life each promised" (p. 19). Axtell discusses incentives and obstacles to conversion (notably the social and moral crises provoked by contact), the differential success of the French and English enterprises, and the "secular" consequences of religious change. Of special interest are sections discussing how

Iroquoians and Algonquians comprehended Christian teaching, since they raise the issue of what constitutes "successful" conversion. Axtell concludes by identifying revitalization movements—distinguishing relatively nativistic from relatively Christian-oriented types—and describes them as responses which both preserved identity and facilitated adjustment to the colonial experience.

Bruce Trigger's *Natives and Newcomers* [69] focuses largely, but not exclusively, on Huron religious change, arguing that traditional practices helped the tribe survive both epidemics and first contact. Initial conversions, he argues, were motivated primarily by utilitarian concerns. Only by the end of the 1600s did conversion become a spiritual adjustment to political and economic debility. Elsewhere in the book Trigger discusses methods of conversion, factionalism consequent upon religious disunity, and the problem of how literally Christian teachers were understood. Daniel Richter's "Iroquois versus Iroquois: Jesuit Missions and Christianity in Village Politics" [45] parallels some of Trigger's concerns and conclusions, arguing that conversions were often initially pragmatic in the 1600s and that literal acceptance of Christianity followed inevitably from compromised sovereignty. Annemarie Shimony's "Conflict and Continuity: An Analysis of an Iroquois Uprising" [54] demonstrates how a recent conflict between political factions resulted in accusations of witchcraft/sorcery that in turn motivated increased recourse to traditional curers and heightened awareness of the value of Iroquois social identity.

Olive Dickason's *The Myth of the Savage and the Beginning of French Colonialism in the Americas* [11] covers somewhat similar ground with respect to the Jesuit enterprise, emphasizing especially the linkage between converting and civilizing. James Moore's *Indian and Jesuit* [40] is a somewhat partisan account of the Jesuit missionary enterprise that documents expertly both the priests' adjustments to Indian life and their sometimes relativistic coordination of Christian and Indian practices. Despite its sensitivity in those areas, however, Moore's work makes too little of Jesuit hostility towards indigenous religious complexes and slights the priests' interest in cultivating the usual secular indices of "civility" (sedentism, agriculture, monogamy, and so on). Nancy Bonvillain's "Missionary Rule in French Colonial Expansion" [7] is a briefer but more balanced and contextualized discussion of the Jesuit project.

Jordon Paper's "The Post-Contact Origin of an American Indian High God: The Suppression of Feminine Spirituality" [44] argues the politically attractive but evidentially improbable thesis that an aboriginal complementarity between earth (female) and sky (male) was displaced historically by new European ideas: a single masculine "supreme being," male domination, and a hierarchical social structure. Although the aboriginality of "high god" concepts is an important issue, Paper's Algonquian reconstructions are unconvincing; the author's argument rests on a simplistic cosmological "reflection" of altering social designs.

Aside from Axtell's book, John Grant's *Moon of Wintertime* [19] is the most significant recent discussion of Indian conversion to Christianity. Tracing the history of missionaries in Canada from the 1500s to the present, Grant notes that conversions in these regions were necessarily voluntary and that *acceptance* of white religions was and is more enigmatic than rejection. Grant traces conversion to the sufferings attendant upon the contact experience but argues this familiar thesis with unusual sensitivity to the distinguishable and often concurrent attitudes towards new religions within Indian communities. Grant examines orientations toward white religion(s) as conscious breaks with the traditional. Christianity, he argues, was a source of syncretic innovation or of a compartmentalized adjunct to indigenous practice. It was a faith only nominally accepted ("the 'yes' that means 'no' "). Grant also identifies apparent contradictions between the nativistic (or antiwhite) and Christian orientations of most revitalization movements. Grant's work provides an example of the lack of common discrimination in Indian religious movements between Christian teachings and white values. In the native view, the rejection of white goods could be a prerequisite to accepting the Christian concept of salvation.

John Grant also addresses the definitional problem of conversion. Since missionaries, with negligible exceptions, saw white and Indian religions as mutually exclusive, how "genuine" are Indian converts who compartmentalize the two, synthesize them, or unconsciously construe Christianity according to indigenous premises? Grant concludes that Canadian Indians were typically receptive to Christianity but that they received it in a way that was humiliating and destructive. Syncretic religions should be seen, therefore, as transformations or creations of an indigenous Christianity consonant with Indian dignity and social identity.

Southern New England and the Great Lakes

A number of recent publications have brought new attention to a region many have considered "empty" of Indians and Indian religious history. William and Cheryl Simmons's *Old Light on Separate Ways: The Narragansett Diary of Joseph Fish* [59] provides important insight into the day-by-day conduct of missionary work in a Narragansett "praying town." A companion volume, William Simmons's *Spirit of the New England Tribes: Indian History and Folklore, 1620–1984* [58] offers a view of the Indian side of the historical encounter. *Spirit* is a unique and meticulous examination of Algonquian (Wampanoag, Mashpee, Gay Head, Mohegan, Narragansett) folklore and folkloristic narratives in relation to the historical experiences of conquest, missionaries, reservations, allotment, and Indian political activism. The book draws on extensive documentary and field material, tracing native traditions as well as influences from Afro-American and Anglo-American folklore. Neal Salisbury's *Manitou and Providence: Indians, Europeans, and the Making of New England, 1500–1643* [49] takes up aspects of Algonquian and Iroquoian religious change in a more focused time frame. Perhaps most important from a religious standpoint, Salisbury demonstrates the sociopolitical meanings Micmacs attached to conversion and shows how epidemics validated the spiritual claims of the Jesuits.

Concerning the Great Lakes area, R. David Edmunds suggests in *The Shawnee Prophet* [12] that the prophet Tenskwatawa's role in the trans-Appalachian Indian rebellion has been overshadowed by historians' fascination with the exploits of its military leader, Tecumseh. Edmunds suggests that disease, rapid social change, and loss of sovereignty reduced the Shawnees by 1805 to a condition of cultural disintegration marked by alcoholism and a fear of witchcraft. Tenskwatawa responded to those events with a vision that combined explicit nativistic and antiwhite teachings (which prohibited social interaction with whites, prophesied white destruction, and rejected white goods) with exhortations toward peace with "all mankind." The prophet also urged the acceptance of a variety of European ideas: monogamy, temperance, and the renunciation of shamanism. Edmunds's study provides detailed coverage of Tenskwatawa's prophecy and the rebellion led by Tecumseh, but he does not examine the interplay between the two.

Melburn Thurman's "The Shawnee Prophet's Movement and the Origins of the Prophet Dance" [67] argues for continuity between Tenskwatawa's teachings and the prophetic religions of the Amero-Canadian Plateau. Contrary to the premise that Plateau movements were independent, Thurman's reanalysis of an 1813 movement among (Subarctic Athapaskan) Chipewayns indicates that the doctrines of the Shawnee Prophet were introduced into the trans-Mississippi west by an immigrant Ojibwa berdache. Additional information regarding the origins and spread of the Shawnee prophet's message can be found in R. David Edmunds's "Main Poc: Potawatomi Wabeno" [13]. That article discusses the influential religious and political leader who disseminated the Shawnee Prophet's message while rejecting the latter's proscription of alcohol and inter-Indian warfare.

In "Kenekuk the Kickapoo Prophet: Acculturation Without Assimilation" [21], Joseph Herring argues unpersuasively that Kenekuk, the Kickapoo civil and religious leader, prevented the expulsion of the Vermilion band from Kansas. Despite its weakness, however, the study documents one of the more interesting syncretic movements on record. Kenekuk's religion combined Christian elements (notably self-flagellation which "strengthened tribal unity," [p. 297]) with selective retention of indigenous concepts. The Kickapoo was yet another nativist who advocated social accommodation to the majority society. Kenekuk nominally welcomed missionaries, but he passively resisted them after their arrival. Perhaps he saw them as rivals. He was also exposed—through the person of the itinerant preacher Jane Livermore—to a more millennial brand of Christianity. Livermore's teachings had great dramatic appeal. Among other things she predicted the resurrection of Napoleon Bonaparte as the anti-Christ, the end of the world, and the assumption of herself and the Kickapoos into Heaven.

Martin Zanger's "Straight Tongue's Heathen Words: Bishop Whipple and the Episcopal Mission to the Chippewas" [76] demonstrates the limitations of missionization as an instrument of directed acculturation and suggests that White Earth Chippewas creatively redefined Christianity as a means of sustaining their own identity. Zanger introduces also the useful distinction between motivated conversion and anomic receptivity to directed change.

Thomas Vennum's *The Ojibwa Dance Drum* [71] is a rich study which provides a thorough discussion of the inception and attenuation of the Drum Dance Religion (elsewhere Big Drum, Powwow,

Dream Dance) in Minnesota and Wisconsin Ojibwa communities. The discussion is particularly valuable in detailing the consequences of attenuation. Vennum shows precisely what such labels as "religious loss" can mean by describing the dwindling membership of the group, the sale of drums for fast money, absence, lateness, vanishing ritual offices, errors, and songs performed in the wrong sequence. Vennum also explains the attrition of membership by referring to generational boundaries, persecution by missionaries, competition from the Native American Church (peyotism), and the copious demands of the Drum on the time and resources of members. Despite such obstacles, the Drum persists in the 1980s as an integral expression of faith in some communities and as a potential for renewed faith and identity in many others.

Anastasia Shkilnyk's *A Poison Stronger Than Love: The Destruction of an Ojibwa Community* [56] deals peripherally with aspects of Ojibwa religion in detailing the effects of mercury poisoning and relocation on the Grassy Narrows (Ontario Ojibwa) band, but its description adds greatly to our picture of a society that has lost its spiritual underpinnings. Christopher Vecsey's *Traditional Ojibwa Religion and Its Historical Changes* [70] is a broader study. It contains a summary of missionary enterprises, a discussion of factors favoring and obstructing conversion, and descriptions of such historically emergent movements as the Wabeno, the Drum, and peyotism. Vecsey's principal thesis is that missionary pressures destroyed the integrity and coherence of the indigenous religious complex. His description of Ojibwa social anomy is perhaps overly general, but his study contains important data. Like Shkilnyk [56], for example, Vecsey discusses Grassy Narrows, providing valuable statements by band members regarding the subversive effects of religious persecution on their community.

Subarctic and Arctic

Little appears to have been written on subarctic or arctic religious history of late. One exception is Jennifer Brown's "The Track to Heaven: The Hudson Bay Cree Religious Movement of 1842–1843" [8]. Brown's article contains an expert reconstruction of the syncretic movement led by "Abishabis." The cargo-like aspects of the doctrine and its probable connection with the Cree syllabary introduced by James Evans are of particular interest. Berke's "Chisasibi Cree Hunters and Missionaries: Humor as Evidence of Tension" [5] demonstrates that the acceptability of the Anglican Church, now considered an aspect of "traditional Eastern Cree culture; turns in large upon conceived resemblance to the indigenous complex." Crees characteristically saw symmetry and consistency where missionaries saw incompatibility; as one priest plaintively observed, "You show more respect to those black bears than you do to the good lord!" (p. 5). The article also makes clear how humor expresses tensions provoked by the priests' antagonism to persisting traditional practices and beliefs.

Although not specifically concerned with processes of religious change, Janice Sheppard's [53] meticulous and sensitive comparative analysis of Tahltan, Tsetsaut, Carrier, and Dogrib versions of "The Dog Husband" provides the specification of shared and variant elements that can permit temporal arrangement of myth along the lines indicated by Levi-Strauss (1982, pp. 151–62). Robert Gessain's "Dance Masks of Ammassalik" [18] provides yet another example of missionary destructiveness in describing Greenland Eskimo masks and the airport art that has succeeded them; the article is accompanied by excellent plates.

Northwest Coast

Sergei Kan's "Russian Orthodox Brotherhoods among the Tlingit: Missionary Goals and Native Response" [26] is a superb account of the "indigenization" of the Russian Orthodox Church by the Tlingit. Tlingits, motivated by practical and spiritual considerations, as well as a characteristically Northwest Coast concern with being seen as "civilized," adapted the introduced religion to their own purposes; the orthodox brotherhoods, introduced by the priests as agents of social change, paradoxically became vehicles perpetuating Tlingit culture. Kan also pursues this general theme in "Words That Heal the Soul: Analysis of the Tlingit Potlatch Oratory" [25] which discusses continuity in Tlingit oratory. In this article, Kan describes the selective incorporation of Christian elements into religious and secular oratory. L. L. Langness's "Individual Psychology and Cultural Change: An Ethnohistorical Case from the Klallam" [29] picks up the theme of "indigenization" in its description of the Klallams, who, again desirous of being thought civilized, built in 1880 the only

Christian church in their county. They did this, however, without themselves becoming Christian.

Joyce Wike turns to a less "civilized" aspect of the region's religious life in her "A Reevaluation of Northwest Coast Cannibalism" [74]. By reconstructing beliefs concerning the poisonousness of certain human body parts, Wike argues, contra Boas, that the cannibal complex existed among Wakashan speakers as early as the sixteenth century. Wike asserts that such beliefs motivated cannibal displays by prestige-seeking leaders as well as the experimental and hostile (or mischievous) offerings of lethal viands to visiting Europeans. The observations of John Ledyard are especially interesting. Ledyard tasted a human arm out of curiosity but then expressed to the Nootka his "disapprobation of eating it on account of its being part of a man like ourselves" (p. 247).

Jay Miller's "Tsimshian Religion in Historical Perspective" [38] is a general essay which offers an excellent overview of religious change. Miller discusses successively indigenous shamanism, the syncretic religion introduced by the Carrier prophet Bini, and the introduction of Christianity. He discusses the psychological costs of conflicting commitments to Christian and indigenous beliefs and also the persistence of the latter (sometimes disparaged as "low class") into the present.

Great Basin

Continuity is a prominent theme among the recent studies of religion in the Great Basin. Jay Miller has also produced two fine interpretations of Numic belief. "Numic Religion: An Overview of Power in the Great Basin of Native North America" [36] and "Basin Religion and Theology: A Comparative Study of Power (Puha)" [37] demonstrate the continuity of Shoshonean religion. Power, conceived as weblike currents associated with water and mountains, is understood as available to those who make themselves attractive to it. Also of importance are Miller's emphasis on the feminine (exemplified by the being Ocean Old Woman), his remarks on mining and the MX missile complex as motivating renewed interest in power, and the nonexclusivism of Shoshoneans who seek power simultaneously from indigenous practice, the syncretic peyote religion, and Christianity.

Exclusivity and mutual suspicion are more apparent in Edgar Siskin's excellent *Washo Shamans and Peyotists* [57], which discusses
the antagonism between "traditional" shamans and peyote adher-
ents. According to Siskin, Washo peyotism offers both alternative
medical procedures and security from the threatened sorcery of traditional shamans. His analysis has considerable *in situ* credibility
even though it does not address the problem of why some groups
view different persisting complexes as complementary rather than
exclusive.

Among more historical studies of the region are L. George Moses'
"The Father Tells Me So! Wovoka, the Ghost Dance Prophet" [41]
and Floyd O'Neil's "The Mormons, the Indians, and George Washington Bean" [42]. Moses searches for the sources of Wovoka's message, and finds them in the Washani religion preached by Smohalla
and the Shaker religion of the Nisqualli Indian John Slocum. O'Neil
situates Bean's missionary endeavors within the broader context of
Indian dispossession in the West and demonstrates that the importance of the "Lamanites" in Mormon theology was not expressed in
concerted missionary work or advocacy.

Russell Thornton's recent work rounds out studies of this region
even though the Cherokee sociologist's interests stretch beyond the
Great Basin region. His "Demographic Antecedents of Tribal Participation in the 1870 Ghost Dance" [65] and "Demographic Antecedents of a Rivitalization Movement: Population Change, Population Size, and the 1890 Ghost Dance" [64] use statistical methods to
argue that population size was negatively correlated with participation in the two movements. The doctrine of returning ancestors was
welcomed by groups desiring to compensate for high mortality rates
linked to introduced diseases. (At the time of this writing, Thornton's
fuller study of these movements is in press [66]).

Plateau

Studies of the Plateau continue to focus on the prophetic movements
which have played so important a role in that region's Indian history.
The fullest recent study of native religion in the Plateau is *Prophetic
Worlds: Indians and Whites on the Columbian Plateau* [35] by Christopher Miller. Miller juxtaposes plateau prophetic movements focused on intrusive whites with white views of Indians as potential converts. He suggests that epidemics and warfare engendered

a transplateau prophetic movement in the late 1700s. Lewis and Clark, David Thompson, and Ignace's Iroquois band, which united with the Salish ("Flatheads"), were thereafter seen as worldly tokens of the prophetic message promising both power and trade goods from the east. Miller profitably employs Wallace's [73] concept of "revitalization" to the movement, but the book is sketchy on its doctrine and practice.

"Smohalla, the Washani, and Religion as a Factor in Northwestern Indian History," [68] by Clifford Trafzer and Margery Beach, provides another view of Smohalla. They emphasize the prophet's doctrines (notably his rejection of Christianity and of individual land-ownership) as factors in Plateau resistance to acculturation. Their article also discusses the derivative Dreamer religion among the Nez Perces and Palouses. Beach's "The Waptashi Prophet and the Feather Religion: Derivative of the Washani" [4] discusses a little-known synthesis by the Klikitat prophet Jake Hunt of Smohalla's teachings with the Shaker religion. That movement included apparent "ecstatic" dancing, healing and initiation rites, and the rejection of alcohol.

The sole recent study of missionization in the region is Robert Carriker's "Joseph M. Cataldo: Carrier of Catholicism to the Nez Perces" [9]. In his essay, Carriker describes the career of a Jesuit who, like many of his brethren, mingled a provisional relativism with aspirations of civilizing the Nez Perces through education.

California

Most studies of this area continue to focus on the mission experience. Harry Kelsey's "European Impact on the California Indians, 1530–1830" [27] suggests that many conversions in the 1800s were motivated by practical considerations and that literal acceptance of Christian teaching was problematic. Kelsey does not discuss the attenuation of indigenous religion but asserts, perhaps too categorically, that the cumulative effort of acculturation on the Mission Indians was "total." Florence Shipek's "California Indian Reactions to the Franciscans" [55] takes a similar point of view. She argues that the guns and pointing habits of priests led to their interpretation as witches and that they were seen as both the source and the remedy for introduced epidemic diseases.

Not surprisingly, the only cited work *not* on the mission theme focuses on northern California, the area beyond the reach of most Spanish friars. Al Logan Slagle's "Tolowa Religious Shakers and the Role of Prophecy at Smith River, California" [60] also examines a relatively recent phenomenon. He argues that the nineteenth-century Shaker religion became a focus of Indian identity among this coastal California tribe.

Plains

The drama of plains culture continues to attract serious scholars. Fred Voget's excellent monograph *The Shoshone-Crow Sun Dance* [72], for example, combines detailed descriptions of earlier and later conditions of the ceremony with consideration of the ambiguous tension between religious accommodation and resistance. Voget demonstrates that accommodation—or syncretism—allows for concurrent membership in the Sun Dance and the Peyote church while resistance—or exclusivity—preaches the differences between "Indian" and "white" ways. As one Crow leader observed, "The White man's religion is for the White man and the Indian belief is for the Indian" (p. 130). The combination of elements of both resistance and accommodation is expressed among the Crow in their defense of religious autonomy: the Sun Dance and peyotism are legitimized by appealing to both their traditional meaning and their similarity to Christianity.

Voget indicates factors that motivated Crows to borrow the Sun Dance from Shoshones (deprivation, illness, concern for relatives in service) and reaches the credible conclusion that sun dancing and peyotism maintain a separate Crow identity while bridging at the same time conflicts between perceived "traditional" and "modern" models of social obligation. The book benefits from a wealth of contextual data on the persons and events involved in the reintroduction of the Sun Dance.

Some irony accrues to the revelation that Black Elk, for many whites the apotheosis of the numinous Indian, was a Catholic catechist. In "Black Elk's Relationship to Christianity" [22] Clyde Holler observed that, under reservation conditions, Sioux religious leaders had to confront Christianity if they wished to continue in their roles, and he demonstrates that Black Elk's conversion entailed not substitution but creative biculturalism. Of particular interest are

Black Elk's conception of the two systems as similar (suffering for others, for example, being common to both) and his conscious strategy of combining the two for their mutual improvement. Holler touches also on the effect of syncretism on traditional symbolism; the color black, for example, was disassociated from war and generalized as a symbol of evil.

Raymond DeMallie's careful introduction to *The Sixth Grandfather* (10) offers a fuller view of Black Elk's life and suggests that "conversion" was a complex process for the Sioux. Given the exclusive attitudes of the priests, it is not surprising that Black Elk's conversion was followed by a nominal rejection of traditional practice and ambiguous feelings which continued until his meeting with Niehardt in 1930. Pragmatic motives ("My children had to live in this world" [p. 47].) as well as convictions of the lessened efficacy of Sioux religion ("The spirits do not come to help us now. The White men have driven them away" [p. 92].) undoubtedly contributed to conversion. At the same time, the Christian elements in Black Elk's visions and teachings demonstrate the syncretism discussed by Holler. Finally, Black Elk's return to forbidden religious dancing in his old age shows the persistence of Sioux religion. DeMallie's essay makes evident the importance of examining changing orientations towards existing and introduced religions during an individual's entire life.

As in other western areas, studies of missionaries are relatively scarce in the recent scholarly literature on the plains. Moreover, the one prominent example of a missionary study, Bruce Forbes's "John Jasper McThuin: Missionary to the Western Tribes" [16], provides further documentation of themes expressed in the work of Voget, Holler, and DeMallie. Forbes shows that McThuin shared the "exclusive" attitude of most Christians, while the Kiowas he encountered were remarkably ecumenical. Thus, even though his focus is a Christian missionary, Forbes provides an analysis that is sensitive to the dynamics of religious change within the tribal context.

Southwest

It is striking that so vital an area of contemporary Indian culture has produced relatively little new scholarship on religious change. Of the work that has appeared, the bulk of it focuses on the Navajos and emphasizes the persistent vitality of religious systems in that large tribe. Sections of Stephen Kunitz's *Disease, Change and the Role of Medicine: The Navajo Experience* [28] deal with the relationship of indigenous to introduced medical practices. Despite the ready use of Western medicine, faith healing, and peyote curing in Navajo culture, Kunitz finds little syncretism between old and new. He posits the correspondence in Navajo thought of "traditional" practice with the *causes* of disease and of other systems with the treatment of symptoms. This dichotomization contrasts with the partitioning, encountered elsewhere, of health disorders into two exclusive groups treated respectively by traditional and introduced practices.

Carol Jopling's "Art and Ethnicity: Peyote Painting, a Case Study" [24] also addresses contemporary religious variation in Navajo communities. Her article deals peripherally with peyote doctrines in the course of discussing stylistic variation and indicates that the paintings are sometimes understood by their creators as vehicles for conveying peyote values to outsiders. Eric Henderson's "Kaibeto Plateau Ceremonialists: 1860–1980" [20] describes another source of variation: history. Henderson relates the decline in ceremonial learning by Navajos to competition from peyotism, logistical incompatability with wage labor (as against the livestock economy), and the fragmentation of the residential kin units forming the usual context for instruction. Similarly, Karl Luckert's "Toward a Historical Perspective on Navajo Religion" [31] turns to historical factors to specify sequences in Navajo ceremonial development. Luckert's method, following upon ideas presented by Sapir [50], resembles the linguistic reconstructions used so effectively in other contexts.

Other scholars have tried to place Navajo beliefs in a broader historical context. Mary Shepardson's "Changing Attitudes Toward Navajo Religion" [52] is an excellent overview of white stereotypes and policies regarding Navajo religion from the characteristic repression of the early 1900s to the inception of the American Indian Religious Freedom Act. Shepardson also nicely documents the compartmental orientation of many Navajos: "I have a great respect for white doctors; there are things they can do that we cannot. . . . There are certain sicknesses that a doctor can never cure that we can" (p. 203). Aberle's "The Future of Navajo Religion" [1] is a succinct and penetrating discussion of the interplay between "traditional" religion, peyotism, Mormonism, and evangelical Protestant sects.

Aberle relates Navajo religious experimentalism to the need for access to new sources of power, both sacred and secular, and emphasizes the doctrinal and logistical competition between coexisting religions while demonstrating the nonexclusivist orientation of traditionalists and peyotists. Aberle sees decreasing contexts for ceremonial training, problems in Navajo language maintenance, and overt competition from exclusivist introduced religions as at least short term threats to traditionalism and peyotism. At the same time, he predicts that the latter will continue to assume both spiritual and political importance in contexts of resistance to external pressures and disruptions.

Southeast

Writing on Indian religious history in the Southeast follows the pattern evident in other culture areas. Studies of missionary activity share the bibliographical spotlight with work on prophets, the persistence of native beliefs, and the intricacies of religions change. Examples of the first two genres are the works by David Baird and Frank Owsley. David Baird's "Cyrus Byington and the Presbyterian Choctaw Mission" [3] is a somewhat partisan account of Byington's work among Choctaw in Oklahoma, emphasizing the fashion in which his Choctaw writing system enabled a "bicultural" adaptation to the majority society. Frank Owsley's "Prophet of War: Josiah Francis and the Creek War" [43] discusses the career of the Creek warrior and prophet but provides little information on religion beyond Francis's involvement with the teachings of Tenskwatawa, the Shawnee Prophet. A very valuable discussion of the persistence of traditional belief in the contemporary Southeast is provided in Thomas Blumer's "Wild Indians and the Devil: The Contemporary Catawba Indian Spirit World" [6]. Beliefs in "wild Indians" with trickster/abductor attributes persist but have become less relevant with occupational shifts of Catawbas towards towns; the images suggest convergence with probable early historic Catawba interpretations of the scriptural Devil.

As in other aspects of Southeastern Indian studies, most writing on the region's religious history has focused on the Cherokees. Ronald Satz's "Cherokee Traditionalism, Protestant Evangelism and the Trail of Tears" [51] is a careful examination of Cherokee reactions to Protestantism; it provides a striking profile of the details of Christian conversion in the nineteenth century. Satz documents a pragmatic or "secular" orientation to introduced religions, exemplified by the ready acceptance of missionaries as educators and the manipulation of conversion as a politically advantageous symbol of civility. He also cites instances of spiritually motivated conversion predicated in part upon perceived resemblances (for example, the significance of immersion in water) between evangelical and Cherokee systems.

McLoughlin's *Cherokees and Missionaries, 1789–1839* [32] and *The Cherokee Ghost Dance* [33] both contain a wealth of data on the effect of Christian missionary activities on sacred and secular aspects of Cherokee society, and they provide an elaboration of the approach outlined above by Satz. McLoughlin's two works should be consulted simultaneously, since some issues relating to religious change are taken up in more detail in the collected essays [33] than in the narrative [32]. McLoughlin argues that social/psychological stresses accompanying the contact experience and loss of sovereignty induced pragmatic and spiritual receptivity to Christian messages as well as two distinguishable nativistic movements. The first "Ghost Dance" of 1811–13 emphasized the value of traditional custom (to the point of proscribing white clothing at ceremonies) while making provision for limited social change. White Path's movement of 1823 opposed acculturation more categorically. Both movements were overtly antiassimilationist and also politically oriented. Together with McLoughlin's coverage of Christian coversion, the discussion of the two movements provides valuable detail regarding the predictably ambivalent religious reactions of Cherokees to encroaching whites.

Fogelson's "Who Were the Anî-Kutánî? An Excursion into Cherokee Historical Thought" [15] is a unique contribution to folk history which explores Cherokee knowledge of a prehistoric revolt against a superordinate priestly class or clan. Although Fogelson is primarily concerned with the legend's relation to contradictory stratificational and egalitarian aspects of Cherokee society, the article concludes with a valuable discussion of how Cherokees themselves comprehend the historic attenuation of their traditional religion. Fogelson's work is a necessary reminder that some of us should be writing or recording Indian historical consciousness of Indian religious history rather than simply studying the conventional history record.

General

A few studies defy classification into a regional framework. Robert Michaelson's "We Also Have a Religion: The Free Exercise of Religion Among Native Americans" [34], for example, is a useful discussion of the American Indian Religious Freedom Act (AIRFA) which addresses all of contemporary religious practice. In the same way, Steve Talbot's "Desecration and American Indian Religious Freedom" [63], although assuming unrealistic notions of religious homogeneity in Indian society, provides a good discussion of AIRFA in relation to sacred lands and museum holdings. Both articles correctly emphasize the self-evident but often overlooked fact that listening to what Indians (as against archives or social scientists) have to say is often the key to understanding the legal implications of American Indian religions.

Michael Steltenkamp's *The Sacred Vision* [62] addresses the heady problem of the relevance of Indian spiritual knowledge to non-Indians. Steltenkamp feels that Indian and non-Indian religions are compatible and susceptible to synthesis, and he discusses syncretic Indian religious movements that developed historically in the course of the acculturation experience. Although it is important to make clear that Indian religions have neither disappeared nor everywhere become attenuated, Steltenkamp's assertion that "whether Native or Christian, rural or urban, Indian religious constructs are intact" (pp. 117–18) would be questioned by many Indian practitioners.

Summary Remarks

The thumbnail characterizations outlined above fall far short of communicating the scholarly acumen exhibited in recent writing on American Indian religious history and religious change; they may, however, indicate the broad range of topics and issues currently under consideration. A synthesis of recent contributions to such areas of concern as the conversion experience and the inception of revitalization movements, although badly needed, would, in this context, do justice neither to the scholars nor to their subjects. Instead, our concluding discussion is limited to some summary observations and to a characterization of one influential branch of social theory that may usefully orient future research.

The archaeological and documentary records concur in demonstrating that religious borrowing and synthesis existed both prehistorically and independently of white proselytizing. It is therefore probably unnecessary to point out that a dichotomous retrospective assumption of precontact religious stasis followed by a postcontact religious dynamism is illusory. Indian groups exchanged religious complexes, and parts of religious complexes, long before Europeans introduced Old World religions and other disruptions into the native environment. From this point of view, it should be clear that Indians are not "less Indian" because they worship in churches whose doctrines originate from the Old World or because they participate in syncretic religions incorporating Christian elements. Experimentation with Old World religions would be simply one more instance of a traditional receptivity to religious innovation.

There is, therefore, nothing "non-Indian" in the *event* of religious change, although the circumstances of white-Indian interaction provide contexts in which adherence to different religions both creates and reflects different cultural orientations. These different orientations are certainly affected as well by the cultural diversity of the native world and the coercive quality of the majority society.

Paradoxically, of course, the characteristically "Indian" receptivity to new sources of spiritual experience can cause not only the attenuation of "traditional" practice, but also its disappearance. Thus, although it is both politically and factually correct to remark the persistence of "traditional" religions in some areas, or the "indigenization" of Christianity in others, we need to appreciate very real instances of ultimate cultural loss—rituals for whose offices there are no candidates, myths no longer remembered. Such instances are part of the subjective historical awareness of many Indians. Neither should we emphasize exclusively how Indians consciously and creatively negotiated their own religious transformations. When, to take just two Subarctic examples, sacred drums were burned to ashes by a missionary or when irreparable rifts in the intergenerational transmission of religious knowledge followed from the imposition of culturally genocidal boarding schools, it is difficult to escape the conclusion that much (not all) religious change proceeded independently of the volition of those who experienced it.

The encounter of Indian societies with Old World religions could not, of course, be *only* another instance of exposure to novel spiritual doctrines and practices since the circumstances of the encounter had, to say the least, no precedent. Indians experienced Christianity as the faith of their conquerors and expropriators. The doctrines themselves were fundamentally opposed to existing Indian religious knowledge in many respects. And although proselytizing was probably not the unique franchise of the Europeans, Indians had surely never before experienced classes of religious entrepreneurs whose *raison d'etre* was the destruction (as against the augmentation and replacement) of existing systems. Thus much (not all) historic Indian religious change has been motivated *in relation* to Christianity and the contact experience, whether this change took the form of accepting, selectively incorporating, or rejecting the missionary message.

Obviously then both different orientations toward Christianity and the inception of revitalization religions need to be understood and explained within the historical contexts of Indian-white contact. Recent scholarship makes this conclusion obvious. Throughout much of this literature, the "explanation" for accepting or rejecting Christianity and/or for the inception of revitalization movements is identified as the social, cultural, and psychological disruption caused by the contact experience. That suffering and deprivation explain religious experimentation and innovation seems to be taken readily for granted by both historians and ethnologists.

Without questioning the undoubted catalytic effect of suffering and deprivation in religious innovation, the very diversity of the innovated religious behavior revealed in the literature under review suggests serious limitations on the explanatory adequacy of suffering *per se* as an explanation for the particularities of American Indian religious response. Putting this another way, epidemics, loss of sovereignty, perceived deprivation, land theft, and other aspects/concomitants of the colonial project explain particular trajectories of religious change to the same degree that nutritional and energetic requirements explain the specific content of socially differentiated cuisines. While it is self-evident that needs for intelligibility and relief in the face of suffering prompt religious innovation, the specific character of the innovation cannot be predicted or understood by referring only to the brute facts of suffering.

Restricting the discussion only to the encounter of indigenous systems with Christianity, we need to ask whether the diversity of Indian responses to missionary entrepreneurs—sincere and "literal" conversion, nominal conversion, categorical rejection, indigenous Christian movements, self-consciously syncretic movements, unconsciously syncretic movements, compartmentalization, exclusivism, and the like—can be read either from suffering itself or, even more specifically, from the specific circumstances attendant upon the contact experiences. Given the complexity and variation evident in situations of religious change, we should be reluctant to propose transcultural correspondences between particular socioeconomic or political factors and particular categories of religious response.

Anthony Wallace [73, p. 276], whose landmark elucidation of revitalization was a necessary corrective to earlier and less flexible typologies, suggests that varying degrees of political domination explain a continuum of religious innovations. I am somewhat skeptical of our ability at this point to devise the appropriate scale for a comparative examination of this hypothesis in North America, but data drawn from the papers and books discussed above provide a rich picture of variation. This picture is further complicated by the "Janus-faced" orientation—to employ Worsley's well-turned phrase [75, p. iv]—of many Indian responses to religious change. This is the simultaneous and ambivalent valuation and disparagement of both the traditional and the innovative. Despite some points of comparison, however, broad generalizations are extremely difficult to defend. For example, when the Shawnee Tenskwatawa and the leaders of the Cherokee movement of 1811–13 independently proscribed white clothing, it would seem obvious that we had observed the same religious response in two settings. For these two instances to count as examples of the same response, however, it would be necessary to identify resemblances in the meanings ascribed by Shawnees and Cherokees to the proscription. This in turn would require consideration of the contextual circumstances of contact in each case as well as consideration of the ways Shawnees and Cherokees experienced and acted upon these circumstances.

The preceding remarks, which take the existing sociocultural orders of Indian societies rather than the precise content of their several contact experiences as basic to the interpretation of religious response, draw explicitly from Sahlins's [46, 47, 48] influential recent works on the relations between cultural orders and historical events. Sahlins's writings are already well known, but there seem to exist as yet no applications of his ideas to problems in American Indian religious history. The *précis* outlined here is not, of course, a directive intended to align all such research within the spheres of semiotic anthropology but rather to delineate, in very broad terms, a theoretical paradigm that takes cognizance simultaneously of the complexities and contradictions entailed in the interpretation of cultural systems. Such interpretation must also be aware of the gap between behavior and practice, the complexity of historical events, the difficulty of cultural reproduction, and the continuous presence of cultural transformation.

Sahlins's writing on Polynesian history take as basic the Saussurean principle of semiotic arbitrariness; cultural categories, rules, and propositions are comprehended, "in the last instance," as meaningfully organized systems encompassing but not encoding objective "natural" discontinuities, biological requirements, or material circumstances. The linguistic prototype is the Saussurean sign itself, an entity whose meaning is specifiable not through its denotative relationship to extralinguistic experience but rather through its oppositive relations to other signs that reciprocally define and differentiate each other. As with the particular lexical distinctions of individual languages, so with historically constituted cultural orders: the particular system of categories and rules is never the only one possible, given the material coordinates of demography, technology or environment. Sahlins's approach derives not simply from a refinement of Saussurean arbitrariness into semiotic (or structural) anthropology but also in innovations that alter Saussure's (and arguably Levi-Strauss's) exclusion of motivated system change and pragmatic human behavior from semiotic interpretation. Although actors reproduce in their behavior the categories and rules of the socially shared cultural order, and thereby necessarily reproduce that order through time, distorting relationships between the pragmatic orientation of different sets of actors (male/female, noble/commoner) or between the actors' culturally presupposed categories and the characteristics of novel situations engender innovations that eventually transform the cultural order.

History is culturally ordered, differently so in different societies, according to meaningful schemes of things. The converse is also true: cultural schemes are historically ordered, since to a greater or lesser extent the meanings are revalued as they are practically enacted. [48, p. vii]

The complexity of a semiotic reordering, entailing novel relations of signs *vis à vis* both other signs and unfamiliar referents is best examined in the original [cf. 46, pp. 33–72]. Here it is only necessary to indicate that the approach traverses such classic oppositions as cultural order/behavior and structure/history. It also permits both the understanding of how cultural meanings motivate events and how events reciprocally reproduce and transform cultural meanings.

One very brief example may suffice to indicate applications to problems of change and persistence in American Indian religion. Before the late 1800s, the Rock Crees of the Churchill River drainage in Manitoba pursued during winter a predominantly nomadic or transhumant regime of frequent movement from camp to camp. Consultants pointed out that preservation of food supplies (dried fish, dried meat, frozen fish and meat, pemmican products) was logistically incompatible with this movement because of problems of transport. They also emphasized that stored food was "unlucky" in the bush because spirit beings regulating human access to animals would interfere with this access if the hunters already possessed food. Food on hand and food not yet captured were thus in a kind of complementary distribution, incapable of existing simultaneously in the same context. Around 1900, experimentation with dried fish and the availability of flour from traders made possible a transition to a semi-sedentary regime in which hunting groups maintained log cabin settlements as main camps throughout the winter. This regime did not come into being *ex nihilo*; relative winter sedentism of this kind was formerly made possible by occasional large-scale caribou kills.

Food storage thus emerged as a central aspect of Cree production, rendering the earlier nomadism simultaneously unnecessary and impractical. Both the storage and the sedentism were "transformations" in which what were technological potentials became predominant practices. For whatever reason, relative sedentism and storage were positively revalued; nothing in the earlier circumstances of production rendered them impossible. However, the doctrine that preserved food may interfere with successful hunting persists into the 1980s, an alternated "reproduction" of the structure of prehistoric and early historic subsistence. Some trappers will not take meat with them when they leave their villages or camps for the trapline, citing the antagonism of spirit beings as explanation. Two individuals of my acquaintance extended this rule to include *all* forms of food, a practice that exposed them on at least two occasions to periods of debilitating although not life-threatening hunger for the duration of the foray. Food storage, and indeed dependence on commercially prepared store food have long since become basic aspects of Cree subsistence in town or in camp. The traditional proscription persists, however, restricted spatially and temporally to the sphere of the bush and transient movement through it.

Insofar as most students of American Indian religious history would reject both a monolithic cultural order existing apart from worldly events and a meaningless succession of contingent events unaffected by the constructions of the historical actors, the theoretical scheme sketched here is self-evident. This is all the more the case since Sahlins himself identifies culture contact as the context within which the cultural encompassment of events and the historical reordering of culture are maximally observable. Further, since the scheme illuminates reorderings that cross our conventionally partitioned "social," "economic," "religious," "productive," and "political" aspects of analysis, it provides the basis for a fresh approach. Understanding religious change in terms of a semiotic reordering of culture can show how religiously motivated behavior reciprocally reacts with and constrains other analytically distinguishable spheres of action.

References

1. Aberle, David. 1982. "The Future of Navajo Religion." In *Navajo Religion and Culture: Selected Views*, pp. 219–31. Ed. David M. Brugge and Charlotte Frisbie. Santa Fe: Museum of New Mexico Press.
2. Axtell, James. 1985. *The Invasion Within: The Contest of Cultures in Colonial North America*. Oxford: Oxford University Press.
3. Baird, W. David. 1985. "Cyrus Byington and the Presbyterian Choctaw Mission." In *Churchmen and the Western Indians, 1820–1920*, pp. 5–40. Ed. C. Milner and F. O'Neil. Norman: University of Oklahoma Press.
4. Beach, Margery Ann. 1985. "The Waptashi Prophet and the Feather Religion: Derivative of the Washani." *American Indian Quarterly* 9(3): 325–33.
5. Berkes, Fikret. 1986. "Chisasibi Cree Hunters and Missionaries: Humor as Evidence of Tension." *Actes du Dix-Septième Congrès des Algonquinistes*. Ed. W. Cowan. Ottawa: Carleton University.
6. Blumer, Thomas J. 1985. "Wild Indians and the Devil: The Contemporary Catawba Indian Spirit World." *American Indian Quarterly* 9(2): 149–68.
7. Bonvillain, Nancy. 1985. "Missionary Rule in French Colonial Expansion: An Examination of the Jesuit Relations." *Man in the Northeast* 29:1–14.
8. Brown, Jennifer. 1982. "The Track to Heaven: The Hudson Bay Cree Religious Movement of 1842–1843." *Papers of the Thirteenth Algon-*

quian Conference, pp. 53–64. Ed. William Cowan. Ottawa: Carleton University.

9. Carriker, Robert. 1985. "Joseph M. Cataldo, S.J.: Carrier of Catholicism to the Nez Perces." In *Churchmen and the Western Indians, 1820–1920*, pp. 109–39. Ed. C. Milner and F. O'Neil. Norman: University of Oklahoma Press.

10. DeMallie, Raymond, ed. 1984. *The Sixth Grandfather: Black Elk's Teachings Given to John G. Neihardt*. Lincoln: University of Nebraska Press.

11. Dickason, Olive Patricia. 1984. *The Myth of the Savage and the Beginnings of French Colonialism in the Americas*. Edmonton: University of Alberta Press.

12. Edmunds, R. David. 1983. *The Shawnee Prophet*. Lincoln: University of Nebraska Press.

13. ———. 1985. "Main Poc: Potawatomi Wabeno." *American Indian Quarterly* 9(3):259–271.

14. Evans-Pritchard, E. E. 1962. *Social Anthropology and Other Essays*. New York: Free Press.

15. Fogelson, Raymond. 1984. "Who Were the Anî-Kutánî? An Excursion into Cherokee Historical Thought." *Ethnohistory* 31(4):255–64.

16. Forbes, Bruce D. 1985. "John Jasper Methvin, Missionary to the Western Tribes." In *Churchmen and the Western Indians, 1820–1920*, pp. 41–73. Ed. C. Milner and F. O'Neil. Norman: University of Oklahoma Press.

17. Frake, Charles. 1969. "A Structural Description of Subanun Religious Behavior." In *Cognitive Anthropology*, pp. 470–87. Ed. S. Tyler. New York: Holt, Rinehart, Winston.

18. Gessain, Robert. 1984. "Dance Masks of Ammassalik." *Arctic Anthropology* 21(2):81–107.

19. Grant, John W. 1984. *Moon of Wintertime: Missionaries and the Indians of Canada in Encounter since 1534*. Toronto: University of Toronto Press.

20. Henderson, Eric. 1982. "Kaibeto Plateau Ceremonialists: 1860–1980." In *Navajo Religion and Culture: Selected Views*, pp. 164–75. Ed. D. Brugge and C. Frisbie. Santa Fe: Museum of New Mexico Press.

21. Herring, Joseph B. 1985. "Kenekuk, the Kickapoo Prophet: Acculturation Without Assimilation." *American Indian Quarterly* 9(3):295–307.

22. Holler, Clyde. 1984. "Black Elk's Relationship to Christianity." *American Indian Quarterly* 8(1):37–49.

23. Horton, Robin. 1970. "African Traditional Thought and Western Science." In *Rationality*, pp. 131–71. Ed. B. Wilson. New York: Harper Torch Books.

24. Jopling, Carol F. 1984. "Art and Ethnicity: Peyote Painting, a Case Study." *Ethnos* 49(1–2):98–118.

25. Kan, Sergei. 1983. "Words That Heal the Soul: Analysis of the Tlingit Potlatch Oratory." *Arctic Anthropology* 20(2):47–59.

26. ———. 1985. "Russian Orthodox Brotherhoods among the Tlingit: Missionary Goals and Native Response." *Ethnohistory* 32(3):196–223.

27. Kelsey, Harry. 1985. "European Impact on the California Indians, 1530–1830." *Americas* 41(4):494–511.

28. Kunitz, Stephen J. 1983. *Disease, Change and the Role of Medicine: The Navajo Experience*. Berkeley: University of California Press.

29. Langness, L. L. 1984. "Individual Psychology and Cultural Change: An Ethnohistorical Case from the Klallam." In *The Tsimshian and Their Neighbors*, pp. 255–80. Ed. J. Miller and C. Eastman. Seattle: University of Washington Press.

30. Lévi-Strauss, Claude. 1982. *The Way of the Masks*. Seattle: University of Washington Press.

31. Luckert, Karl. 1982. "Toward a Historical Perspective on Navajo Religion." In *Navajo Religion and Culture: Selected Views*, pp. 187–97. Ed. D. Brugge and C. Frisbie. Santa Fe: Museum of New Mexico Press.

32. McLoughlin, William G. 1984. *Cherokees and Missionaries, 1789–1839*. New Haven: Yale University Press.

33. ———. 1984. *The Cherokee Ghost Dance*. Macon, Ga.: Mercer University Press.

34. Michaelson, Robert S. 1983. "We Also Have a Religion: The Free Exercise of Religion Among Native Americans." *American Indian Quarterly* 7(3):111–42.

35. Miller, Christopher. 1985. *Prophetic Worlds: Indians and Whites on the Columbia Plateau*. New Brunswick: Rutgers University Press.

36. Miller, Jay. 1983. "Numic Religion: An Overview of Power in the Great Basin of Native North America." *Anthropos* 78(3): 337–54.

37. ———. 1983. "Basin Religion and Theology: A Comparative Study of Power (Puha)." *Journal of California and Great Basin Anthropology* 5(1–2):66–86.

38. ———. 1984. "Tsimshian Religion in Historical Perspective: Shamans, Prophets, and Christ." In *The Tsimshian and Their Neighbors of the North Pacific Coast*, pp. 137–47. Ed. J. Miller and C. Eastman. Seattle: University of Washington Press.

39. Milner, Clyde A., II. 1982. *With Good Intentions: Quaker Work Among the Pawnees, Otos, and Omahas in the 1870s*. Lincoln: University of Nebraska Press.

40. Moore, James T. 1982. *Indian and Jesuit: A Seventeenth Century Encounter*. Chicago: University of Chicago Press.

41. Moses, L. G. 1985. "The Father Tells Me So! Wovoka, the Ghost Dance Prophet." *American Indian Quarterly* 9(3):335–51.

42. O'Neil, Floyd. 1985. "The Mormons, the Indians and George Washington Bean." In *Churchmen and the Western Indians, 1820–1920*, pp. 140–76. Ed. C. Milner and E. O'Neil. Norman: University of Oklahoma Press.

43. Owsley, Frank L. 1985. "Prophet of War: Josiah Francis and the Creek War." *American Indian Quarterly* 9(3):239–94.

44. Paper, Jordon. 1983. "The Post-Contact Origin of an American Indian High God: The Suppression of Feminine Spirituality." *American Indian Quarterly* 7(4):1–24.

45. Richter, Daniel K. 1985. "Iroquois versus Iroquois: Jesuit Missions and

Christianity in Village Politics, 1642–1686." *Ethnohistory* 32(1):1–16.
46. Sahlins, Marshall. 1981. *Historical Metaphors and Mythical Realities: Structure in the Early History of the Sandwich Islands Kingdom.* Ann Arbor: University of Michigan Press.
47. ———. 1982. "Individual Experience and Cultural Order." In *The Social Sciences: Their Nature and Users*, pp. 35–48. Ed. W. Kruskal. Chicago: University of Chicago Press.
48. ———. 1985. *Islands of History.* Chicago: University of Chicago Press.
49. Salisbury, Neal. 1982. *Manitou and Providence: Indians, Europeans and the Making of New England, 1500–1643.* New York: Oxford University Press.
50. Sapir, Edward. 1949. "Time Perspective in Aboriginal American Culture: A Study in Method." In *Selected Writings of Edward Sapir*, pp. 389–462. Berkeley: University of California Press.
51. Satz, Ronald. 1985. "Cherokee Traditionalism, Protestant Evangelism, and the Trail of Tears." *Tennessee Historical Quarterly* 44(2–3): 285–301, 388–401.
52. Shepardson, Mary. 1982. "Changing Attitudes Toward Navajo Religion." In *Navajo Religion and Culture: Selected Views*, pp. 198–208. Ed. D. Brugge and C. Frisbie. Santa Fe: Museum of New Mexico Press.
53. Sheppard, Janice R. 1983. "The Dog Husband: Structural Identity and Emotional Specificity in Northern Athapaskan Oral Narrative." *Arctic Anthropology* 20(1):89–101.
54. Shimony, Annemarie. 1984. "Conflict and Continuity: An Analysis of an Iroquois Uprising." In *Extending the Rafters: Interdisciplinary Approaches to Iroquoian Studies.* Ed. M. K. Foster, J. Campisi, and M. Mithun. Albany: State University of New York Press.
55. Shipek, Florence C. 1985. "California Indian Reactions to the Franciscans." *Americas* 41(4):480–92
56. Shkilnyk, Anastasia M. 1985. *A Poison Stronger Than Love: The Destruction of an Ojibwa Community.* New Haven: Yale University Press.
57. Siskin, Edgar E. 1983. *Washo Shamans and Peyotists: Religious Conflict in an American Indian Tribe.* Salt Lake City: University of Utah Press.
58. Simmons, William S. 1986. *Spirit of the New England Tribes: Indian History and Folklore, 1620–1984.* Hanover: University Press of New England.
59. ———, and Cheryl L. Simmons, eds. 1983. *Old Light on Separate Ways: The Narragansett Diary of Joseph Fish, 1765–1776.* Hanover: University Press of New England.
60. Slagle, Al Logan. 1985. "Tolowa Indian Shakers and the Role of Prophecy at Smith River, California." *American Indian Quarterly* 9(3): 352–76.
61. Spiro, Melford. 1966. "Religion: Problems of Definition and Explanation." In *Anthropological Approaches to the Study of Religion*, pp. 76–113. Ed. N. Banton. London: Tavistock.

62. Steltenkamp, Michael. 1982. *The Sacred Vision: Native American Religion and Its Practice Today*. Ramsey, N.J.: The Paulist Press.
63. Talbot, Steve. 1985. "Desecration and American Indian Religious Freedom." *Journal of Ethnic Studies* 12(4):1–17.
64. Thornton, Russell. 1981. "Demographic Antecedents of a Revitalization Movement: Population Change, Population Size, and the 1890 Ghost Dance." *American Sociological Review* 46:88–96.
65. ———. 1982. "Demographic Antecedents of Tribal Participation in the 1870 Ghost Dance Movement." *American Indian Culture and Research Journal* 6:79–91.
66. ———. 1986. *We Shall Live Again: The 1870 and 1890 Ghost Dance Movements as Demographic Revitalization*. New York: Cambridge University Press.
67. Thurman, Melburn D. 1984. "The Shawnee Prophet's Movement and the Origins of the Prophet Dance." *Current Anthropology* 25(4): 530–31.
68. Trafzer, Clifford, and Margery Ann Beach. 1985. "Smohalla, the Washani and Religion as a Factor in Northwestern Indian History." *American Indian Quarterly* 9(3):309–24.
69. Trigger, Bruce. 1985. *Natives and Newcomers: Canada's "Heroic Age" Reconsidered*. Montreal: Queen's-McGill University Press.
70. Vecsey, Christopher. 1983. *Traditional Ojibwa Religion and Its Historical Changes*. Philadelphia: American Philosophical Society.
71. Vennum, Thomas. 1982. *The Ojibwa Dance Drum: Its History and Construction*. Smithsonian Folklife Studies No. 2. Washington, D.C.: Smithsonian Institution.
72. Voget, Fred. 1984. *The Shoshoni-Crow Sun Dance*. Norman: University of Oklahoma Press.
73. Wallace, Anthony F. C. 1956. "Revitalization Movements." *American Anthropologist* 58(2):264–81.
74. Wike, Joyce. 1984. "A Reevaluation of Northwest Coast Cannibalism." In *The Tsimshian and Their Neighbors*, pp. 239–53. Ed. J. Miller and C. Eastman. Seattle: University of Washington Press.
75. Worsley, Peter. 1968. *The Trumpet Shall Sound*. New York: Schocken Books.
76. Zanger, Martin. 1985. "Straight Tongue's Heathen Words: Bishop Whipple and the Episcopal Mission to the Chippewas. In *Churchmen and the Western Indians, 1820–1920*. pp. 177–214. Ed. C. Milner and F. O'Neil. Norman: University of Oklahoma Press.

The Contributors

Robert A. Brightman is Associate Professor of Anthropology at Reed College.

George S. Grossman is Director of the Law Library in Northwestern University, Chicago.

Dennis F. K. Madill is Research Officer at the Treaties and Historical Research Centre, Indian and Northern Affairs Canada, Ottawa.

Melissa L. Meyer is Assistant Professor of History at the University of California at Los Angeles.

Douglas R. Parks is a Research Associate in the Department of Anthropology, Indiana University.

James Riding In (Pawnee) is a faculty member in the School of Justice at Arizona State University.

Willard Rollings is Associate Professor of History at the University of Nevada at Las Vegas.

Russell Thornton (Cherokee) is Professor of Sociology at the University of California at Berkeley.

Ronald L. Trosper (Flathead) is at the University of Northern Arizona.

Deborah Welch is a historian at Elon College.

Colin G. Calloway, formerly Assistant Director/Editor at the D'Arcy McNickle Center, is Associate Professor of History in the University of Wyoming.

Frederick E. Hoxie is Director of the D'Arcy McNickle Center for the History of the American Indian, the Newberry Library, Chicago.

Index

Note: Page numbers printed in boldface type are to the reference lists that follow each essay. Coauthors are listed individually.